THE ART
OF THE
POSSIBLE

Photo Karsh, Ottawa

THE AUTHOR

THE ART

OF THE

POSSIBLE

THE MEMOIRS

OF

LORD BUTLER

K.G., C.H.

HAMISH HAMILTON

LONDON

First Published in Great Britain
by Hamish Hamilton Ltd 1971
90 Great Russell Street London W.C.1

SBN 241 02007 7

Printed in Great Britain by
Western Printing Services Ltd, Bristol

TO

MOLLIE

FOR HER CONSTANT CARE

CONTENTS

LIST OF ILLUSTRATIONS

Cartoons by David Low, Vicky and Giles appear on
pages 129, 163, 166, 197, 215 and 261

PREFACE

THE TITLE of my Romanes Lecture at Oxford in 1967 was *The Difficult Art of Autobiography*. I quoted Virginia Woolf who had found no one in literature capable of expressing his whole self except Montaigne, Pepys and Rousseau. I cited numerous attempts that have been made to produce a good autobiography, giving praise to Chateaubriand, who could not resist publishing his *Mémoires d'outre tombe* during his lifetime.

I have decided to publish this book before I am too old since as Duff Cooper (one of the few successful practitioners) says 'Old Men Forget'. I feel that I have not in myself the power of being what Goethe called *'hübsch subjektiv'*. I cannot dilate like Rousseau, nor talk of my escapades like Pepys. I have therefore sought to bring in some of the dispassionate approach which only a biographer can assume by seeking the assistance of one who, while knowing me for thirty years, has had experience as an author and historian. Peter Goldman has helped me review and edit the whole of my political papers. Clearly, coming from these papers and from recorded interviews, the book represents my own attitudes but he has brought his special skill and judgement to bear.

I have eschewed the current autobiographical fondness for multi-volume histories, and have preferred a single book which is not too heavy for anyone to hold up and doze over in bed.

Politics is the Art of the Possible. That is what these pages show I have tried to achieve—not more—and that is what I have called my book.

R.A.B.

ACKNOWLEDGEMENTS

I AM indebted to those to whom I had given the bulk of my political papers, and the copyright therein, for making these papers available to me and to Peter Goldman, and for dealing with the business aspects of the publication of this book.

We are indebted to Lucia Santa Cruz for assisting with historical aspects, especially in the chapter on the Munich period, and to Robin Allen for research work, particularly in connection with the reform of the Conservative Party after the defeat of 1945, also to Michael Fraser for political advice. I make grateful acknowledgements to the many others who have kindly read individual chapters and commented upon them. My secretary, Julia Fish, has provided much help with the preparation of the sheets for publication, and to her too I offer my gratitude.

For permission to reproduce cartoons by David Low, Vicky, Giles and Ernest Shepard I am obliged to the David Low Trustees, the *Evening Standard*, the *Daily Express*, *Punch* and Associated Newspapers Ltd.

CHAPTER ONE

EARLY INFLUENCES

THE HONOURS examination in my University is described as the Tripos. I have spent the whole forty years of public life that are recalled by this book perched, whether in circumstance of ease or of discomfort, on just such a *tripos*. One of its legs has been planted in academic groves, another in the arena of politics, the third in what was once our great Raj and is still culturally a microcosm of the world. The span of the metaphor is no more extended, the hint of acrobatics no more marked, than the record will justify. For it would not only be too simple to describe my career as having been divided, like Caesar's Gaul, into three parts; it would also be untrue to the manner in which each of the three—Cambridge, Conservatism, India—has proved a constant or a recurring factor. If all my work has shown intolerance of any concept of Conservatism that is not sympathetic to progress, I have childhood in India and studies at Cambridge to thank. If I am remembered for any post-war contributions to the new Conservatism in theory and in practice, I would not wish this to be at the expense of the two principal legislative achievements with which I was fortunate enough to be associated—the India Act of 1935 and the Education Act of 1944. If there is one long-standing political ambition whose non-fulfilment can still give me the sharpest of pangs, it is that I never became Viceroy. And if there is one period of my life in which I have found a perfect and unalloyed happiness, it is now, since my home-coming as Master of Trinity.

My family has a very long academic record, described by Sir Francis Galton and by Dean Inge. We have maintained a consecutive tradition at Cambridge as dons since 1794 when my great-grandfather, George Butler, was Senior Wrangler as well as being high on the classical side. He was a Fellow of Sidney

Sussex and is credited with making an abortive attempt to become Master of that College in his twenties. He was soon appointed to be Headmaster of Harrow and later Dean of Peterborough. My grandfather, Spencer, and his brother, Montagu, were both at Trinity. Montagu also became Headmaster of Harrow at an early age, following this with the Mastership of Trinity from 1886 until 1918. His namesake, my father, was a Fellow and later, on retirement from public life, Master of Pembroke.

My father's political gifts, and any I may possess, came from his mother, Mary Kendall of Pelyn, Lostwithiel, Cornwall. At Trinity I have Reynolds' portrait of Mary Kendall's direct ancestor of the same name. Reynolds painted this in 1744 when he was still learning from Hudson, near Plymouth. Mary Kendall of that day went out to her sittings in a carriage from Pelyn. Gilbert in his *History of Cornwall* says, 'This truly respectable family is of considerable antiquity in the county of Cornwall and has perhaps sent more representatives to the British Senate than any other in the United Kingdom. Richard Kendall, the first of the name which is preserved on record, was seated at Trewndy in the parish of Dulce and served in Parliament for Launceston in the reign of Edward III, anno 1368. His descendants had the honour of representing in succeeding Parliaments, the boroughs of Liskeard, Lostwithiel, East and West Looe in the county of Cornwall, together with several towns in the county of Devon.' The last Member was the old Squire Nicholas who sat for East Cornwall from 1852 until 1868. He was a Liberal and organized the West Country for Gladstone. The main Kendall phalanx had sat before the Reform Bill and mostly at a time when Cornwall had been granted by the Tudors no less than forty seats. This family, like many others, were part of the unsung band of country gentlemen who have served England throughout many generations without attracting attention in history books. One was beheaded in the reign of Henry VIII, another was Governor of Barbados in the time of William III, and Nicholas Kendall was Chief Magistrate of Gibraltar. Surprisingly, the family was never ennobled.

Lord Dunboyne, the genealogist of the Butler family, tells me that we are related a very long way back to the Butlers of

Ireland. It was suggested that I take Saffron Walden into my name to distinguish it from the old Butler titles.

It was probably the Kendall blood which influenced my uncle, Sir Geoffrey Butler, to become Burgess, or M.P., for Cambridge University, and I was to follow him into the House as Member for Saffron Walden and my son Adam as Member for Bosworth. We were the first Butlers to take to politics rather than sticking to academic life, just as my father and his elder brother, Harcourt, were the first Butlers to go to India as members of the I.C.S. Both eventually became Governors of Provinces—Harcourt of the United Provinces and also of Burma, and my father of what were then known as the Central Provinces. But that was not until 1925. At the date of my birth, on 9th December, 1902, he was Settlement Officer of Campbellpur District.

The residence allotted to this young functionary was an ancient *serai*, which means inn or rest-house, attached to the fort at Attock where

> 'The Kabul and the Indus meeting
> Splash with the music of their greeting.'

The fort had been built by the Mogul Emperor Akbar as a stopping place on his journeys to Kashmir. I was told by Lord Slim that he lived there when he was a Gurkha Captain, and in the hot weather used to take his little riflemen to sleep on the bridge and be cooled by the night airs coming down the gorge. We were visited at Attock by my mother's eldest brother, George Adam Smith—later Principal of Aberdeen University and Moderator of the Church of Scotland—who wrote a poem for me as the newest arrival. It contained the topographical couplet cited above, and ended with the lines:

> 'Rulers win their right to rise
> By service and by sacrifice.'

I quoted this excellent sentiment, though execrable rhyme, in a speech when I was Chancellor of the Exchequer. But the Press were bored.

My father spoke and wrote the main languages of India and could get along in a number of local dialects. His classical training gave him a clear mind which quickly grasped political problems and legal tangles. He was extremely well up in Indian history, though untouched by the arts. I have never known a human being with quite such an acute sense of responsibility; it made him morose and anxious, but it was used at all times for the good of the people of India as he saw their needs. They repaid him with friendship and love. As for his personal life, this was happy because of his partnership with my mother, which span out its ideal course till they died within months of each other in 1952 and 1953. We children depended chiefly on my mother since in India my father was often away. I do not know whether it is trite to describe oneself as the devoted son of a loving mother. But I certainly was. My father used to get bored at times by her cutting out and putting in a series of volumes called the Rab Books all references to me from the earliest days, as long as she lived. I certainly found it good to have someone whose love was permanent and all-surrounding. She supported me in all my ventures with grace and shrewdness.

The Indian tradition on my mother's side was already two generations old when I was born. Her father, George Smith, an early editor of the Calcutta paper then called *The Friend of India*, now *The Statesman*, originally went to India from the port of Leith to teach in a school for Eurasian boys. He came under the influence of two notable missionaries, Carey and Marshman, who had a number of interests at Serampore, near Calcutta, including a college and the publication of a daily newspaper. He married a woman of brains and character, Janet Adam, and they had ten children who were sent home in batches to live with 'the aunts' on the shores of the Firth of Forth. Everything the Smith family did seems to have been original. Uncle Will kept a tame bear in his tea-garden in Assam and went all the way to Lahore to buy a tombstone for his wife's grave. Uncle Charles, Resident in Gilgit and known as 'Smith of Asia', conducted an almost independent far-frontier policy to the great annoyance of Simla. Aunt Kate was baptized by a missionary called Mr. Jagadisha Battarcharjia. Uncle Dunlop was Private Secretary to Lord Minto and his diaries, edited by Martin Gilbert, have been published under the title *A Servant of India*, to which I have written a preface and an epilogue. All these sagas were woven into our childhood, mixed up with *Stories of Indian Gods*

and Heroes with which we were as familiar as with Hans Andersen
or Grimm; also tales about Akbar, Babar, Humayon and, best of
all, the wonderful legends of Rajasthan. So that when we went
to live in Kotah State we felt completely at home.

My father was Settlement Officer at Kotah for about five years.
The work entailed camping throughout the cold weather,
moving from village to village to assess the land. We all went
to camp, with a train of camels carrying tents, furniture and
crockery. My sister Iris and I travelled in a cart pulled by two
ponies called Peter and Polly; our parents rode everywhere and
sometimes changed to elephant transport for crossing rivers.
The tents were pitched by a grove of trees and we were let loose
to wander in and out of tent-ropes and to climb the tent sides
and slide down them. We went quite near the table placed by the
office where father sat to receive petitions and give judgement
and settle quarrels. Thus we witnessed the grass roots of government. Before sunset, the parents took a ride round looking at
crops and land boundaries. In the very early morning, when the
sun rose in a pink blaze over the edge of some huge plain, we
were taken from our beds, wrapped in dressing-gowns, and
bundled into the cart to drowse till the breakfast stop, where
we all paused to eat and dress properly till the camel train
caught up with us. I remember the unfenced fields stretching
away endlessly, dwarfing my puny gaze, and little realized that
I would for many years (thirty-six in all) live and breathe in the
wide spaces of the wheat-fields of Saffron Walden.

The Maharao of Kotah was known to his people as Andatta,
the Breadgiver, and we called him that too. He gave us four
splendid stuffed animals on wheels; their names were Bear,
Lion, Elley and Dog. Lion had an apparatus on his back similar
to an old-fashioned pull-up lavatory plug and, when you pulled
it, Lion growled. The Andatta was a kindly figure, a happy man,
an enlightened ruler. His title was no empty one, so how was it
possible for us to grow up feeling foreign, let alone superior,
when such a romantic father-figure formed part of our childhood memories? When I compare notes with my sister, Iris
Portal, who was next to me in age, we feel that India will always
be with us—the rich smells of wet marigolds round the neck,
when we were greeted after a journey, the burning dung fires in

the evening, the stone bathroom, the tent and rope smells, the horses and ponies, the deluge of the monsoon, the brilliant-coloured shrubs coming out after the rains. But this is to speak a Rupert Brooke recital, 'These I have loved'. What is enduring is that we children ever after regarded Indians, and by extension all coloured people, as friends. We were never infected by the Memsahib complex of 'keeping them in their place'. My time as a small child in Kotah made me sympathetic by instinct and in my innermost being when in later life the Indians were seen to seek and expect self-government.

Even after so many years—and I can only have been seven at the time—I can remember the change of atmosphere when we left Rajputana for Lahore, then the capital city of the Punjab. It was here that my youngest sister Dorothy was born. She has always been my close friend in the family. We moved from a Hindu country to an Islamic one and from the sixteenth to the nineteenth century. The year must, in fact, have been 1909; for my father then became Deputy Commissioner of Lahore District. Though he still did much district work, we camped no longer and lived in an urban or suburban climate, and the steel frame of the administration closed around us. We went to parties with other English children, and for picnics to beautiful formal Mogul gardens, with sheets of water reflecting domes and minarets. Here there was no dust, no dancing horses, no hyenas running near the camp in the early morning. India drew back a little and only came near if we went to the canal area when the waters had been withdrawn, and played in the sand, watching troops of little slit-nosed donkeys carrying burdens to and fro and slow bullock carts weaving along the road. Thus the seasons rolled around and from Lahore, as from Kotah, every spring we took the big train to Kalka in the Himalayan foot-hills, and changed into what I called the 'Little Ill Train' because we were always sick in it as we jerked up the gradients and round the bends to Simla. Simla was like a garden city plastered on the side of huge mountains. Either you looked down over vast precipices, or away to distant peaks with a tremendous snow-line which appeared as the ramparts of heaven. We walked along the hill paths with a pony on a lead in front and the rickshaw trailing behind. Great masses of rhododendrons and dark deodars marched up the hills and there were bright flowers with red tongues and cobra-shaped hoods. We were told they would poison us if we touched them, but they were just outsize lords-and-ladies.

We did not have an Indian enclosed childhood such as Kipling describes in *Something of Myself*. We had Nanny, who was of Aberdeen granite and who organized every detail of our lives and of the household in general. We did not learn to speak the vernacular freely and the Indian scene was filtered through Nanny's astringent personality. Ghokal, our father's bearer, was of the Bearer caste, the people who originally only bore palanquins. It is a high caste and Ghokal had to have three hours off in the middle of the day to take his midday meal and perform the necessary purifications connected with it. Mother explained this to us and we accepted it as perfectly normal behaviour. It even occurred to us that Ghokal had to purify a great deal because of his contacts with us—technical untouchables. He was a stately man, not genial at all, and a strong ally of Nanny's.

One day when out riding round Jakko, I ordered my *sais* to let go of the reins. Galloping round a corner, I was thrown and hopelessly broke my right arm. The *sais* did not catch up and the first to pass was a Sikh who 'passed by on the other side' and left me. All my life, especially when I was Under-Secretary for India, I was quite unjustly cautious of Sikhs. Eventually I was picked up and taken to the Walker Hospital where I suffered a big burn on my arm from a hot-water bottle while I was being X-rayed. Later my arm got Waltman's Contraction and I had to spend many years having it massaged and treated. My father's sorrow was terrible. He was brought up in the public school tradition and felt that my whole future as an athlete would be prejudiced. Indeed this proved to be so.

A penalty of British rule in India was the non-continuance of the family residence. The adults went home at sixty, or stayed in some now neglected grave. The children all left abruptly about the age of eight, sometimes never to see the East again and to be segregated, as Plato may have wished, from their parents and brought up to be, if possible, philosopher kings. I went to a typical preparatory school at The Wick, Hove. The

Headmaster was a remarkable man related to Thring of Uppingham, but I remember less of him than of his sister, who was very stern with us. The Captain Scott tragedy happened during my early time there, and if ever we were careless with our food, Mary Thring would say: 'Captain Scott would have given his eyes for that egg.' We became less and less appreciative of the great explorer.

The 1914 War started when I was eleven. We were walking down from Bourton House to church on that August Sunday. The harvest was early and I can remember passing a big rick already collected. We were told proudly that the B.E.F. had landed in France. I was at Marlborough, nearly sixteen, when the war ended. Did I realize then, as I do now, how nearly I had missed that, to so many, overpowering experience? At the Wick I simply noticed that the masters were leaving, in several cases never to return. At Marlborough I realized more because my cousin Charles Sorley was killed after only five months at the front, and George and Beppo Adam Smith were also killed in action. George was a close friend of Walter Elliott's at Glasgow University. I remember his Gordon kilt when he stayed with us on leave at the Manse at Bourton and my mother's pride in him. He would certainly have come into public life and made his name. Young as I was I gained the impression of the irreparable loss bequeathed to us by those years. When I first entered the House of Commons in 1929 the cloak-room attendants zealously and persistently called us all by military titles. I was ashamed not to have earned my title but as they were so determined I bore it for a year or two until I became a Minister. But of course no one in the House was under the illusion that I had served. The politics of the 'thirties and 'forties would have been very different in Britain but for the sacrifices of the First World War. Certainly those of us who were called to office would not have come to the front so early and with so little experience.

My sister and I spent most of our holidays in the war years with Uncle Dunlop, Sir James Dunlop Smith, then retired from India and Political A.D.C. at the India Office. He lived at 25 Ovington Square in a comfortable household run by his sister, Aunt Minnie. On Sunday evenings those of the Indian Princes who were in London, either on leave from the war front or arranging assistance to the cause from behind the lines, came to supper and we were allowed to be at the meal. They talked in Hindi with Uncle Dunlop—deep voices making a soft thunder —and though sombre in khaki uniform, they were magnificent-looking men: Sir Ganga Singh of Bikaner; Sir Pertab Singh; also the rulers of various Moslem states, the latter with subtle differences of dress and cast of features from the Hindus, which Uncle Dunlop explained to us afterwards. He also read aloud Henry Newbolt's poem about Sir Pertab Singh defying caste rules in order to carry to burial the corpse of a young Englishman who had died in Jodhpur. This because the boy's father had been Sir Pertab's friend.

By this time I had got to be known by my initials Rab which my father had deliberately designed as a useful sobriquet for life. I fancied myself for an Eton scholarship, and so did my mother, but my schoolmaster was very discouraging. However I went up and sat the papers. At the end of the second day a man in a gown read the names of those who were requested to stay and continue. Mine was not included. I went and spoke to him, asking if there had been a mistake; he said there had not. My mother, who met me on the bridge in the High Street, hid her disappointment and cheerfully insisted that we must buy a camera immediately. So I took a picture of her on the bridge, but this did not come out either, due to faulty exposure. The question then was: where was I to go? The family indicated Harrow, where a place was reserved for me, but the House had a Butler housemaster, a Butler head of the House and some others including a cousin with whom I was to share a room. My Uncle Montagu and my great-grandfather had both been Headmasters at the age of 26 and it was regarded as a definite rebellion when I refused to go. We looked around and chose Marlborough since it was near Bourton, my Uncle Cyril Butler's family home, and because my cousin Charles Sorley, the war poet, had been there. His mother was my mother's liveliest sister and his father the Professor of Moral Philosophy at King's. Marlborough was most accommodating: one of the housemasters, Colonel Wall, had been at Trinity with Montagu Butler and offered me a place. I accordingly went there in the autumn of 1916.

Marlborough had many advantages, especially the Downs and

the Forest. During my time Cyril Norwood came as Master and revolutionized the curriculum, so that the school came right to the front in obtaining scholarships at the universities. When I meet John Betjeman we sometimes discuss our time at Marlborough and feel we have not contributed enough. But what I found difficult was the very slight provision made in my day for debating and literary activities. I helped to revive a society for the former, and attended the rare occasions when the Literary Society met; all this has now been considerably changed and improved. The advantage of day school education, such as my mother's family had enjoyed in Scotland, is that the children are half the time in the world: the great need of a public school is to look outward and not into its monastic self. There is no doubt that Norwood made Marlborough a very good school of its type. But, as Charles Sorley wrote in his *Letters from Germany and from the Army* (which had been printed privately and given to a few personal friends):

> 'The penalty of belonging to a public school is that one plays before a looking-glass all the time and has to think about the impression one is making. And as public schools are run on the worn-out fallacy that there can't be progress without competition, games as well as everything degenerate into a means of giving free play to the lower instincts of men.'

Certainly in my day games were everything; a boy had only to shine at games to come to the top and be encouraged by the masters to assert himself. I did manage to play cricket for the House. My arm made me an expert in blocking, so I was put in first and exasperated the bowlers. I never made many runs so did not get my colours, but considering my inevitable lack of prowess at games I think I was very fairly treated in being made a prefect early. It must, however, be said that when I became Minister of Education and Home Secretary I had not much personal knowledge of corporal punishment since I could not use a cane even if I had wanted to.

My last year at Marlborough was a more intense and satisfying experience: for I then changed from classics to modern languages, literature and history. Leonard Whibley, brother of Charles Whibley, who was my father's tutor at Pembroke, said that he divided his pupils into those 'clever with an interest' and those 'clever anyway'. He advised me to stick with the former group, since it was not only legitimate but wise to be captivated by your subject rather than to do it as a duty. I had found classics as taught at Marlborough very unrewarding. I started in the Classical Shell with a master called Trilby Turner, whose method was to give rapid exercises and then to yell 'Square your marks.' There were six exercises, so if you got only two you made four, and a respectable result of four gave you only sixteen out of thirty-six. It followed that demotion, or even being reported for caning by one's housemaster, was a common occurrence. Although I reached the Classical Fifth before providentially changing, I never knew about the death of Socrates, never read Aristophanes or Euripides, and never studied the oratory of Demosthenes and Pericles or the philosophy of Plato and Aristotle until much later in life. No doubt in the Classical Sixth I would have learned, like Charles Sorley, to appreciate the *Odyssey* and to be able to quote from the *Iliad*, Achilles speaking: 'Died Patroclus too who was a far better man than thou.'

Sorley had been shot in the head as he led his company at the 'hairpin' trench near Hulloch after the opening of the battle of Loos. I went to Marlborough under his inspiration and have tried to assess his importance to the poetry of the war. Earlier critics, like Robert Nichols in *An Anthology of War Poetry* and Robert Graves and Laura Riding in *A Survey of Modernist Poetry*, gave very special praise; the former comparing his temperament with that of Corneille, the latter bracketing his name with Rosenberg and Owen. I agree with John Press, who did as much as anyone to keep Sorley's memory alive and who wrote in 1966 in the *Review of English Literature* that he had great potential, but being killed at twenty he had not the time to compete with Owen. He would undoubtedly have had a fine career at Oxford and might then, before returning to drama and poetry, have turned to social work—for he had very strong views on social reform, including the provision of greater opportunities in education, which I much admired. I was probably more influenced at the time by the Marlborough poems than the war verse. I found running on the Downs a great joy and change, and I used to quote to myself his lines from 'The Song of the Ungirt Runners':

> 'We swing ungirded hips,
> And lightened are our eyes,
> The rain is on our lips,
> We do not run for prize.
> We know not whom we trust
> Nor whitherward we fare,
> But we run because we must
> Through the great wide air.'

Within sight of the Downs my Uncle Cyril, oldest of my father's family, had his estate and guarded his rich collection of Chinese treasures and modern pictures. The former, products of his Far Eastern tours, were mostly stored away, except for Ming and Tang horses and bowls. But the modern English pictures occupied every wall. He was himself Chairman of the Contemporary Art Society and made Bourton a home for painters. They were very glad to have a weekend to relax, to walk on the Downs, to get their clothes washed in his laundry, which was under my room in the north wing, and to take home vegetables. Many a sketch and drawing was left behind and many an oil painting purchased. Wilson Steer was in the dining-room with portraits of the family. Sickert and McEvoy filled in the gaps. McEvoy was especially represented and enjoyed painting in the downland country. Augustus John left endless drawings, many of his high women, along the first-floor passages. Tonks, who was then head of the Slade, had pride of place with a cat playing with a necklace in the library, and a birdcage in the hall. He was frequently there for weekends. Derwent-Lees painted the rock garden and the drive before instability intervened to check his course. His pictures of the South of France were also in the music room. When my Uncle Cyril died his collection was gradually sold. I wish I had had the wit to buy. But I was lucky enough to acquire some drawings and paintings by John, Sickert and Tonks which my fond Aunt May parted with.

While just eighteen I left Marlborough and soon afterwards was to be found *chez* M. le Pasteur Vernier du Pontet in a manse residence at Abbeville. I had made two decisions. The first was to learn French properly. Each day I read Gautier, whose vocabulary is the widest of any French writer I know, and wrote down all the new words. I then rehearsed these with the Pasteur the next day. My second decision was to go to the local Collège Courbet as a pupil. I was put in the 'classe de philo' and was rapidly learning the classics by heart, particularly La Bruyère and Corneille. The form-master's name was Biendîné, which led to obvious and easy jests which he ignored. There was a terrible smell in the class-room, and only later did I discover that one of the town latrines was on the wall right outside the window. A great spirit of *égalité* and *fraternité* swept through the school. The sons of officers and of bourgeois mixed with the tradesman's family and the artisan's. We shook hands mostly with our left hands in the early morning. My particular friend's father was at the signal box at Abbeville station and I was allowed to watch nostalgically as the Grands Express Européens roared by from Calais and Boulogne, hauled by their majestic steam engines swaying on the points after gliding through the free fast run of the bloody valley of the Somme. I was very lonely in the cramped small-town surroundings of Abbeville and the railway station seemed a point of contact with home and with the wider world.

It was therefore a blessed relief to receive an invitation to go as tutor to Alain, the son of Robert de Rothschild. Alain had no intention of spending his vacations overworking. I did try to initiate him into the legends and romance of Greece and Rome but he appeared to know more about this subject than I did. So we passed two idyllic summers at Les Fleurs, Bênerville par Blonville, Calvados, and at the Château de Laversine near Chantilly. There we went for September. We rode in the woods and very often in the evenings, when the children had gone to bed, I went to my room and set about an original work on the 'Esprit Gaulois' which I submitted to the Baron Robert for ruthless criticism. My knowledge of France and the French was electrically advanced in this friendly, family atmosphere.

Meanwhile I had been home to Pembroke and sat for an exhibition at my father's college. This I obtained, and for two years studied French literature and French thought under the benign influence of Professor Oliver Prior. He was a new head of the Department, and laboured to make it a success by staying up all night before his lectures so that he might bring them to perfection. His wife became a lifelong friend and they looked after me on many a vital occasion. To write a book that would carry forward his tradition remains one of the unrealized ambitions of my life.

In the summer of 1923, after getting my First in French and being made a scholar of Pembroke, I decided—since at that time I was destined for the Diplomatic Service—that a little German might also be useful. I got much more than I bargained for. My time in Austria was spent with the Stolberg-Stolbergs, fugitives from their own State at Wernigerode at the foot of the Harz Mountains in Germany. The whole of the Krems Valley was populated by émigrés of whom the Windischgraetz family were our nearest neighbours. I thought of Hardy's poem about the man 'harrowing clods' and 'thin smoke without flame' rising from the burning couch-grass. He concludes that 'this will go onward the same—though Dynasties pass'. Dynasties had passed all round in Germany and in Austria and here I was with them gathering in the hay and cleaning out the byres. The Graf was a war casualty and had been advised to work out of doors. He was bitterly anti-French and one day seized a cock with a great shout of 'Gallia' and threw it right over the farm-house. The Gräfin was a Prinzessin Reuss and took me to visit her brother the Prinz at Ernstbrunn on the Danube. Regina was a remarkable woman of an intelligence quite out of the ordinary and a great power of affection. I felt at first that with her four children she was of a much older generation, but this was not really so and we became warm friends. Seeing how difficult life was for her in exile, I brought her a breath of the outer world; in turn she provided me with a family home while my parents were still in India. I also became very attached to her younger sister, Ola, at Ernstbrunn, where we explored the castle and the woods, later to be taken over by the Russians. Life was very sweet and the language came easily. We climbed the great Kremsmauer and found fire lilies on the heights. We visited Vienna and tasted the inflation which was then raging. So we turned back to the farm and its simple hospitality.

I returned from Austria to Bourton and then up to Cambridge as Secretary of the Union. My studies were not such as to alarm me. I had decided to stay up for four years in all, partly to avoid taking a second tripos too soon and partly because of the likelihood that I would be President of the Union during 1924. My third year was, therefore, to be devoted to the sort of general education which ought to be recommended for everybody. A course on 'the weather' was attended by sporting young men in very large-squared plus-fours, usually with their arms round a young woman's waist and accompanied by retrievers. A course on Germany kept up the progress I had made in Austria. I also attended Sir James Frazer's lectures on his masterpiece of anthropology *The Golden Bough*, and looked in occasionally on lectures on philosophy.

Politics and the Union claimed an increasing share of my time. I had joined the University Conservative Association of which my uncle, Sir Geoffrey Butler, was the architect and for years the President. He was the author of *The Tory Tradition*, a book first published in 1914 and still relevant, which drew precepts from Bolingbroke, Burke, Disraeli and Salisbury and, more important perhaps, illuminated, within the context of history, their political habits of mind. Geoffrey's own subtle and interesting mind left a considerable impact on the young men of his generation, and he did much to bridge the gulf between leading Parliamentarians in London and 'the young idea' in Cambridge. Everyone seemed to wish to come to his rooms at Corpus Christi—and how greatly stimulated we undergraduates were by the lavish entertainment we received and the celebrated people we met. I well remember the day that Winston Churchill came, full of his new constituency of Epping which, he said, had 'a little bit of all England in it'. He had just been to Ireland and, with characteristic *brio*, had somehow managed to travel on the bridge of a destroyer.

I became an official of the Association and shared duties with Geoffrey Lloyd, Charles Smythe, later to be Canon of Westminster, and my great friend Willie Wolfson. Willie was a Russian who had been rescued from the revolution by the British Navy at Novorossiysk. He had aristocratic leanings and political views several miles to the right of mine. But thrown into Pembroke among rowing blues, rugger blues, cricket blues, and other hearties who would knock over your mug of beer as soon as say 'good morning', the charm and elegance of Willie's intellect, manners and appearance constituted an oasis of college civilization. Though he went into business and not politics we remained good companions for thirty years until one day, in 1954, he flew out with me to Australia when I was Chancellor of the Exchequer and warned me that if a window gave way or the structure failed, we should all be swept out in a great blast. It was a premonition of death. On his return journey something like this happened in the Comet off Elba.

Conservatism at the Union was strong, and the debates were lively. Patrick Devlin, then as now, was the wittiest extempore speaker. Selwyn Lloyd was a Liberal. Michael Ramsey, also a Liberal, showed no archiepiscopal tendencies. Geoffrey Lloyd so impressed Stanley Baldwin that he was recruited straight into the Private Office at No. 10. I had a different effect on the Prime Minister. On 11th March, 1924, during the brief nine-month period in which he had been out of office, the Union debated the motion 'That this House has the highest regard for Rhetoric'. Baldwin spoke last against the motion and Mitchell Banks, K.C., spoke in favour. I was in the chair as President for the first time. Baldwin followed his accustomed line, saying that rhetoric had done great harm in the world and that it was the harlot of the arts. The voting came out exactly equal. Considering that the Union lived by rhetoric I gave my casting vote against Baldwin and the motion was carried. When I saw the great man off at the station next morning he took me over to the bookstall and bought me a shocker, saying that the sin of intellectualism was worse than death. He besought me to remember this in my future public life. This was indeed a vicarious tit for tat. For Baldwin had suffered from my great-uncle, Montagu Butler, both as Master of Harrow and of Trinity. Indeed, he had once been discovered with an indecent book in his room at Harrow and was never allowed to forget it.

The Union was a wonderful training ground and simply should not be missed by those at the University aiming at public life. The contact with members of opposition parties is not at all unlike the House of Commons and the oratory is if anything more spiced. I was never able to make a speech of unrelieved humour, but very often a little seriousness succeeds as well. One reward of being President in 1924 was that I was invited to visit America in the company of A. P. Marshall and Gerald Sparrow. We debated two main motions, one asserting that democracy was not consistent with personal liberty and the other favouring closer relations with the Soviet Union. Both were designed to shock and so to attract audiences. We started in Nova Scotia eventually reaching McGill at Montreal, where I met H. A. L. Fisher, little realizing that twenty years on I was to follow his Education Act. Debating was not the strong point of the eastern universities with the exception of the girls' college at Vassar. We usually spoke extempore, while the others, notably at Cornell, sat with a team of nine—three speakers, three librarians, and three trainers. The job of the trainers was to see that the speakers had a good steak before the debate and to watch over their health. The librarians sat with card indexes behind the speakers and, if moved, passed a card with an apt quotation for immediate use. These varied from the classics to Lloyd George's latest utterance. It was not surprising that with all these ministrations the opposition speakers were somewhat stilted.

I had now a heavy final year before me so as to pull off a First in History. I had thought long about my special period—a typical Cambridge system—and had decided on the four years of Peel's premiership which culminated in the repeal of the Corn Laws. A third of my time was spent on this fascinating subject, reading all the standard works, the old issues of *The Times* and the *Annual Register*. I used to know by heart many of the names in the division list when Disraeli defeated Peel on the Irish Coercion Bill. Several of the names repeated themselves in my time in the Commons. Peel's heart was wrung when he saw the Tory squires trooping in against him. My sympathies were for Peel against Disraeli. But there was far more to learn than partisanship—monetary policy, relations with the Queen, the penalties of splitting a party.

My other main decision was to read International Law with Professor Pearce Higgins. I was introduced to Whewell's notebooks by Geoffrey Butler who also let me see his notes for his own book on International Law. As the examination approached my health deteriorated for the second time in a year and I got jaundice. Ashley Clarke[1] ferried me out to see his father, a doctor in Norfolk. He said that I must take the exam in spite of my illness and recommended moving to stay with the beloved Oliver Priors, taking champagne twice a day and some special pills. He said that after the exam this treatment must be countered by going for a definite cure to a spa. I saw Will Spens and Geoffrey Butler who were very doubtful about my taking the papers but admired my resolution. When I got in the great Arts School I found Peel quite congenial, but at half-time on the International Law had made no progress. I tore up all that I had written, took six sheets of foolscap and wrote six answers, one on each page. I later heard that I came first in International Law and in the first division of the Firsts for the whole tripos. Immediately I was bundled off to Strathpeffer Spa by my mother and kept there for several weeks, my only solace being a number of heart-warming messages from Geoffrey Lloyd, Pat Devlin, Willie Wolfson, the family *in toto*, and what pleases me to look back on today, Harry Hollond of Trinity, Sheppard the Provost of King's, Arnold now Lord McNair, Anderson the Master of Caius and many others. But the best letter of all came from Will Spens of Corpus who as a result of the exam wrote offering me a Fellowship there to operate from the autumn. This I readily accepted since it meant that I should be immediately independent and earning my own living. Corpus had a small and distinguished high table including Arthur Goodhart, later Master of University College, Oxford, my uncle Geoffrey Butler, and my contemporary Charles Smythe. I combined my two subjects by lecturing on Modern French History, namely the Third Republic, and considering that the hour was 9 a.m., I had quite a reasonable sprinkling of attendance.

That summer of 1925 I was invited to Norway by Sydney Courtauld who had been at Newnham while I was at Pembroke. She was cousin of my friends John and Arthur Pedder who had been at my prep school with me. My first introduction to her had been at her home at Stanstead where the Pedder boys were often invited. We became firm friends at Cambridge meeting frequently in the plays and meetings of the French Society of

[1] Sir Ashley Clarke, G.C.M.G., sometime Ambassador in Rome.

THE AUTHOR, AGED SIX AND THREE-QUARTERS, WITH HIS BEARER (*right*) AT LAHORE AND (*below*) AT NEWSTEAD, SIMLA.

AT PREP SCHOOL

THE AUTHOR'S PARENTS
SIR MONTAGU AND LAD
BUTLER

which I was the Secretary. Her mother Lil and Sir John Atkins, the senior members of the party, fished all the best pools and we were left to go on expeditions down the fjords in a paddle-steamer called the *StaatsRad Ridderwold*. I had never heard of this statesman, but hoped that the political career I plotted would also result in a paddle-boat being called after me. The romance of the fjords helped to develop into love a friendship which had started in Cambridge. On return we announced our engagement. My future mother-in-law, a formidable Irish-woman, appeared to accept me for two reasons: first, that I was a member of the Carlton Club; and second, that when carving I could make a partridge do six. My father also approved. He said that Sydney supplemented sides of my character which he thought deficient, and referred repeatedly to her 'astringent spurs'—if this adjective and noun can go together. Next April we were married at a Corpus church, built by Wren—St. Mary Abchurch—by the Master, Pearce, later Bishop of Derby. Geoffrey Butler was best man. Lil gave a function at the Ritz and then despatched us to Cambridge.

My parents-in-law were then living at 20 Portman Square. We stayed there on one occasion for the night and later atten-ded two or three typical London 'socialite' functions. At one of these Sam Courtauld took Sydney and me aside and said, 'I hope you will both understand if I give this house and its contents to the nation.' We, being young and appreciative of his high notions, warmly agreed. The house has for long since been the Courtauld Institute and the great majority of the pictures are under London University in a lonely gallery in Woburn Place. When I breakfasted in the dining-room Manet's 'Bar' was above the mantelpiece and the 'Pavayeurs' close beside. Gauguin's 'Never More' was in Lil's room and the drawing-room was filled with Monet and other treasures. Arthur Lee, Lord Lee of Fare-ham, insisted on the pictures going to London University in-stead of the Tate or the National Gallery as I wanted. Sam had a great eye for the pictures. He was helped by Lee mostly over his English collection and by Percy Moore Turner over his French. He gave comparatively reasonable sums for the great impres-sionist masterpieces.

I had long intended to go into politics. I therefore made the decision to give up the Fellowship at Corpus and to go round the world for a year as a preparation for entering public life. The opportunity of seeing my parents in India after so many years of separation had a powerful effect. In addition, my health had not completely recovered, and Sir John Atkins thought that a year away with sea voyages would make all the difference. Accordingly we set out in September of 1926 to visit my parents in the Central Provinces of India. Before leaving I called on L. S. Amery, then Secretary of State, to obtain introductions in Australia, New Zealand and Canada.

This was the time that I supplemented my classical deficiencies, though only by reading translations. I was impressed by the lead that Plato gives to education, but could make little progress with Aristotle. I travelled with Xenophon across Asia Minor and was easily absorbed in Herodotus. I studied Cicero and Demosthenes for style—only to find that I got more from a four-volume edition of the speeches of the younger Pitt which themselves came from classics. I took Macaulay's *History* with me, and read the lot, Doughty for the Red Sea, Froude for *Oceana*, Robert Louis Stevenson's *In the South Seas*, and many new authors in Australia and New Zealand on the experiments in state organizations and profit-sharing. While in India I read books on Dufferin, Curzon and William Bentinck, and there conceived or admitted the great ambition of my life which was to be Viceroy of India. I could think of no position in the world which so well combined administration, concentration, diplomacy and presence.

To stay at Government House, Nagpur, and to indulge in *shikar* parties in Kipling's own jungles was memorable. I shot a tiger by good luck, so that was a Sheerkhan, and sitting up at night I got Bagheera, the panther. The latter was shot through the heart and galloped away to be found dead in the scrub. But this meant a night of being accused of missing, a dawn patrol and the driving of a herd of bullocks before us until we found the body. The jungle camps were arrayed in the most princely way with fine tents and huge bonfires on which we heaped the local 'tendwa' wood.

In his province of Central India my father was a pioneer in bringing Congress representation into Government. But he paid for his advanced views, and was never given the honour or distinction he deserved, although serving the best part of ten years as Governor. I studied and enjoyed his patient methods of administration and his subtle intrigues with Congressman Tambe. But about my own political future he seemed to have some very strange views, which we discussed in lonely mountain walks at Pachmarhi. He thought that it was not in my line to take strong personal executive decisions. My forte was to be friends with all, impartial and diplomatic. He was in favour of my entering Parliament, but only for the purpose of becoming Speaker, a course he strongly recommended. When touring Delhi I did buy a book called *The Speaker of the House of Commons* by Dasent. But I didn't fancy the job. Indeed, at that time I thought it rather a soft option, little realizing the continuous strain to which the occupant of the chair is submitted, as was evidenced by the lasting fatigue experienced by W. S. Morrison.[1]

When we arrived at Sooke Harbour, British Columbia, there was a letter waiting for us from my wife's eldest cousin, William Courtauld, saying that the sitting member for the Saffron Walden constituency, William Foot Mitchell, was unlikely to stand at the next general election and that therefore the association would be looking for a new candidate from the autumn. He was of the opinion that I should put my name forward and he said that the family would support me. As we had made arrangements to be home by mid-September we stuck to our programme of crossing Canada by degrees, staying notably at the Emerald Lake Chalet and riding in the Rockies. We had some fine days out with guides and got some conception of the grandeur of the mountains.

About six weeks after we had returned home I was asked to attend a selection committee of the Saffron Walden Conservative Association at a hall in Great Bardfield in Essex. Unlike the crush of today there appeared to be no other candidates except a rumour that Sir Montague Barlow, sometime Minister of Labour, would like to be considered. I made a short speech, the main point of which was that we would choose our home in which to live in the constituency. I also said that I would devote full time to the job of nursing and representing. The hall was in

[1] The late Lord Dunrossil, sometime Governor-General of Australia.

a barn and Sydney and I were asked to withdraw to an outhouse. It appears that there was considerable doubt about my tender age and attainments. But after some delay we were summoned back and I was chosen as prospective candidate. When I look back on the good fortune that attended my youth, I must really count this one of the luckiest developments of my career.

During the year 1928 I set about as systematic a task as learning French at Abbeville. There were at least eighty villages and twenty or more greens and ends, together with four or five small towns in the Saffron Walden constituency. I visited two or three of these villages a night during the dark evenings accompanied by a film outfit from which I showed films of our Empire tour. These interested the villagers much more than political speeches and I usually followed up the show by a visit to the local pub. There I accepted beer, and stood a round only when eager faces showed that I had accepted enough. It is a great mistake for candidates, even years away from an election, to go into a pub and offer drinks all round immediately. It is better to receive half a pint than to give twenty. By the time I had done the round of villages, some of them more than once, I had gained quite a name as a friend. When the films were finished I asked for grievances and wrote them down in a book. During the summer months I went out just before dark with a mobile cinema. In the dark the agricultural labourers who normally did not attend political meetings sidled up and asked questions. The worst way to canvass is to conduct an old-fashioned political meeting with a Union Jack and a bottle of water.

Saffron Walden had been a Liberal seat. It had been in fact the seat of Jack Pease, later Lord Gainford, the Liberal Whip. The seat was always radical but also personal. However what really clinched my holding it with moderate majorities for thirty-five years was the organization. I fully believe that, when I left, this was one of the best in England. Every village had a small majority in my favour and these small margins made up a general majority. My first agent was the son of a publican. P. A. Hunt was most careful of the Women's Organization with the most attractive of whose members he had discreet affairs. This greatly advanced the cause since women are the key to success. I then had a genius, B. T. Powell, who brought the village organization to the highest pitch and got rewarded by becoming an area agent. Finally, I was lucky to be served by Kenneth Baker who helped my successor Peter Kirk to the well-assured position he deserved.

It was inspiring to feel the loyalty of over 10,000 subscribed members who only had to bring one person with them to make a victory certain. It was also refreshing to tour the undulating uplands of North Essex, waving with corn in the summer, shorn to stubble in the autumn, clothed with blue-green in the spring. The autumn elms have a deep blue-indigo colour. They stand begging to be painted with their brushy pantaloons festooning their lower trunks. I prided myself on knowing every by-road between these hamlets that I loved so well. I noticed that the local hunt and some sporting activities thrived on internecine strife, but for all the time I was in Saffron Walden, I had almost the same officers, my principal Chairman, Sir Reuben Hunt, lasting for twenty-four years. Nor was I ever accused of the sin of intellectualism, which Baldwin had assured me was a fate worse than death. I spoke simply and directly at village meetings.

The only time I came near to being defeated was in 1945—the election at which, as I describe later, I warned Churchill that we had no organization. That was precisely our trouble in Saffron Walden as elsewhere. Everything during the war had come to a standstill and I got home with only a thousand to spare over my jovial opponent and friend Stanley Wilson. Otherwise I was always respectably cushioned and in 1931 and 1935 had enormous majorities.

This was the happy seat from which I approached the Election of 1929. The Baldwin administration and the Churchill Chancellorship had not gained the full satisfaction of the public. It was not that there was anything particularly wrong. What was evident was a lack of initiative and a general sense that it was time for a change. There was a feeling that the Tories were persisting on too traditional lines and this gave an opening for the Labour Party. Besides this the Conservatives had not foreseen that the new rate demands would coincide with the most critical fortnight of the election. The fact is that I as a new candidate was fighting against the tide. As I darted from village to village, past the chestnut trees in full bloom, pink and white in the May of that year, I wondered anxiously what the result would be. I ended up with a 5,000 majority and was declared the proud victor from the steps of the Town Hall at Saffron Walden. Richard, my eldest son, had been born the January before. And my friends, the drovers from the Cattle Market, as they carried me to the Conservative Club, shouted, 'We'll make you Premier—or yer biby.'

CHAPTER TWO

THE LONG HAUL

'The Foreign Secretary rose to his feet and stared with gravity at the middle distance. His hearers waited uneasily; the question hung poised in the air. In the mind the lights were going out all over Saffron Walden. "The situation is not good," said the Minister, "and it is well it should be faced. I have done what I could. . . ." He paused, and made a gesture of resignation. "Yet the water-main has not yet come to Pebmarsh. Nor the sanitation. We have some way to go in north Essex. But" —he raised his eyes squarely and bravely—"we shall go forward, and be not dismayed. With a Conservative administration you shall see." The Rt. Hon. Richard Austen Butler, P.C., C.H., M.A., F.R.G.S., H.M. Secretary of State for Foreign Affairs, was back in his bailiwick, stumping the hustings of his own constituency. . . . This is the correct case of the local boy who made good—or at any rate goodish. The highest office may have eluded him, but he could say to Pebmarsh: "I did get my own house on the water-main after twenty-five years. *And* the sanitation." '

NO POLITICIAN should mind having his leg pulled a bit when it is done with such grace and humour as was shown by James Cameron, covering for the *Sun* my last election campaign in 1964. I had, as he indicates, kept my promise to the local association to make a permanent home in the constituency. Sydney and I lived for the first few years at Church Hall, Broxted, and moved in 1934 to Stanstead Hall, Halstead. I was churchwarden in both parishes over a period of thirty-six years. This is a long service in very small parishes where the churchgoers can be numbered on two hands, and provided an honourable apprenticeship to my dignified position

as Master of Trinity sitting in a fine stall untroubled with the
numerous and painstaking duties of warden. The various vicars
I nurtured were perplexed with problems of accommodation
and underpayment. The church fabric was in almost constant
need of repair. Our organ at Greenstead Green became infested
with mice, causing the incumbent of the day to place traps
baited with fragrant cheese. One Sunday I was distracted when
kneeling at the rails to find my right foot painfully seized in a
powerful clamp. However, I liked very much the simplicity
of the quiet village services and have never yet got used to
more elaborate ritual.

In the constituency and in London we brought up a family of
three sons and a daughter. Richard, in whose future the drovers
of Saffron Walden had shown such a jocular interest in 1929, is
now Deputy-President of the National Farmers Union. Adam,
born in 1931, followed me into the House of Commons by cap-
turing Bosworth in the 1970 general election. My youngest son
James has thrived in television and public relations activities.
Sarah, now married to Anthony Price, was born in wartime
during my period as Minister of Education. I was fortunate
indeed in having such a background and stimulus to my public
life; even more fortunate, after the tragedy of Sydney's death in
1954, to have discovered abundant happiness and support in my
second marriage.

My earliest preoccupation in politics was with the agricultural
interest, and this stemmed from Saffron Walden. I made my
maiden speech on a private members' day in October 1929 and,
in urging the need for action to assist home farming, stressed
the grave social consequences of unemployment in my own
constituency. All parties had made mass unemployment the
main issue of the election. But the Labour government of Ramsay MacDonald presided over a rapidly worsening situation.
Assuredly it was as much the victim of international circumstances as of its own domestic shortcomings. But both it, and its
Conservative critics, were accused of myopia and bad faith in a
long, magisterial letter to *The Times* from Harold Macmillan.
This letter, published on 27th May, 1930, expressed the hope
that Oswald Mosley, who had just resigned office because of the
rejection of his unorthodox programme to deal with un-

employment, would receive applause and support. Mosley, wrote Macmillan, wished to change the rules of the party political game; if they were not changed, 'many of us will feel that it is hardly worth while bothering to play at all'. At that time I had joined hands with Lord Lymington, Harold Balfour and Michael Beaumont in a band known as 'the boys' brigade' and we immediately penned a brief reply which was published in *The Times* next day and caused chuckling in the Opposition Whips' Office:

> 'Sir—We have read with interest and some surprise Mr. Harold Macmillan's letter published in your issue of today. When a player starts complaining "that it is hardly worth while bothering to play" the game at all it is usually the player, and not the game, who is at fault. It is then usually advisable for the player to seek a new field for his recreation and a pastime more suited to his talents.'

It is surprising to look back and remember how seriously Mosley was taken forty years ago. There was a yearning among some of the young and some of the intellectual for a more dynamic approach than was or could be provided by the Labour government up to 1931 or even the National government afterwards. I remember Mosley writing from the South of France to say, 'I am sitting on a rock by the sea, waiting for it all to come my way.' We stayed one weekend at Blickling with Philip Lothian. Felix Frankfurter, the American jurist, was there in a thoroughly gloomy mood, seemingly impressed that England was about to renounce her belief in liberty and throw herself into the follies of Fascism. Lothian declared that, although a life-long Liberal, he would have chosen a Fascist dictatorship rather than a Communist had he been compelled to make the choice, because the former would at least have preserved his property. This, Frankfurter said, summed up a point of view he had found expressed at Oxford. We both tried to reassure him that England was not made up of Oxford common rooms. But the episode troubled me profoundly. I wrote to Lord Brabourne: 'Evidently America and the world flatter us by believing that we are the last stronghold of representative institutions and fear that we shall jump into Mosley's arms, and that those who talk about reorganization and planning or the corporative state necessarily believe in Fascism.' Fortunately, from my angle of vision, the Mosley movement went through disorder and disrepute to ridicule and pantomime; those who had nosed round him and his policies having long before disengaged.

My own attitude to politics, as I have made clear in writing of Cambridge days, had been strongly influenced by my uncle Geoffrey Butler's essays on *The Tory Tradition*. In his preface to these, written in 1914, he had declared, 'Resistance to predatory attacks upon property, and the like, will always form important items in the Tory programme. But Tory doctrine loses all that is ennobling in its appeal, if it confines itself to these; if it fails, that is, to get down to the principles which lie beneath all such resistance. The great Tory leaders of the past challenge us to something more, and by their challenge show us the secret of their own irresistible example. The captains of Toryism in the past can be made the instructors of Toryism in the present: and the Tory tradition is the Tory hope.' Many years later I wrote my own preface to a revised edition of the book in which I sought to identify the legacy of these captains of Toryism. What they had left us, I insisted, was not a collection of causes for which we were obliged to die in the last ditch, nor a set of premises by whose consistent application we might infallibly regulate our conduct, but a mature tradition of political thought and behaviour which is neither fixed nor finished. This tradition at its best is responsive to the demands of each new age, empirical as to method, resourceful in expressing itself in popular idiom, though deeply conscious that the 'councils to which Time is not called, Time will not ratify'.

In attempting to conduct my own political career in con- formity with this tradition, as I interpreted it, there were periods —notably my years at the Treasury during the Churchill government—when the policies I applied were heartily approved by the entire party. But there were others when I was obliged to stand out as a champion of progress against substantial sections both in parliament and in the country. This was true of my pre- war work as a junior Minister for Indian self-government and, to a much lesser degree, of the negotiations I conducted as an elder statesman for the orderly achievement of African aspira-

tions. Similarly, there were some who regarded both my Education Act of 1944 and the Industrial Charter of 1947 as 'pink
socialism', while at the Home Office I incurred opprobrium for
eschewing the use of birch and cat. In no instance, however, did
I attempt to push politics beyond the limits of the possible—to
repeal some latter-day Corn Laws, so to speak, at the risk of
splitting my party irreparably or sending it for years into the
wilderness. Indeed I stopped short at 'the possible' in 1963, on
the very brink of Premiership, since I wished above all things to
preserve party unity. Clem Attlee once told me I had been 'too
good'. I might well have answered 'Tu quoque'. My temperament is that of a reformer, not of a rebel, and each of us must
act according to his character.

Peel was my mentor among historical figures, Stanley Baldwin among living statesmen. From him I learned both 'the
patience of politics'—the importance of biding one's time before
action—and the need in our modern democracy to associate the
Tory party with progressive and humane causes. Like many
political figures of the first order S.B. was much influenced by
his wife: I have heard her say to him in a moment of indecision
'Go on, Tiger'—what the wine merchants would call *une appella-
tion contrôlée*. By some of his colleagues, particularly the younger
and more irreverent, he was called Bonzo. During the financial
crisis of 1931 which led to the formation of the National government, Geoffrey Lloyd who was then in Baldwin's entourage
rang me at Broxted about the Leader's longed-for return from
Aix, and to confuse the local exchange gave me his message in
atrocious French: '*Le livre est foutu—le Bonzo va revenir demain.*' On the
other hand, with close friends like the Cunliffe-Listers, the
Bridgemans and the Davidsons, it was permissible to speak of
S.B. as 'God'. This got us into trouble whenever Edward Halifax
appeared, because he had ideas about who God really was.

Of all the Prime Ministers I served, and there were seven, I had
the most affection for Baldwin. He visited Stanstead and spoke
at a great fête in our grounds in July 1935. When one of our dogs,
whom he approached sympathetically, nipped his finger, he
said calmly: 'I quite understand how you feel; I want to do that
to every supplementary question in the House at this time of
year.' He then took an iodine pencil out of his pocket and

painted the scratch. The meeting was held beyond the tall elms in the park (which in the war I was pathetically to regard as a shield against low-flying aircraft). I had besought the P.M. to attack Lloyd George, but he replied sagely, 'That is exactly what he wants me to do.' I also asked him to speak about the Tithe, but he said that that was too controversial. It was, however, a masterly speech which greatly complimented our neighbour-hood because it addressed itself to all our local problems and showed his usual uncanny knowledge of the countryside, in-cluding the novels of Mary Webb, which in his idiosyncratic fashion he had both fingered and sniffed in my library. Waiting for the train at Kelvedon station he gave me some advice: 'I am so glad to have seen you at home in the country. You must go on coming down every weekend. Life in the country makes you see things whole and will enable you, like me, to steer between Harold Macmillan and Henry Page-Croft: then you will be on the path to Leader of the Conservative Party.'

I had been given a very different view of this 'steering' by Mac-millan himself, with whom I had a long talk one evening in March 1934. He then told me how regrettable and frustrating he found it that the left of the party, with which he associated himself, was always being played off against the right. 'You bring me and my friends down to the House to vote against Page-Croft and the die-hards on India, and then you get them along to vote against us on children's allowances.' This, he said, could not go on for long. Eventually one or other side would get fed up, and it was quite possible that those who held his views might turn in sheer desperation to the right and say, 'If you give us national reconstruction for the domestic economy, you can do what you like about the coloured races of India.' In the end Macmillan abandoned the Conservative party for a time on yet another issue, and his evident talents were not to be utilized in office until Churchill formed his first administration in 1940. I trod a different path, serving the establishment with patient if un-glamorous tenacity. This is not a sure recipe for success in achieving the highest political rewards. As I invariably inform young men who now come and ask me about politics, the lives of leaders the world over have frequently been advanced by colourful rebellion or resignation. This is not quite what Bacon

meant when he observed that all rising to great place is by a
winding stair. But, in their different ways, Churchill, Eden, Macmillan and, on the Labour side, Harold Wilson, have exempli-
fied the advantages of *reculer pour mieux sauter*.

My own career, by contrast, exemplifies the advantages of the
long haul, namely the steady influence one may exert by being
at all times on the inside. Of the thirty-six years that I served in
the House of Commons, the Conservative party was in power,
either alone or as the dominant partner of a coalition, for almost
twenty-seven. And with the exception of a few months at the
beginning of the National government I was a Minister of the
Crown whenever my party was in office. This span of twenty-six
and a half years was slightly exceeded by Churchill, and is of
course far less than Palmerston's record in the nineteenth century. It does, however, mean that I was a practitioner of the art
of the possible as long as anyone living in Britain today. I have
frequently been asked which post I enjoyed the most. If I am to
measure this by lasting achievement, the answer must be the
Ministry of Education. If I am to measure it by contemporary
and potential importance, the zenith was certainly reached at
the Treasury. It may be that had I had several years at the
Foreign Office in which to advance from the ballroom to the
casino, from the stately figures of 'the Lancers' to the poker-
faced bids of the gaming table, these retrospective reflections
might have been different.

Austen Chamberlain, at the end of a distinguished career,
brought four years at the Foreign Office to the climax of
Locarno. I was vouchsafed rather less than twelve months. The
Foreign Secretaryship, for which I asked in 1957 and could again
have expected in 1960, was withheld from me by Macmillan
throughout his Premiership. He chose instead to heap upon me
the honours of Pooh-Bah, crowning me simultaneously with the
cricketing cap of the Leader of the House, the policeman's hel-
met of the Home Secretary and the top hat of the Party Chairman. I found it very uncomfortable wearing these three pieces
of headgear at once and advise no one else to make the experiment. The House of Commons prefers to have as its head prefect
someone who is not in the very forefront of the party fray: the
party lieges who wish to be organized and influenced by their

chief resent his outside activities: and the government department which may be combined with the Chairmanship tends to suspect him of total partisanship.

A few years earlier I might have been unable to sustain this triple burden and clash of responsibilities. But 1959 was a turning point in my life. In that October Mollie Courtauld and I decided to get married. From that date I have felt that my personal strength and happiness were such that no political appointments or disappointments could disturb them. My main regret in leaving politics six years later was that it took her away from a sphere in which her grace and perception had found special fulfilment. A warm heart, excited by any manifestations of wrongdoing or oppression, enriches her talent for public affairs. We had known each other for years and lived as neighbours. Neighbourly love soon developed into devotion not only to each other but to our families. These were well known to Falkner Alison, then Bishop of Chelmsford and later of Winchester, who had helped us both in our previous trials and bereavements. We were married by him in Ashwell Church, Hertfordshire, in the presence of my four children and Mollie's six, who all joined in a family reception afterwards at the home of Mollie's daughter, Perina Fordham. Since the Commons was meeting almost immediately we had only four or five days' interlude in Rome. We spent each day outside the city, visiting Tivoli, the Villa Adriana and the Etruscan necropolis. I think our favourite place was Ostia since we could enjoy not only the excavated city but also the pine groves and the sea.

We have a great love of the sea and next year we made an expedition to Mull where we acquired Frachadil, a sixteenth-century cottage expanded during the nineteenth century. It is on the north coast overlooking Rhum, Skye, Eigg and Muck, and on occasions we find the sea as blue and the islands as sparkling as Greece. The labour of this book would not have been possible without the peaceful holidays of Mull. As I work on the manuscript I let my eyes wander over the sharply rising glen, the reddening bracken, the white and grey tinted rocks, the bending alders and the firs stunted by the wind. These are subjects for the brush as well as for the pen, and so they have proved.

I began painting when I was at Marlborough, and it has remained my principal hobby. The best amateur painters who
have also been Ministers of the Crown are, in my opinion, Patrick Buchan Hepburn (Lord Hailes) and the late Lord Alexander.
The former was properly trained and the latter had a simplicity
of talent which matched his character. My own pictures, with
one exception, are not allowed in the main public rooms of our
various homes, though some have reached the bedroom in the
Master's Lodge. They are almost on a line with those framed
views which you see in old-fashioned railway carriages and
which I have always found to beguile the journey. This is particularly true of my reproduction of the inlets and mountains
of Mull. I have a certain facility with skies and would be on
speaking terms with Boudin, though he would soon have
broken off the conversation. My own favourite artist is Bon-
ington who, alas, died so young. I do not think that my best
pictures are worse than Winston Churchill's and he did not
think so either. But mine are neither so valuable nor so profuse.
I painted more than once with Winston, notably at Cap d'Ail.
On one occasion he commanded me to 'take the mountain'
while he would 'take the sea'. Detectives prepared the palette
and easel. The palette was of glass surrounded by paints already
squeezed out, including the most terrible pinks and mauves.
On the surface stood bottles of whisky and soda and a bowl of
turps and oil mixer. One dipped one's brush and drank in-
discriminately, in the midst of choking fits. While I was in the
process of rounding off the mountain, Winston approached
accompanied by his detectives and aides. He surveyed my effort
and said, 'That is too good, *I* must do the mountain. There is
nothing for me in the sea.' He and his assembly then sat down
in front of me obscuring the view. My mountain, although
cherished, therefore remains unfinished, but still it is now in
our London flat, hanging in the drawing room where it has
been mistaken for an Impressionist. I was also obliged to leave
the whisky since paints in drink are lethal. Winston's essay on
painting is hard to excel. He is quite right about the difficulty of
covering the canvas which he likens to a military operation. I
think his best pictures were painted at Chartwell, his least successful with blue water and green trees on the Italian lakes.

There is little intellectual content in his work. It was thus, as it was meant to be, a complete recreation and comfort in the periods when his tumultuous career provided intermissions.

During the time when I was Churchill's Chancellor of the Exchequer, Charles Morgan proposed me as President of the Royal Society of Literature. I was to succeed Archie Wavell whose finely chosen anthology *Other Men's Flowers* made me realize how suitable *he* had been for the post. My suitability also lay in an appreciation of other men's flowers rather than in the cultivation of my own. But thanks to a happy suggestion of Sydney's I asked Lord Birkenhead, whose literary and bio-graphical talents were already renowned and have now become pre-eminent, to be Chairman of the Council. Ever since then he and his wife Sheila, as well as being my best friends, have worked to raise the standards of the Society founded by George I to a very high level of taste and modernity. In this they have been much helped by the Poet Laureate, Cecil Day Lewis. They hold a series of first-class lectures and poetry readings, and a selection of the lectures are published in the Transactions of the Society. These include a contribution on Proust by Mollie who, well-versed in the English and French classics, appreciates every facet of human nature exhibited in *A la recherche du temps perdu*. My own contribution is on the subject of 'Indirect Auto-biography', by which I mean those works in which authors draw from their own experience to create a novel or work of art. The greatest exemplar, perhaps, is Tolstoy whose *Anna Karenina*, *War and Peace* and the grim *Kreutzer Sonata* depend upon a high de-gree of self-confession or autobiography. Conrad and, later, Ernest Hemingway similarly drew upon their own lives, and so frequently do D. H. Lawrence, Somerset Maugham—and, of course, Dickens, George Eliot, Meredith and Proust himself. I only wish I had the talent to write indirect autobiography which is greater than autobiography *tout court*, even in the hands of such literary masters as I paraded in my Romanes lecture on *The Difficult Art of Autobiography*. But 'few autobiographies of statesmen and politicians can claim distinction on literary grounds, though quite a few are well written', observes Professor Pascal.

With this stern and daunting judgement to enjoin a due sense of modesty, I now resume the narrative of my own life in the year 1929, when I was first elected to Parliament to represent Saffron Walden, found a flat near the House with a division bell, and proceeded to obey the instructions of the Conservative Chief Whip, the immaculately clothed Sir Bolton Eyres Monsell.

CHAPTER THREE

GOVERNMENT OF INDIA

FIVE MONTHS after I entered the House of Commons, the Viceroy of India issued his controversial Declaration concerning Dominion status. The Viceroy was Lord Irwin, heir to the earldom of Halifax, and later my chief at the Foreign Office. He had been persuaded much against his personal inclination to go out to India in 1926—partly from a sense of duty, partly by the blandishments of his great friend Stanley Baldwin, and partly through the strong-willed insistence of the Secretary of State, Lord Birkenhead. With Birkenhead his relations were superficially easy, but in temperament and philosophy the two men stood poles apart. 'I remember so well', he was to say long after, 'how bloody it was serving under F.E.' The Conservative Viceroy therefore viewed the loss by his party of the 1929 general election with a certain equanimity, and welcomed the accession to the India Office of the Labour leader Wedgwood Benn: 'He was always rather a friend of mine in the House of Commons, and I have no doubt I shall get on with him.' This prophecy proved accurate. Both men were equally, and in my judgement rightly, anxious to make a strong and memorable gesture of friendship to the Indians and so to restore faith in the ultimate purpose of British policy.

Since the war the tide of nationalism had been rising ever higher in British India, and already in 1917 the Coalition government had defined its historic goal as 'the progressive realisation of responsible government in India as an integral part of the British Empire'. This policy had been justified in the eloquently liberal Montagu-Chelmsford Report and the first stage in its realization embodied in the Act of 1919. But the Act was not a success. The powerful Indian National Congress became, under the leadership of Mahatma Gandhi, a quasi-revolutionary body pledged to immediate *Swaraj* or self-rule, and accordingly refused to co-operate in working the Act. At the same time, mounting communal divisions and antagonisms between Hindus and Moslems prevented the system of 'dyarchy'—under which certain functions were transferred to Indian Ministers responsible to their Provincial legislatures—from leading (except in Madras) to any genuine party parliamentary system. The working of the new Constitution was due to be examined by a Statutory Commission after ten years. But Birkenhead was leaving nothing to chance. In 1927 he appointed a small Parliamentary Commission, composed exclusively of the conventional and the then obscure, and chaired by the highly legalistic Liberal Sir John Simon. It lacked Indian representation, was saluted by Indian crowds bearing banners inscribed 'Simon Go Back', was cut dead and boycotted by most Indian leaders, and after two and a half years of labour produced a magisterial report which, as Sam Hoare pointed out, left the central questions unanswered and had been overtaken by events.

For Birkenhead had underestimated Irwin. The Viceroy was only too well aware of the trend of the proposals the Commission would make, and knew how little favour they would find with Indian political opinion.

In the summer of 1929, therefore, he suggested to the new government two immediate announcements. First, that a Round Table Conference, representative of British political parties, all sections in British India, and the Indian Princely States, should be convened following publication of the Simon report. Secondly, that Dominion status for India was considered to be implicit in the Coalition government's declaration of 1917. The first suggestion was acceptable to the Simon Commission, but in the second suggestion they declined to involve themselves. Both statements were issued in the *Indian Gazette* of 31st October. It was upon the second that political attention focused:

'In view of the doubts which have been expressed both in Great Britain and India regarding the interpretation to be placed on the intentions of the British Government in enacting the statute of 1919, I am authorized on behalf of His

Majesty's Government to state clearly that, in their judgement, it is implicit in the Declaration of 1917 that the natural issue of India's constitutional progress as there contemplated is the attainment of Dominion status.'

Whilst I was myself fully aware of the political significance of this announcement and of the political rumpus it would cause, I could not regard it, as a student of history, to be more than the admission of an always undeniable truth. For the 1917 phrase about 'the progressive realization of responsible government in India' had itself been a terse and precise description of the rise of the self-governing Colonies—from Canada onwards—to Dominion status.

Nevertheless, the British Parliament exploded at once with anger and indignation. In the Lords, Birkenhead and Reading, the former Viceroy, launched a massive onslaught. In the Commons, I well remember an able and mischievous attack by Lloyd George being loudly cheered by Winston Churchill—'to the concern of some of us', as Eddie Winterton later wrote in an uncharacteristic under-statement. Churchill repudiated Irwin's Declaration and set off on his own road to independence: a road which was to lead him to dizzy heights of superb oratory but forcefully exclude him from any share of government decisions for the next ten fateful years and, worst of all as far as India was concerned, so to retard the process of constitutional development as to embitter the Indians and help pave the way for those who were most deeply distrustful of British motives. For the next six years India remained a central, perhaps the central, issue in parliamentary life—'in certain moods', said Eustace Percy of Baldwin, 'he would talk in private about nothing else'. For four of those years I was myself intimately and officially involved, and it was a painful experience to find the main lines of debate and battle drawn not between parties but within my own party. I did not then think I had gone into politics for that.

My intervention on the 1930 Finance Bill won a double-edged compliment from Baldwin: 'That was a good speech, Rab. But I got damn bored. You went too fast; you need not think everybody has a quick brain.' Baldwin could certainly never be accused of going too fast. His rupture with Churchill was not immediate. Over the Irwin Declaration indeed he had found himself in considerable difficulty, since he had made his prior acceptance of it conditional on that of the Simon Commission. But he refused to join Lloyd George in a motion of censure on the government and, though mildly critical of the Declaration, spent the major part of his speech in eloquent philosophizing, about 'the split migration of the Aryan peoples', the need for Britain's pledges 'to be honoured in the letter and in the spirit' and the imaginative hope that those 'who will be putting the coping-stone upon this building may not be unforgetful of those of us who built in faith among the foundations'. Writing to my parents in India, I said, 'The public are right to think that Baldwin has a political mind in the way that he moves from decision to decision according to the most expedient moment, but they are wrong to credit him with any lack of vision and foresight, which are his great and historical characteristics.' After 1930, say his most recent biographers, Keith Middlemas and John Barnes, he had made up his mind irrevocably that India was to be his great mission. Early in 1931, following the Delhi Pact by which Irwin had released political prisoners in exchange for cessation of civil disobedience and Gandhi's participation in the second session of the Round Table Conference, Lord Lloyd went to urge on Baldwin the necessity for a change back in Indian policy. Lloyd told me about this the following evening after he had addressed a meeting on Moslem aspirations under the auspices of my uncle Jack Courtauld. Baldwin had listened gravely and politely, and then he replied, 'Well, you are so much more last ditch than I am, that I cannot agree; and *then there's Edward.*'

'Then there's Edward' was really the key to Baldwin's India policy. He was devoted to Irwin. When Birkenhead had suggested appointing him Viceroy, Baldwin's first reaction, as he later told the House of Commons, was 'I cannot spare him.' And then he added, 'He is one of my most intimate friends, not only politically but personally, a man whose ideals and views on political life approximate most closely to my own, a colleague to whom I can always tell my inmost thoughts. On reflection I felt that India must have the best that we could send. That was the reason why I agreed. I will only add that if ever the day comes when the party I lead ceases to attract to itself men of the calibre of Edward Wood, then I have finished with my party.' I myself always admired Edward this side idolatry. Yet I do not doubt that his viceroyalty was the greatest episode in a varied and distinguished career, and that the comprehending and enlightened policy he pursued, culminating in his Pact with Gandhi, was both realistic and right. Churchill, alas, saw it otherwise. It was, he thundered, 'alarming and also nauseating to see Mr. Gandhi, a seditious Middle Temple lawyer, now posing as a fakir of a type well-known in the East, striding half-naked up the steps of the Viceregal Palace, while he is still organizing and conducting a defiant campaign of civil disobedience, there to negotiate and to parley on equal terms with the representative of the King-Emperor'. Irwin's release of Gandhi marked the breaking-point in Churchill's relations with the leadership of the Conservative party. He resigned from the Opposition Business Committee and left the front bench to establish himself on the corner seat below the gangway, from where he continued in Baldwin's phrase to speak 'as George III might have done had he been endowed with the tongue of Edmund Burke'. This was, as I have already suggested, a misfortune for Indian constitutional development and a tragedy in Churchill's own career. But it was more than that. In the shrewd judgement of Robert Rhodes James, 'By the violence of his speeches and the exaggeration of his images he had grievously debased the coinage of alarmism. Many of Churchill's phrases used in the India controversy were to be subsequently repeated in another context, with inevitably a lesser impact. . . . The description of the Indian nationalist leaders . . . was striking, but was not likely to make comparable descriptions of genuinely evil men more credible.'[1]

During the summer of 1931 I was, for the first time, to see both 'the representative of the King-Emperor' and the 'half-naked' nationalist in action. In June I attended a meeting in the House of Commons of the India Committee, normally composed of those Conservative back-benchers with a special interest in Indian affairs. It was a sign of the times that most of the party had turned up. Irwin, gaunt and sombre, was flanked by

[1] *Churchill, A Study in Failure 1900–1939* (Wiedenfeld and Nicolson).

Winterton, Lloyd and Churchill. His replies to their questions were agile and tinged with irony. But his speech, apparently unprepared and certainly unpolished, seemed disappointing, even disillusioning. He asked us to keep the account private, for fear of embarrassing Lord Willingdon, who was to be his successor as Viceroy. Despite this, the *Daily Telegraph* came out next morning with striking headlines. The speech in its entirety had, however, been even more striking. It began with references to the growth of nationalism and to the fact, as he put it, that owing to the Russo-Japanese war and the looseness of Western women as depicted in films, our prestige in the East was gone. An incredulous gasp greeted this sacrilege, and I noted at the time: 'It was like the scene in *Stalky and Co.* where "the jelly-bellied flag-flapper" offends the boys—only inverted.' After this display of courageous naïvety, he altered course and, when he came to his Pact with Gandhi, explained that it would ensure the loyalty of the older politicians in India, those on the side of 'conservatism'; whereas the great agrarian forces, always latent in the Indian situation, were harnessed by the younger Nehru and would cause the serious problem of the future. What his policy had done, he maintained, was to build a breakwater against these dangerous waves. No doubt such sentiments were intended to reassure conservative feeling, but they frankly disturbed me, since I knew that what had failed to capture the young mind of India could not endure. 'It was probably the most important meeting at which he will ever address the Conservative party, although of course personalities and events will change', I wrote to my parents. 'I thought he spoke of Gandhi in much too matter-of-fact a tone, considering that one had supposed that he dealt with him as one mystic deals with another. . . . It is disturbing to me to see him fall short, in the breakwater statement, of the ideals for which I had given him credit.'

A week later Sir John Simon spoke to an almost identical gathering. His monumental report had, of course, been thrust to one side and the first session of the Round Table Conference, presided over by Ramsay MacDonald, had taken place between November 1930 and January 1931. The Congress boycotted it; but the Princes came, and from this emerged its one seeming success—their agreement that the States should come into an all-India federation of the future. Simon rather pooh-poohed this. In his view the introduction of responsible government at the centre had to await developments in the Provinces, and if this was so, then the final federation of all India was a still more distant consummation. Federalism was going to make the problem of central government more and not less difficult. To settle the individual problems of the Provinces was a more suitable method of proceeding than to have what he called 'a ready-made federal suit tried on at once'. He felt that the problem of communal difficulties was intensified by the prospect of power falling into the hands of one or other section; a further argument for providing a strong central executive. 'I think', he said in conclusion, 'we should encourage these people to come together to solve their communal difficulties, rather than adopt the policy of "divide and rule".' The contrast between this speech and Irwin's was singular. Simon was a good spokesman of lucid brain, taking a high moral line in the best tradition of British rule; Irwin was a great moralist, taking or obliging himself to take a line of political expediency by talking about breakwaters against a future deluge. Simon kept his head, evaded answers to bald questions, and alluded to Irwin's character throughout with marked courtesy. I was vividly struck by the fact that Simon's had been the better performance. But the substance as distinct from the tone of his argument—with its dominant note of 'gradualness' and (like his report) its total absence of any reference to Dominion status—seemed too cautious and tentative to match the needs of the new situation. I agreed with Baldwin that Simonism was not enough and that 'if we were to keep India within the Commonwealth, we must be prepared to go much further and faster'.

Before the summer of 1931 was out, we were being put to the test. By a series of dramatic events which do not require any retelling here, a National government of all three parties came into being in August to deal with an economic crisis hitherto unprecedented in severity. It was meant to be temporary but, as I wrote at the time, 'The Opposition have got few personalities, and the worse things are, the more likely the National government will recruit better and better leaders, and stay longer and longer.' Irwin, fearing that he was unacceptable to the right wing of his party, declined the Foreign Office which then went to Reading—a Liberal of outstanding brain and unusual charm, but the same man who had attacked Dominion status for India two years earlier. Fortunately the India Office itself was entrusted to Sam Hoare who conceived it to be his duty from the very start to 'convince the Indian delegates that I was as strongly in favour of all-Indian federation as any of them'. I myself was suddenly hoisted into this high endeavour, so close to my interests and congenial to my ideals, by an invitation to become Hoare's Parliamentary Private Secretary. In this capacity I attended the second session of the Round Table Conference which began in September and lasted three months. It was the only session to which Gandhi came, and his personality made an even deeper impression than his performance. On the first occasion he spoke I was sitting in a window of the conference room in St. James's Palace, with the warm sun streaming through. Outside the Guards Band played, and inside a portrait of William IV, familiarly known as 'Silly Billy', gazed down from the wall over a chubby gartered calf upon the assembled wealth of political intellect from east and west. Gandhi was just in front of me, on the left of the Lord Chancellor, and that morning I witnessed his personality expand. Toothless and dressed in his habitual *khaddar*, he talked rapidly, in a low voice and at inordinate length; but his utterance was impressive. He insisted that Congress alone represented political India; that the Untouchables, the lowest of the Hindu castes, could not be segregated from the main body of Hinduism; and that Hindus and Moslems could and should live together in a united India without separate electorates or special safeguards for minorities. He was also quick to introduce the economic argument, saying that a *free India* would be more helpful to an England struggling with her financial difficulties.

It was in fact true that Gandhi himself controlled to a greater extent than anyone else the seething population of which India was made up. In October I had a personal talk with him in which he said that the British were more capable of self-delusion than any other people. He knew the British very intimately, both from his time in South Africa, and then from his long fight in India, and he felt we were capable of lulling ourselves into the belief that we were doing the right thing by Congress. It is indeed rather extraordinary that while I was working away against Conservative opposition to obtain Indian self-government in the India Bill, I certainly did not spend as much time on the Congress and on the realities of Indian politics as I should have done. The fact we must face, arising out of Gandhi's statement, is that there was a great gulf at that time between Indian nationalism and British 'nationalists' (if I may so describe us) who were desirous of making a peace with India. It is only by looking back that one sees that we should have drawn closer to the Congress movement, and that this great gulf may, as Gandhi said, have been a form of self-delusion.

The second Round Table Conference broke up without any notable result. It had foundered on the issue of recognizing communal claims; those delegates representing minorities having refused to consider any other position unless their demands were granted. 'I have never concealed from you', said MacDonald in his concluding statement, 'that this is above all others a problem for you to settle by agreement amongst yourselves', but he added that if this continued to be impossible, the government would be compelled to apply a provisional scheme of its own, which it eventually did. Meanwhile Congress politics, with Gandhi away in London, were dominated by the Nehrus, father and son. Friction had arisen over agrarian discontent in the United Provinces, and Congress had advised a no-tax campaign. Jawaharlal Nehru, Vallabhbai Patel, and soon after his return from London Gandhi himself, were taken into custody. New ordinances were issued which gave the new Viceroy, Lord Willingdon, widespread, drastic and absolute powers to enforce law and order; and Irwin took occasion to say in public that, had he himself still been in India, he could have done nothing different. In May 1932 Hoare wrote to Willingdon, 'The nearer we get to a Bill the more apprehensive I am becoming about its possible fate. There is no doubt whatsoever that recent events in India have hardened opinion against many of the constitutional changes that we have been discussing.'

However, the renewal of civil disobedience did not prevent the continuance of constitutional preparations. A Franchise

Committee, consisting of both British and Indian representatives under the chairmanship of Lord Lothian the Parliamentary Under-Secretary, toured the whole of India together and made a big impact on Indian opinion. I served on this committee, and formed the strongest respect for Lothian's acute intellect and a warm friendship with young Basil Dufferin whose untimely death at Ava was one of the greatest losses to our generation. He had a first-class brain; among contemporaries today only Quintin Hogg or Edward Boyle are in the same league. Our principal recommendation was an increase in the electorate from seven million to thirty-six million; electoral qualifications being based on property and education. At the time we thought we were taking a great risk of the machine breaking down, and commentators regarded our work as being unusually distinguished for its liberalism. It shows the pace at which progressive ideas developed soon after, that India could pass within fifteen years from our small electorate to universal suffrage. Having received our report, and those of the Federal Finance Committee and the Indian States' Inquiry Committee, Sam Hoare declared in the House in June 1932 that the government intended to give effect to their policy by means of a single Bill, 'which will provide alike for the autonomous constitutions of the Provinces and for the Federation of the Provinces and States'. He proposed the establishment of a Joint Select Committee of both Houses to consider plans for the revision of the Constitution, and to introduce a Government of India Bill.

September brought me promotion to the position of Under-Secretary of State in succession to Lothian. Among other Liberal Free Traders, he found it impossible to agree with the decisions reached at the Ottawa Conference about Imperial Preference. Hoare wrote to Willingdon: 'I am very sorry to have lost Lothian. I think myself that he was exceedingly silly in not stopping on, and in not dissociating himself from Samuel and Samuel's crowd. Anyhow he has left most friendlily disposed towards us and will give us all the help that he can. You will have seen that I have got young R. A. Butler to succeed him. I was most anxious to have someone who knew the constitutional story and who was also in touch with the chief personalities in India. I can depend upon him entirely to do what I want and to work really hard at the terribly complicated questions connected with the constitution.' For me the chance given was exciting and challenging; apart from which Hoare and I were supported by probably the best India Committee that we could possibly have had: MacDonald, Baldwin, Simon, Irwin, Hailsham and Neville Chamberlain. In Parliament the extreme right were beginning to mobilize what Hoare described as 'an extensive attack upon our India policy. . . . It will be a great gain when we have got the whole question safely into the hands of the Joint Select Committee . . . the opposition are going to make a great deal of what they claim to be the reluctance of the Princes to join the Federation.' The Conservative party on the whole were very nervous. I wrote, 'The Winston crowd have been very active with meetings, lunches and propaganda of every kind . . . the attitude of most Conservatives is one of suspended animation. They are waiting to see whether the White Paper really does make the safeguards as effective as possible, and also whether the Federation looks like taking shape.'

In March 1933 the White Paper was published, embodying the greatest measure of agreement obtained at the Round Table Conference, whose third and last session had ended the previous Christmas. With the support of the *Morning Post* and the *Daily Mail*, Churchill launched his attack. He made a great impression on the constituencies, and caused dissension within the National Council of the party. At the half-yearly meeting of the National Union Churchill tried to pass a resolution against the White Paper policy. Hoare found the delegates proved 'very susceptible to Winston's propaganda . . . the hall was full of his partisans and a great many people were wobbling towards him.' Thanks to Hoare's speech 'we just won. . . . But it was a touch and go affair . . . it does prove conclusively the strength of the doubts and suspicions that are in many people's minds. There was the makings of a first-class crisis and the breakaway from the Centre of three-quarters of the Conservative party.'

There was a three-day debate on the government's motion to appoint a Joint Select Committee of both Houses 'with power to call into consultation representatives of the Indian States and British India . . . to consider the future government of India', and to examine the White Paper. I opened for the government on the third day of the debate. I recalled my early days spent in India and could not refrain from a warning to Churchill. 'Many a time I have sat in the jungle in Central India watching a bait, in the form of a bullock or calf tied to a tree, awaiting the arrival of the Lord of the Forest, and put there as a trap to entice him to his doom. On this occasion I have exactly the same feelings as those of the miserable animal whom I have so often looked upon in that position, and, if I compare myself to that bait, I may compare my Rt. Hon. friend the Member for Epping to the tiger. I hope that Hon. Members and the Rt. Hon. gentleman himself will remember, however, that there is waiting for the tiger a pair of lynx eyes and a sure and safe rifle to ensure his ultimate fate. . . .' And I concluded: 'This plan is not born of expediency or fashioned in haste, or the result of any political compromise. As we have worked upon it, we have come to know and to believe in our hearts that it is the best. It combines in a practical manner the two ideals of British Imperial policy described by Lord Lloyd, responsibility for the welfare of the people, and evolution towards self-government and ultimate political independence.' Churchill subsequently spoke: 'The Montagu-Chelmsford reforms have failed . . . by every test, moral and material, which can be applied. . . . Instead of contentment, these reforms have aroused agitation and disloyalty. Instead of bringing peace between jarring races and rival religions, they have only wakened old passions which were slumbering, under the long Pax Britannica. . . . It is a tragedy that the greatest gift which Britain has given to India was not the gift that India needed most. During the last fifty years the population of India has increased by 100 million. The 100 million new human beings are here to greet the dawn, toil upon the plains, bow before the temples of inexorable gods. They are here. You cannot desert them, you cannot abandon them. They are as much our children as any children could be. They are actually in the world as a result of what this nation and this Parliament have done.' This was fine, colourful and brilliant stuff, but the House was not carried away, when it came to constructing a new Constitution, by appeals of this sort. Winston was entranced by his own imagery; he loved to hear himself, as he knew others did, but whereas he was profoundly moved by his own words, others were not. It did not stop him from haranguing the House; but it meant that in desperation Winston turned from the House to the machinery of the party. This was his second line of attack; if he could capture control of the party, he could bring down the government; but he had to do this outside the House. The organization of the Conservative party, tradition-ally more to the right than the parliamentary party, nearly fell to him: that it didn't was due partly to the fact that even the party managers would not accept Winston as their leader. In the end, Winston could only delay, obstruct, hinder, fight a guerrilla war; and in so doing he caused considerable damage, not only to the party, but to the implementation of the Govern-ment of India Act once it had finally been passed.

The previous month I had had an interesting talk with W. S. Morrison on the state of party feeling over India. As Chairman of the 1922 Committee he was in a good position to test the feeling of the new Parliament. I was impressed first of all by the fact that the 1931 Parliament, being totally different from the previous one, was only slowly finding its character. New types were coming to the front and it was difficult to find exactly which personalities had a 'public'. Morrison considered that the two great fears, which he regarded as typically Conservative, were, first, that we were handing over India to a set of agitators who were not the real leaders of the people, and, secondly, that we were not taking proper steps to safeguard our trade. He reiterated that trade was the vital question, especially to the large contingent of Lancashire members, who were in politics for that. If we could satisfy them on that point, they would swing on to other interests. We both agreed that the best way to spike the Churchill lunch and dinner parties that were going on over India was to get Sam Hoare himself to appear before the Committee to state his position and allow questions to be put to him.

Discontent, however, was not only to be found at Westmin-ster. In early March, in a letter to my parents, I described a women's conference in the Eastern Area, which I addressed one morning: 'A woman from Bedford with a determined voice said it was wrong to give votes to naked men with bows and arrows

instead of keeping all power in the hands of the British government. She was seconded by a woman who declared she had just
got up from a bed of laryngitis, which appealed strongly to the
women's audience. She in her turn was succeeded by a woman
of fighting disposition, who lived up to her name by saying that
Great Britain had always persecuted the Irish and obviously
were persecuting India, and so must clear out. This, from a
speaker against a resolution condemning any sort of progress
in India, was greeted with vociferous howls. Blood was seen
streaming from the ears of several of the audience, and at that
juncture a loud-voiced and broad-bosomed Irishwoman leapt
up on the montagne, that is, the high benches at the side,
saying that the whole of Ireland would be delighted to be forever
under the British heel, and that they demanded nothing better.
The audience was now in a state of ecstasy. Mrs. Davidson, who
was in the chair, then turned to me to get up and oppose the
resolution. She introduced me as my uncle's son, and one who
had made a tour of India. I was listened to with quiet. There was
a slight ripple of approval at the idea that it was rather contrary
to British impartiality and justice, of which we had heard so
much talk during the speeches on India, for Britain now to
propose a resolution condemning any advance before the
government's plans had ever been seen. However, this temporary triumph, aided as it was by my assurance that Gandhi
was still in jail, did not serve to dim the enthusiasm of this
democratic assembly, which accordingly passed a sweeping
resolution condemning democracy itself. The voting was very
unscientific, half the audience did not put their hands up, and
the majority of the rest voted for the resolution opposing
reform.'

This sort of thing happened fairly frequently. I talked to
Findlater Stewart, the Permanent Secretary, about it, and he
said, which was true, that these reforms are moulded by great
forces, and that naturally we were feeling the impact of the
Great British Public at this moment. He agreed with me that
whatever happened to any of us politically, 'the scheme we are
now working on at the India Office must go through in some
form, since the wit of man can devise no other'.

After the government motion to approve the White Paper

had been passed by 449 votes to 43, discussions took place about the size and membership of the Joint Select Committee. Hoare found this to be an unpleasant and difficult job since there were so many interests to represent. He conducted negotiations through the Chief Whip and Hailsham, and also Salisbury whom he saw three or four times a week. Salisbury was offered the chairmanship, but turned it down. The final choice fell on Peel, because he knew the stuff, and because it meant that Hoare's influence could be maintained. At the last minute, however, there was a crisis. Peel had a severe attack of phlebitis and had been ordered to bed. Linlithgow was hurriedly persuaded to be Chairman and Salisbury was conciliated with difficulty. Thus Linlithgow worked extremely hard for India before he was ever thought of as Viceroy and Governor-General. He had done a great agricultural review of India. He served with distinction on the Joint Select Committee, and he became fully versed in Indian affairs. He made a statement that he had five children and never showed them any preference. By that he meant that he was not going to show any preference to the various races of India or to the various communities: to that extent, Linlithgow was as true as his word. He was, in fact, an honest but a rigorous man, and his honesty and rigour were both needed.

The Joint Select Committee gathered together much of what was most old-worldly and noble in the public scene of the day. Lord Lytton was a proconsular type with a grace of sentient feeling which may not have given a dynamic impression, but which seemed to perpetuate British Imperial standards. Lord Derby was there with immense three-inch collars and cuffs, looking as though nothing would disturb him, including his own bulk which he carried without complaint. Lord Rankeillour seemed ever ready for a technical or legal battle. The Archbishop of Canterbury was an historic Prince of the Church, eager for finesse on any point. At about eleven o'clock in the morning at least two or three of the above would sneak out and order each other a dock glass of port. I sometimes had the honour to be invited, unless, as Under-Secretary, I was too busy 'on the bridge'. I enjoyed meeting Austen Chamberlain, the uncrowned Prime Minister, who is said to have been born in a

THE FRANCHISE COMMITTEE, INDIA, 1932
In front, Lord Lothian (Chairman). At the back, Lord Dufferin and the author

AT STANSTEAD, JULY 1935
Seated (*centre*) Mr. and Mrs. Stanley Baldwin
Seated (*left*) Sydney Butler, (*right*) Mrs. Malcolm Sargent
Standing (*left to right*) Dr. Malcolm Sargent, Mr. Samuel Courtauld, Lord De La Warr,
the author and Sir Geoffrey Fry

red government Despatch Box. If anyone had the 'allure' of a statesman it was he. He was always ready to take a line and to argue it, yet one had the feeling that he was an actor—a sincere one—and that Neville was the tough businessman. It is a pity that Neville did not borrow some of Austen's Foreign Office experience. We occasionally exchanged views with Lord Sankey, the Lord Chancellor. Whenever I looked at him he reminded me of the gloomy Sankey and Moody hymns, with which presumably he had nothing to do. On one occasion he showed some of us a letter from an Indian—a Magdalen man, he said sadly—which started with the words 'You bloody brute'. We all chortled with delight, and Irwin added to the merriment by saying that laughing made his lumbago worse.

In 1933 I was very busy trying to organize some publicity campaign against Winston. This later came to be known as the 'Union of Britain and India'. But initially it was very difficult to find anyone willing to join it. We started with the idea of having a façade of distinguished ex-Governors, putting their signature to a letter to the papers. Irwin and I saw Goschen and Harcourt Butler, but both refused. They were nervous of getting mixed up in rather venomous politics. It was thus sporting of three personalities, Sir John Thompson, Sir Arthur Watson and Sir Edward Villiers, to agree to set up a small publicity committee whose object was to organize counter-propaganda and arrange meetings. Winston in opposition made the party organization his principal target, and wrought a good deal of havoc. I was not unhopeful at that time, though, that he might have shot his bolt, particularly as he had started at such an early date. Winston had money from various sources and had enlisted the Duke of Westminster, Salisbury and others. 'The trouble is', Hoare wrote, 'that our case is a complicated case of detail, whilst the attack is an attack of headlines and platform slogans.' Winston was hoping to capture the Conservative organization. We thought it doubtful that he would succeed, even though the magnitude of the task of piloting a Bill of several hundred clauses through Parliament, with half the Conservatives in the House of Commons doubtful or hostile, and the House of Lords suspicious of almost every detail, impressed us deeply. Thus our people had to put their best foot forward. I held many a meeting

of the U.B.I. in my flat and was aided by my friend Lord Brabourne, Hoare's Private Secretary, who was Treasurer. It is rare
in politics for two sides in the same party to organize meetings,
campaigns and articles against each other, but if we had not
organized the Union of Britain and India with its activities all
over the country, we should have gone down.

On 29th July a meeting took place at the Friends' House where
it was clear that Baldwin had still a considerable hold on the
women of the country and on the more thoughtful of the men.
I wrote next day:

'The Berry press this morning has a very striking picture of
Baldwin puffing a pipe against a notice of "No Smoking". This
is all to the good. The meeting yesterday was impressive in that
it exhibited the organized tactics of the opposition. Lloyd,
Wolmer and Davidson sat at a great table piled with documents
on constitutional reform which I now, alas, know so well.
Churchill again got rattled speaking. I could not find a seat,
so sat on the steps quite near him. He looked suffused as if by
some stimulant. Before lunch Page Croft's ringing tones about
the legions coming home "to go on the dole" had caused a
universal clap at his oratory. Churchill rushed out with
Brendan Bracken and appeared very elated by the meeting.
This shows his lack of understanding of the real sentiment of
such a gathering. The final figures gave us a small majority and
I think a fair indication of the actual feeling in the country,
though we are convinced that the show of hands gave us a
bigger majority. Baldwin was obviously very much relieved.
He came and offered a grimy paw to Sydney and me at the edge
of the platform, and said he was hot and excited. Lady Maud
[Hoare] was cool as a cucumber and loudly expostulated
when Lloyd said that we were handing over the means of
communication. Lloyd looked extremely thin and ill and
spoke better in his reply than in his original speech. The
Cabinet turned out well. I franked in Walter Elliott, who
arrived without a ticket, rather breathless, and shortly after
him Neville Chamberlain arrived amid a great ovation. His
presence decided the result of the meeting. I think the form of
resolution adopted will now put off a decision until the Joint

Select Committee reports, and I think that Sam Hoare's tactics have been justified hitherto. He made a very good speech at night to a meeting of MPs at dinner, again repeating his cardinal point about decentralization in India as the new tendency, and explaining his distrust of the present central administration, the form of which had all the weakness of the Duma, which he himself had studied in Russia. He therefore preferred the form of Federal centre which would be more truly conservative and less dangerous. These are two favourite points of his and made a good impression on the audience.'

In a letter to Lord Brabourne, who had gone out to India as Governor of Bombay, I wrote in 1934:

'I find myself more out of sympathy with Conservative principles than I have been for some time, although the tendency has been growing. At our last party conference the audience would have been a credit to the zoo or wild regions of the globe. No ray of enlightenment shone on a single face except the shining pate of Sir Henry Page Croft, who has the merit of looking fairly well groomed. My conclusion is that we have got over a difficult occasion in which the lists were set very badly for us. The audience was bound to be restive and provoked by the argument that this was the last opportunity for the conference to make up its mind.'

The Report of the Joint Select Committee was published in November 1934. The Committee had the advantage, during most of 1933, of sitting in joint session with an almost equally numerous representative Indian delegation, and with a small Burmese delegation. Nineteen members of the Committee voted for the Report. Those in disagreement comprised the four Labour members, who did not think the Report went far enough, and five Conservatives, including Salisbury, on the Conservative right wing. In substance the Report endorsed the scheme put forward in the White Paper for an All-India Federation with full responsibility at the centre for all matters except defence and foreign policy; as well as all dealings with those Princely States which might not adhere to the Viceroy. It contained, however, three important changes from the White

Paper. The concession was made to Austen Chamberlain that for direct election on a limited franchise for the Central Assembly there would be substituted indirect election by the provincial Chambers. This was a concession we were willing to make. Chamberlain's view, strongly held, was that to rely on direct election was to play too much into the hands of Gandhi and Nehru and the Congress, who had done little to help the negotiations: for in July 1933, civil disobedience had been resumed on a large scale. Brabourne himself had had to deal with a serious mill strike in Bombay. There had been quite a cheer in the House when I announced that strong measures had been taken; there always was a cheer when the House learned that people had been locked up or firm action had been taken, involving police protection. Willingdon, the Viceroy, had himself been quite sensible about indirect election and long before had begun to realize how lucky he was to get away with this as the only large amendment. Indeed the second concession made, and the second important change in the Report of the Joint Select Committee, was that provisions against terrorism were strengthened. The third was that restrictions on economic discrimination for political objects were clarified.

On 4th December, 1934, a special meeting of the Conservative Council was held at the Queen's Hall, Langham Place, to consider with the Leader of the Party the Report of the Joint Select Committee on Indian Constitutional Reform. About 1,500 were present. Leo Amery moved a motion that the Council 'approves the general principles and recommendations embodied in the Report of the Joint Select Committee', to which Salisbury moved an amendment. The amendment was defeated by 1,102 votes to 390, and Lord Wolmer's subsequent motion that 'a special Conference should be convened to consider further the question of India' was defeated on a show of hands by an overwhelming majority.

The Report of the Joint Select Committee on the Government of India was debated in the House of Commons on the 10th, 11th and 12th December, 1934. Summing up at the end of the debate, Baldwin addressed himself mostly to the Conservative opposition's proposals. He said: 'I recognize and have recognized the sincere convictions of those who are opposing me. I am not trying to convert them, and I know that no words of mine would do so, but to some of the older ones I would say this: we have fought in many great battles together in the past, and I hope we may be spared to fight in one or two more. I shall bear no malice to anyone who votes against me tonight. I shall refrain, as far as I can, from hard words or from anything which would make more difficult the reunion of that party which I believe still has a great part to play in this country, and whose preservation and unity I believe to be essential to the prosperity of the country. . . .' It was a fighting speech and a fighting climax. The Socialist amendment was defeated by 491 votes to 49, and the government motion was passed by 410 votes to 127. The Conservative opposition joined with the Socialists in voting against the government.

The Bill, based on the Joint Select Committee's White Paper, was introduced into the House of Commons in February 1935. It provided that the eleven Provinces should be accorded full self-government, subject to certain safeguards. A central Government was to be created as soon as a prescribed number of States had agreed to join the Federation. The Bill contained 473 clauses and 16 schedules; Churchill called it 'a gigantic quilt of jumbled crochet work, a monstrous monument of shame built by pigmies'. The 1,951 speeches made on the subject of the Bill filled 4,000 pages of Hansard with $15\frac{1}{2}$ million words. It was long and appallingly complex; but it produced some of the finest debates I have witnessed in the House. Altogether the debates in Parliament on India lasted many years and added up to 20 books the size of the Bible. Hoare himself answered over 15,000 questions and made 600 speeches. At the close of the Second Reading debate, Baldwin referred to the regret expressed by Lansbury that there were not three lobbies so that he and Churchill did not appear in the same lobby, and he reminded Churchill of 'that immortal picture by John Leech representing the little Cockney sportsman saying to the Duke "The beauty of 'unting, your Grace, is that it brings together people who would not otherwise meet."' Baldwin finished with an appeal to reason: 'This Bill stands as a whole, comprehensive, single scheme which cannot be divided, and Federation is an essential part . . . we should be extremely apprehensive about granting the measure of Provincial autonomy that is provided for if it were not for what we believe to be the security in Federation for India . . . let us welcome into our Commonwealth of Nations the Indian people, the majority of whom, I am confident, have no greater ambition than to see their country play a worthy part in the Commonwealth.'

We got through the Second Reading by 404 votes to 133, which was surprisingly good. And then there followed the long Committee stage during which, despite 'flu, Hoare began to assume the same position in the House of Commons as he had done through the Round Table Conference and the Joint Select Committee. None of his colleagues or opponents could keep pace with his continued application, and the care with which he thought out all his encounters ahead. I did not believe that his secret lay, as many supposed, in a complete knowledge of the subject, but rather in his tactful manner of handling deliberative bodies, whether large or small, and in confining himself to the issues that mattered and in clearly exposing them. His method was to hold a meeting of his advisers at the India Office and to run with great speed through the various points which were likely to form the issues of the coming day. He would take down the advice succinctly given to him by Malcolm Hailey[1] or by the faithful Findlater Stewart, and these mines of wisdom would be supplemented by any others who were sitting round. His mind went straight to the political issue in question, and I very often knew him rise to answer points later on without having read 'the document'. That is to say, he did not become cluttered up by the intricacies of the Bill but rather adhered to the issues which the Bill was meant to implement in legal language. The Civil Service therefore did not always appreciate his answers, since they were trained to be accurate and omniscient. The House, on the other hand, stood on the other extreme, and considered that there was in his answers all the material they could have desired.

Sam's general attitude to life was also not entirely appreciated in the Office, but it was an interesting model of the manner in which a modern statesman accomplishes his work. Sam did not usually come to the Office till half-past eleven; he left it at

[1] Lord Hailey.

lunch, and on days when the House was not sitting, never stayed much after half-past five or six. In the morning he participated in the conflict, and very often the suavest of his speeches was preceded by an orgy of mutterings and nervous expostulation on the Bench. There were very few efforts, however, which we subordinates had to ourselves, since he nearly always joined in just as the responsibility appeared to be being taken by oneself. His participation was not due to a lack of confidence in those who served him. He had unbounded confidence in those of his choice, and would always look after them, though he was the first to notice ineptitude in a particular position and would not allow any personal regard to prevent transference to some other position. His activity and concentration obscured his intense interest in the adventure of life, which to him was a chapter in a great Napoleonic biography. He would sit in his 'Empire' library, and before the light of one steely electric fire, he used to work out the roles in the biography for his friends and associates to play. I was amazed by his ambitions; I admired his imagination; I shared his ideals; I stood in awe of his intellectual capacity. But I was never touched by his humanity. He was the coldest fish with whom I have ever had to deal.

The third reading of the Bill came up in early June 1935. Sam Hoare addressed himself, quite rightly, to the two fundamental criticisms of the Bill. The first that nobody in India wanted it, and the second that no one was going to work it. The Labour opposition moved an amendment criticizing the Bill for not containing means for the realization of Dominion status and for putting too much restraint on self-government. Churchill made the best impression that he could, and paid certain tributes: 'The Chief Whip [David Margesson] certainly deserves congratulations, not only for his part in evolving this procedure but on other counts as well. The Secretary of State has had the support of several able colleagues on the Front Bench—and particularly the Under-Secretary, who has distinguished himself greatly and has established a parliamentary reputation of a high order. . . .' The Third Reading was carried by 386 votes to 122.

The First Reading of the Bill in the House of Lords was on

6th June; the Second Reading on 18th, 19th and 20th June, when it was passed by 236 votes to 55; and the Bill was carried without a division at the Third Reading on 24th July. The Lords' amendment substituting 'direct' for 'indirect' election of the British Indian members to the Council of State was accepted by me on the Government's behalf. Churchill referred to it as an effort to conciliate the Liberals. He said of me: 'This is a remarkable episode in the history of the Bill. I am sure that the Under-Secretary has rarely made a better speech than that which he has delivered this afternoon. It was cogent, terse, informative, well-reasoned, and he stated the difficult case he had to make in terms which would be inoffensive in almost every quarter. . . . I really think that if the Under-Secretary had not made such a brilliant success of his parliamentary career this Session he might seriously consider embracing the great profession of the law, and then he would find himself in a position where those admirable gifts which he has of being able at short notice to deliver an equally powerful argument for or against any cause for which he is briefed, would not go unrequited. . . .' The Bill received Royal Assent on 2nd August, 1935.

The Act's great contribution was that it set the seal on parliamentary government as the pattern that would thenceforth be followed. Despite Nehru, who himself mellowed a great deal in the later years, Hindus, broadly speaking, were deeply impregnated with the idea and practice of parliamentary government. Federation was the only way to attempt to bridge the gulf that inevitably would appear when the Governor-General had become simply the constitutional head of State. 'We have', as Baldwin said in December 1934, 'given these people literature and liberty. It is impossible to give people literature that tells them of Hampden, Burke, Fox, Shelley, Mazzini, and Lincoln and expect them to be tolerant of oppression.' Whether the attitude of the Princes, whose refusal to enter the Federation was the reason why the letter of the Government of India Act was never fulfilled, was itself justified by a hardening of the stand taken by the Congress, it is difficult to judge. My own opinion is that this was not possible in the long run because of Jinnah. I never knew Jinnah personally, but, of course, he was as single-minded as Carson was in Northern Ireland; in many ways he was not unlike Carson, absolutely determined on the Moslem future, and determined on Partition. For this reason I do not believe that Congress could have weaned the Moslems away from Partition. Men like Jinnah are not born every day. He had few graces, but he had extreme determination of character, and that determination was destined to create the independent Moslem State. Jinnah was just as definite and firm a character as Nehru himself. In the end, the Moslems would have broken away whatever had happened. But both before and after the Government of India Bill, there is no doubt that Congress should have courted the Moslems more than they did. In March 1937 Nehru claimed: 'There are only two forces in India today, British imperialism and Indian nationalism as represented by the Congress'; to which Jinnah replied: 'No, there is a third party; the Mussulmans.'

The Government of India Act was vastly complicated by the characteristics, physical and political, of the Indian sub-continent. The sheer physical size of British India made any sort of homogeneity an apparently impossible target. Among the eleven Provinces of British India, Bengal alone had a larger population than that of Great Britain, and Madras an area as large as Italy. Among the Princely States, administration was complicated by the fact that there had never been any clear demarcation of powers between the States and the British Crown over foreign affairs, defence and economic affairs, although it was generally understood, in practice as well as in theory, that these areas were the prerogative of the British Crown. The seriousness of any deterioration of relations between Moslems and Hindus was aggravated by the 40 million or more who were numbered among the scheduled castes, by the Sikhs who resented Moslem predominance in the Punjab. In his book *India and Freedom* Leo Amery wrote, at the beginning of the last war: 'What we have overlooked is that our type of Constitution can only work in a relatively homogeneous community in which parties are the machinery for the expression of differences of views on specific public issues, the nuclei round which the main fluctuating mass of the electorate forms and reforms itself, but embody no permanent differences either of way of life, or of underlying loyalties. Unfortunately, these conditions do not exist in India, at any rate, in the India of today.' We tried to overcome this hurdle in the Government of India Bill by resorting to the method of Federation. Unfortunately, as everybody saw, Federation, largely due to the obstinacy of the Princes, was never carried out.

It was perhaps a miracle, but in my view it was also due largely to the patience and realism of Baldwin's government and of Sam Hoare, that in a country where the only unifying factor was the presence of the British and a long tradition of the different peoples in India having accomplished things together and sharing past glories, that the final transfer of power was voluntary. The gradualness of the progress towards self-government meant that Indians themselves had grown used to the daily administration of parliamentary government: that it also at the same time made inevitable the domination of the Congress Party was unavoidable. When, in 1954, I stayed with Nehru in Delhi, he affirmed without hesitation that our Government of India Bill, founded as it was on Dicey and Anson, the two great constitutional lawyers, was the basis of the Independence Bill itself.

CHAPTER FOUR

INTO WAR

JUST BEFORE the completion of the India Bill, Baldwin succeeded MacDonald as Prime Minister and Sam Hoare, my exhausted chief, was promoted to his short and ill-starred tenure of the Foreign Secretaryship. I would have welcomed a change myself, and my restlessness was scarcely diminished by the honour of serving the new Secretary of State for India, Lord Zetland. This distinguished ex-Governor of Bengal and official biographer of Curzon and Cromer was too punctilious to be informal and too straitlaced to be communicative. Interviews with him were not to be had by 'breaking in' to his room, but required to be arranged by correspondence or through the channels of his Private Office. One day when I asked him, in effect, what I could do to improve the sensitiveness of my political antennae, he replied 'Read my books.' I served him for two years. In the end Neville Chamberlain stepped in and said it was time for me to understand the home front. He recommended my going to the Ministry of Labour to serve an apprenticeship for future office, and I was instantaneously offered, and happily accepted, the Parliamentary Secretaryship under Ernest Brown.

Brown as an ex-sergeant-major was *simplicitas* itself, straight, loyal and running on predestinate grooves. We toured the depressed areas of South Wales, Cumberland and the North-East, and for ever after I remembered what Montagu Norman's deflationary strictness at the Bank of England meant in human terms. When as post-war Chancellor of the Exchequer I turned on the apostles of old-style economics and said that 'those who talked about creating pools of unemployment should be thrown into them and made to swim', I was still seeing in my own mind's eye the look of hopelessness in the eyes of the men of the 'thirties standing idly on street corners or queuing drably at the labour exchanges. We learn our lessons better from experience than from books. It was particularly helpful for a young Minister in a difficult and exposed office to serve under the tutelage of Sir Thomas Phillips, a Permanent Secretary with an acute brain and a compassionate heart. He was nearly always in the officials' box in the House when the Department's affairs were under discussion and, though I became more practised and more confident in the answering of parliamentary questions, I measured my success or lack of it by the number of times he used his favourite expression 'excellently well'. I learned from him what great diplomatic as well as administrative potential the Ministry of Labour had. I learned about the first trading estates and the 'special areas' policy, more modest forerunners of what we now call regional development. And since Ernest Brown used the same peroration in every city and township we visited, I also learned that by heart.

Late in February 1938 I was having a meal in the Commons Members' Dining Room and happened for some reason to be wearing a dinner jacket. At the Whips' table in the corner sat David Margesson who was dining Lord Halifax. I noticed them pointing towards me and then engaging in earnest conversation. My heart missed a beat. If they were not criticizing my attire, they were considering my preferment. The latter explanation seemed rather the more likely and much the most disturbing. Next day the Chief Whip sent for me and said that Halifax would like me to be his Under-Secretary in view of all that I had done on the India Bill and that I would be hearing from the Prime Minister. Neville Chamberlain made me a very warm-hearted approach, indicating that I would be the only Foreign Office Minister in the Commons and would be relied upon, in parti-cular, to help him answer questions. There was no doubt where my political duty lay; political advantage was another matter. Both Halifax's predecessors had been violently unseated—Hoare ignominiously, Eden voluntarily—and Halifax himself was known to have accepted the succession with great reluctance. 'I have had enough obloquy for one lifetime', was his observa-tion as he looked back on his period as Viceroy. But in trying to appease Gandhi, we had at least been dealing with some sort of saint. In Europe we were confronted with demons.

What is more, neither Britain nor her possible allies had yet the means, let alone the will, to exorcize them. This was a deplorable fact; it is, nevertheless, an incontrovertible one. From early in my career I had regarded it as self-evident that the foreign politics of a nation with world interests such as ours must largely be determined by its military posture. Diplomacy in order to be effective must be based on strength. Threats as an instrument of policy were not only useless but positively harmful unless backed by the determination and the ability to give effect to them. In 1935, desperately worried by the signs of Italian aggression against Abyssinia and our incapacity to avert it by the sanction of force, I had been one of the Conservatives who fought the General Election above all on the issue of more arms. Chamberlain, then Chancellor of the Exchequer, gave a much firmer lead to us than Baldwin and was pilloried by the Opposition not as an appeaser but as a warmonger. In my own constituency rearmament became the fundamental bone of contention between my Labour opponent and myself. I too was accused of being a warmonger and a militarist because I opposed what seemed to me to be Labour's motto, 'disarm and fight', and recommended instead that, if only we prepared, we might not have to fight. After the election, as A. J. P. Taylor has stated, 'the armament plans were recast in order to prepare for a great war, not merely to fill a few gaps. Effective rearmament began soon afterwards. No doubt it proceeded slowly. Before this time it had not happened at all. Later even the critics could only have speeded it up—they could not have produced results at once.'[1] Certainly the desirable level of preparedness had not been achieved by 1938; indeed in that year, when I joined Halifax at the Foreign Office, our military situation was such that Ironside, later Chief of the Imperial General Staff, wrote that 'no foreign nation would believe it if they were told'.

My first major speech on 'The Issues of British Foreign Policy' was made on 9th April to a formidable array of six hundred notables at Chatham House. I had been warned that these intellectual meetings were attended by very many journalists who used one's material for their articles, that the audience would include foreign attachés, and that the lecture would be

[1] *English History 1914–1945* (Oxford).

printed for distribution throughout the Empire. All this encouraged me to put first things first. 'The Imperial conception of our policy', I said, 'carries with it the need of strength. The interlinking of strength and diplomacy is fully realized by H.M.G. That is what prompts us in our determination to proceed with every aspect of rearmament so that our policy may be a strong one. And in our policy is it necessary to stress again the special importance of preparation in the air and of developing the passive resistance of our population? I am convinced that our policy will be more respected the more undoubted the determination of our people is shown.' During the debate that followed, Bernard Shaw, with whom I had just dined at the Astors', managed in the course of a few minutes to demolish the British Constitution, our parliamentary system, the National government and the Socialist Opposition. This enabled me in my reply at the end to say lightly that I was proud to be bowled over in such distinguished company. What I felt to be no matter for pride, let alone for levity, but rather for the reverse, was that this same distinguished company should be bowled over by the dictators again and again. And why? Because in all parties we had been so lacking in diplomatic foresight and, even in the Conservative party, so tardy in making good our defences and our deterrent power.

Within a few days of my going to the Foreign Office, Hitler had given us one more indication of the shape of things to come by his forcible incorporation of Austria into Germany. The *Anschluss*, I told the assembly at Chatham House, had increased my conviction that 'This country must be strong, strong of purpose and strong in arms. We are living in critical times and it is therefore no more than the plain duty of the government to press ahead with our rearmament programme so that we may have the strength to back our policy and so that in case of need we shall be able to defend ourselves.' Churchill had at last been listened to with rapt attention and respect when he warned the House of Commons that we were confronted with a nicely calculated and carefully timed programme of aggression, unfolding stage by stage. There was general agreement and apprehension that the next stage would involve Czechoslovakia. Accordingly the Prime Minister asked the Chiefs of Staff for a report on the new military situation following the *Anschluss*. They specified that the Czechoslovak frontier of 2,500 miles could not be protected from a German attack, thus confirming Austen Chamberlain's warning in 1936 that 'If Austria goes, Czechoslovakia is indefensible.' They also advised that Britain was not in a position to wage war, particularly in view of our unreadiness in the air. Later in the summer they reported to the Committee of Imperial Defence that it was of vital importance for us to gain time for the completion of the defence programme. The government was therefore faced with a categorical warning that the country was not ready for war, especially if this involved (as was expected or feared) not only a German front, but conflict in the Mediterranean with Italy and trouble in the Far East with Japan.

This was the unpalatable military appreciation which Chamberlain and Halifax gave to the representatives of France—who alone had a direct treaty obligation to the Czechs—when they came to London at the end of April. The main result of these Anglo-French conversations was therefore a decision to make a joint *démarche* in Prague to secure the maximum concessions from President Beneš. It has been wrongly assumed that Chamberlain believed such concessions would inevitably forestall a German military invasion of Czechoslovakia. On the contrary, he was fully aware, as were all the best of our diplomatic advisers, that the Sudeten problem might not be the real issue and that Hitler might have ambitions far beyond the restoration of Sudeten rights. Chamberlain felt that this was a situation which would have to be faced if it came, but that a world war could not be fought to maintain inviolate the ascendancy of seven million Czechs over an almost equal multitude of discontented minorities. The boundaries of Czechoslovakia had been drawn, as Churchill himself testified, in flagrant defiance of the doctrine of self-determination. There is no doubt that the government of the new State kept the three million Germans in a position of political, educational and cultural inferiority, and that bitterness was exacerbated by the economic depression of the 'thirties which hit the German industrialized areas (the Sudetenland) more severely than elsewhere. These grievances were outrageously exploited by the Nazis and their

Sudeten puppet, Henlein; but the grievances were real. In the week of the *Anschluss*, Basil Newton, our Ambassador in Prague, advised us (correctly, as was seen in 1945) that the *status quo* in Czechoslovakia could not be perpetuated even after a victorious war. On 22nd March I wrote to Lord Brabourne in India questioning whether we could defend by force a feature of the Peace Treaties which was in fact indefensible. I indicated that I had tried to get the Cabinet Committee involved to issue a statement saying that we were prepared to seek revision of the Treaties. I also said, 'To summon the League, talk to Litvinov, or act as mediator between Germans and Czechs, is likely to bring down on our heads more trouble than standing aloof.' This letter proved, alas, to be prophetic.

I was not myself a prime mover in the complex and dramatic events of the succeeding months. As a junior Minister I was little consulted about their cause or course. My role was sometimes that of a sceptical spectator, as when I stood in the Foreign Secretary's room in July studying the glass-fronted bookcase and heard Lord Runciman accept his impossible mediating mission to Prague with the words, 'I am being cut off like a small rowing boat from a great liner.' Throughout the fateful weeks of September I was off-stage in Geneva where, however, I conducted two important interviews with the Foreign Ministers of the Soviet Union and of France. The former convinced me that Russia had no intention of coming to the help of the Czechs, even if the Czechs had wanted this, which they didn't; the latter gave me the measure of France's political unreliability. These two factors were interrelated, since a French declaration of war was stipulated by the Russians to be a condition of their own intervention. I am thus convinced that Sir John Wheeler-Bennett's conclusion about the inevitability of the Munich agreement was correct and, in view of his own vehement and sustained reaction to appeasement, all the more creditable to his historical mastery. 'Let us say of the Munich Settlement', he wrote, 'that it was inescapable; that, faced with the lack of preparedness in Britain's armaments and defences, with the lack of unity at home and in the Commonwealth, with the collapse of French morale, and with the uncertainty of Russia to fight, Mr. Chamberlain had no alternative to do other than he did;

let us pay tribute to his persistence in carrying out a policy which he honestly believed to be right. Let us accept and admit all these things, but in so doing let us not omit the shame and humiliation that were ours; let us not forget that, in order to save our own skins—that because we were too weak to protect ourselves—we were forced to sacrifice a small Power to slavery.'[1] In the light of the events of March 1939 the defenders of Munich, of whom I have always been one, cannot be morally blind to the savage impeachment of those concluding words; but in the light of the political and strategic realities of 1938 the critics of Munich, though deserving all respect, persevere in passion by denying its historical inevitability.

More than one of my contemporaries have suggested in their memoirs that the alternative to appeasement should have been for Britain to rally all the League to resistance. Churchill wrote of Arms and the Covenant. However, as was clearly stated by Anthony Eden in January 1938 in his speech at the 100th session of the Council of the League at Geneva, 'By the defection of some of its more important members, the League is now faced with the fact that the area of co-operation is restricted and that its ability to fulfil all the functions originally contemplated for it is thereby reduced. We must realize that in present circumstances the League is not in a position to achieve all that was hoped of it.' We still believed that the League ideals were noble and worthy of our fullest support, and our attitude towards League reform was always positive. I had had a hand in the British government's initiative in this direction in 1938. It was decided at our suggestion to separate the Covenant from the Treaties of Peace, as it was thought this would help to illustrate that the League was not an organization bound up with the *status quo*, but that the Covenant as such had a life independent of Versailles. Yet at the same time there were hard facts to be faced. Of the great Powers, the U.S.A. never had come into the League; Japan, Germany and Italy had left it. It was no more than a plain statement of truth to say that the League in 1938 could not by itself ensure the peace of the world. If the League were called to deal with the Czech situation, it could do no more than pass some pious but quite ineffective resolution

[1] *Munich: Prologue to Tragedy* (Macmillan).

which would do no positive good but rather only inflict on it a still further humiliation. This would prejudice its future, in particular its ultimate reconstruction. Manchuria, Abyssinia and Spain had already brought painfully to light the defects of the League, and by condoning a series of unjust aggressions it had proved that it could not provide automatic security. There was, furthermore, a disastrous fallacy in the attitude of those who clamoured for 'collective security' yet repudiated any notion of an international force outside British control or, like the Labour Opposition, voted against British rearmament.

Collective security on the eve of the Munich crisis was certainly not something that could exist independently of the policies of Britain, France and Russia; and France and Russia were no more inclined to move than we. The official policy of France was to stand by her treaty obligation to Czechoslovakia: but as Lord Strang, then head of the Central Department of the Foreign Office, recalls a very different impression was given by what French Ministers said behind the scenes, whether in social gatherings or to foreign representatives. Thus anyone who confines his reading to the published Documents on British Foreign Policy might easily conclude that when Daladier and Bonnet visited London on 28th and 29th April, they wanted a firm stand and were dissuaded only by the logistic pessimism of Chamberlain and Halifax. If, however, one turns to the Documents on German Foreign Policy, it appears that on 27th April (that is, the day before these talks) Daladier told an agent of the German Embassy in London that he hoped the British 'would themselves suggest that pressure should be put on Prague' so that he 'could acquiesce without seeming to have taken the initiative in the matter'. Daladier, however, was a gladiator when compared with his Foreign Minister, Bonnet, whose fascinating memoirs *Défense de la Paix* do not respond to the test of accuracy. Churchill described Bonnet as 'the quintessence of defeatism' but only, I fancy, because he had already used up the epithet 'boneless wonder' on a fellow-countryman.

On the morning of 11th September, when attending the 19th Assembly of the League at Geneva, I went, on instructions, with Euan Wallace to see Bonnet in his hotel. He at once told us that the situation in central Europe had been made infinitely more serious than before by the *Times* leader of 7th September, written by Geoffrey Dawson, the editor, in which the secession of the Sudeten districts to Germany had been advocated. I am myself convinced that Halifax knew this article was to be written: the two Yorkshiremen were very close and I saw Dawson leaving the Office on the 6th after a long interview with the Foreign Secretary. However, the proposal had been immediately and officially repudiated and I could not see why Bonnet should bring it up now, except that it was characteristic of him to shift the blame for appeasement on to anybody's shoulders except his own. This is, indeed, what he proceeded to do. President Roosevelt, he noted, had told his press conference on 9th September that it was '100 per cent inaccurate' to associate the United States with France and Britain in a front of resistance against Hitler. The Russians, he said, 'rather than engage in war, were wrapping themselves in League procedure'. The Poles had told him that they would try to stay neutral but would definitely resist the passage of Russian troops to assist Czechoslovakia. He hoped that Britain would come in if Hitler used forcible action against the Czechs, but did not press us to define our position. Instead he drew attention to the likelihood of an Italian intervention. In these circumstances for France to envisage a war on three fronts—Italy, Spain and Germany— would be 'equivalent to jumping off the Eiffel Tower'. Bonnet made plain to us that France proposed to do nothing of the kind.

Litvinov, the Soviet Foreign Minister, was at once more affable and more sinister, but scarcely less negative. On 23rd September, in the Sixth Political Committee of the League Assembly, he said that the Soviet government had no obligations to Czechoslovakia in the event of French indifference to an attack upon her. If this situation arose the Russians might come to the aid of the Czechs as the result of a decision by the League. But no one could insist on that help as a duty, and in fact the Czech government, out of practical as well as formal considerations, had not raised the question of Soviet assistance independently of assistance by France. This didn't take us very far, and Halifax instructed me by telegram to try to obtain a precise indication of what action the Russians would take if

Czechoslovakia were involved in war with Germany, and at what point they would be prepared to take it. That night De La Warr and I met Litvinov and Maisky in a glass-fronted committee room in the old League building. The press were able to press their noses against the glass and watch our gestures despite the ushers' efforts to move them on. They were inspired by the idea that Russia was straining to intervene and had to be disillusioned, as did so many at home, when they received a distilled account of Litvinov's actual views.

He began by saying that, since the terms of the Soviet-Czech Pact postulated prior French military assistance, the Anglo-French pressure on Prague to 'capitulate' virtually rendered the Pact a dead letter. Nevertheless if France were to honour her obligations and fight, the Russians 'would take action'. I asked him to develop this further and in particular to say at what stage Russian intervention might take place. Would he raise the matter at the League (which was substantially what the Soviet-Czech Pact provided) and, if so, did that mean that action would be suspended while the League discussion was going on? Litvinov, however, refused to budge an inch from his original generalization. He said his government 'might desire to raise the matter in the League', but this did not alter the fact that the Pact would have come into force. We indicated, as plainly as the language of diplomacy would allow, that what mattered was not the formality of the Pact but the reality of the aid. To what extent was the Russian army mobilized and its air force ready to assist the Czechs? Litvinov said that he could not tell us this: he was not posted on military and air questions 'since he had been away from Russia for such a time'. These matters could, however, be discussed if Britain, France and Russia, together with any 'reliable' small Powers such as Roumania, now agreed to confer away from the atmosphere of Geneva, 'to show the Germans we meant business'.

I was left in no doubt that the Russians themselves did not mean business. Litvinov had been deliberately evasive and vague, except when he had said that if France acted the Soviet would act too. Since his conversations with his opposite number had been far more numerous and dispiriting than mine, this was tantamount to saying that if Bonnet threw himself off the Eiffel

Tower Litvinov would be there to catch him. It seemed to me preposterous for him to pretend ignorance of Soviet military preparations. He was, and gave the clear impression of being, much nearer the centre of power than any other Russian Foreign Minister with whom I have had dealings, and he had been at his desk in the Kremlin in the first week of September. He was perfectly well aware that, in the absence of a common frontier between Russia and Czechoslovakia, the 'barrier' policy of Poland and Roumania would limit Soviet aid to modest air support. Nor is there any evidence that if the railways through the Carpathian Mountains had been available to Russian forces, they would have been capable of rendering effective aid. Appreciations arriving at the Foreign Office from our Embassy in Moscow warned that the great purges of 1937 had had a disastrous effect on the morale and efficiency of the Red Army which, 'though no doubt equal to a defensive war within the frontiers of the Soviet Union, is not capable of carrying the war into the enemy's territory with any hope of ultimate success or without thereby running the risk of endangering the régime'. We now know that precisely similar appreciations were reaching Berlin from the German Ambassador.

Nevertheless, the theory that we deliberately 'excluded Russia from Europe' and that this played a decisive part in the ultimate tragedy was widely held by political opinion at home. It was endorsed after the war by Churchill who, advancing a somewhat medieval interpretation of history, argued that Stalin wanted to help Beneš because in 1936 the latter had revealed a plot against his life. The murders and massacres of his régime hardly reveal Stalin as so warm-hearted a man even in matters concerning his own family. Nor was this hypothetical affection and affinity reciprocal. As Beneš told the French Ambassador in Prague, and as Litvinov admitted more or less explicitly to the League, the Czechs did not wish to accept Soviet intervention unless France acted first. Many Czechs had fought against the Bolsheviks in 1918 and feared Soviet domination. General Jan Syrovy is on record as saying, 'We don't want the Russians in here as we shall never get them out.' Though, in the light of subsequent history, no sentiment compels readier or sadder assent, it was of secondary significance to the British in 1938. For us the criterion was whether Russia intended to oppose the German army, whether indeed she could afford to fight. My interview with Litvinov only confirmed our conclusion that, both on political and military grounds, the U.S.S.R. could not be trusted to wage war in defence of interests that were not bound up with her own security.

It is true that none of the diplomatic negatives I have exhibited were to be any less in evidence in 1939 than they were in 1938. In neither year could any reliance have been placed on the League of Nations to deter aggression. In either year the worm-eaten fabric of French political society and the self-seeking duplicity of the Soviet régime would have combined to leave us alone to face at close quarters the onslaught of the Luftwaffe. But the crucial change that came about as a result of the year's delay was in our preparedness to meet this onslaught. The 'special importance of preparation in the air and of developing the passive resistance of our population', which had been my theme at Chatham House in April 1938, proved indeed to be the key factors. In September 1938 the R.A.F. had only one operational fighter squadron equipped with Spitfires and five in process of being equipped with Hurricanes; by the summer of 1939, thanks to Lord Swinton's earlier tenure of the Air Ministry, it had twenty-six squadrons of modern eight-gun fighters, and a year later forty-seven. Our ground defences against air attack were also substantially strengthened in this period. The provision of anti-aircraft guns was increased fourfold to 1,653, of which more than half were the newer 3.7- and 4.5-inch guns, and barrage balloon defence was completed in London and extended outside. More important was the fact that, by the time war broke out, the chain of radar stations, which during the Munich crisis had been in operation only in the Thames estuary, guarded the whole of Britain from the Orkneys to the Isle of Wight. Meanwhile, the administrative talents of John Anderson had wrought corresponding transformations in civilian A.R.P., and plans for evacuating schoolchildren and finding emergency hospital beds were completed.

These preparations extended to the pace and scope of British rearmament generally, as Professor Postan has described in his official history of British war production. But I stress them here both because they undoubtedly constituted the most important defence achievement between Munich and the outbreak of war and because, though we now know that the figures of German strength quoted by our professional advisers and our critics alike to have been greatly exaggerated, they did provide the indispensable means by which we won the Battle of Britain. On this reckoning Munich was not, in Wheeler-Bennett's phrase, a 'prologue to tragedy', but the pause, however inglorious, which enabled Churchill when his time came to lead the nation through the valley of the shadow to victory. Nor was the military breathing-space the only gain. There were subtler but equally significant changes of opinion at home and abroad. During 1938 it had been possible to argue, and I argued myself, that the principles of self-determination for which the previous war had ostensibly been fought could not be denied to the Sudetens simply because they were Germans or even because they were supported by Nazis. The Treaty of Versailles still weighed heavily. By 1939 the morality was quite clearly all on one side. There could no longer be any doubt in any mind that the ambitions of Germany stretched far beyond its ethnic frontiers and that it had indeed, in Chamberlain's phrase, 'made up its mind to dominate the world by fear of its force'. These considerations affected not only the will and conscience of our own people but the attitudes of Commonwealth governments and of enlightened leaders in foreign countries, most notably in the U.S.A.

On the morrow of Munich, by contrast, world opinion was overwhelmingly in favour of and grateful for peace. In making my wind-up speech for the government in the House of Commons on 5th October, I was able to quote hymns of praise which I had brought back from the foreign delegations at Geneva. These justified me in claiming that, whilst I had been impressed by the depth of critical feeling in the debate, British prestige was still high abroad. Disagreeable as the settlement might be, the alternatives—a forcible imposition of German will or a world war—were felt to be worse. Having just emerged from what I called 'the engine room of the League', I was able to give some indication of the difficulties of employing its machinery either to adjust frontiers or to avoid conflict. About my difficulties with Litvinov (of whom I spoke with studied politeness) and with Bonnet I could at the time make no reference. Next day I received a generous letter from Lord Baldwin, whose own lips had been sealed at an earlier date. This said, 'It wasn't easy or simple to make an effective speech and you managed it.' I hope the last few words were deserved; for the rest of the sentence I can vouch.

'Bobbety' Cranborne had written to me, when I took over from him in February 1938, 'This is a rough tough job.' I held it for more than three years in peace and war, and he was certainly right. Today there is a phalanx of Foreign Office Ministers. Then there were just two—and, until Eden succeeded Halifax at the end of 1940, only one in the House of Commons. In the grim winter of 1938–9 I answered alone an average of seventy-five parliamentary questions a week. The most harassing and embarrassing of these concerned the Spanish Civil War where, in the light of Italian and German support for Franco, we had the greatest difficulty in upholding the government's policy of non-intervention. Lloyd George, who had never been averse from bestowing titles, later awarded me the sobriquet of 'the artful dodger'; and certainly I could have succumbed had I not shown a little skill in parrying the blows which rained upon me. The News Chronicle of 8th December was good enough to say that I had excelled myself during the previous afternoon in the capacity of Stonewaller, 'while the Prime Minister sat silent'. I am portrayed as having gone, during the long hour of questions, through three phases: first, determination combined with an air of injured innocence; second, friendliness with an implied appeal for mercy by the bowlers; third, righteous indignation. My most telling remark was thought to be, 'A certain incident has taken place and a certain answer has been returned.' All this sounds more light-hearted in retrospect than it felt amid the passions of the time.

The League of Nations, which in its contemporary embodiment can involve full-time attention, was then all in the week's work. But I was fortunate from time to time to enjoy the support of some more senior members of the government, and have already mentioned the help of Euan Wallace, a bright, amusing, worldly creature who was always on the target, and of

'Buck' De La Warr, the Lord Privy Seal. Buck once created quite a sensation by wandering about the League lobbies saying, '*Je veux aller au Cabinet.*' Obliging foreigners showed him the necessary doors, but he kept asking for the plane times so that he could return to his duties in England at the Cabinet. He proved a very resourceful member of our small team. One evening we all attended a party given by Diana Duff Cooper on the other side of the Lake. I am alleged to have quoted Lamartine on the balcony ('*O lac! l'année à peine a fini sa carrière*'): at any rate Diana mentions it in her poetic autobiography. We needed such distractions and consolations, for the interviews were legion and the foreign situation disastrous.

In the Office I undertook about half the interviews with foreign diplomats (Halifax was particularly averse from conversations with Russians and Japanese), helped the F.O. symposium whenever the Secretary of State made a speech, and sat on the Appointments Board. I have the happiest memory of my time with the Diplomatic Corps. In my crowded life I used to say that I gave them more time than my own family. At that time there were posted in London some very experienced representatives. Perhaps my most frequent visitor was Jimmy, Duke of Alba. He had with him in the Embassy, Pépé Santa Cruz whom I have therefore known all my life, starting in the difficult circumstances of the Spanish Civil War. We have always been fast friends. One of the most senior diplomatists was Baron Cartier of Belgium. He was full of worldly wisdom and used to say when tired of the diplomatic life one should take a cigar and a bottle of claret and retire to bed without dinner. He certainly looked well on this diet. I also had frequent discussions with Maisky and Shigemitsu, the Japanese. Maisky's memoirs are there for all to read. He was certainly the most pertinacious of all foreign representatives.

I had been warned by Cranborne not to expect graces from the Foreign Office. What I could expect and did get as Under-Secretary (and, much later in my career, as Secretary of State) was the most devoted and expert care and attention. I was served by a perfect Private Secretary, Peter Loxley, who was tragically drowned in a plane disaster in the Mediterranean long before he could realize his potential. He was gifted and vivacious and, had he survived, would surely have risen from the modest post with me to the top of the Office. I was fortunate in having as his successor Geoffrey Harrison, later to be our Ambassador in Moscow. As P.P.S. David Margesson advised me to choose 'Chips' Channon. This appointment, according to his Diaries, 'made his life'. It also provided me with much diversion, colour and friendship. I began in ignorance of having, to use Winston Churchill's remark about Philip Sassoon, 'attached a first-class restaurant car to the train'. But I was always aware that, however late he went to bed, he would be writing an account of his impressions in his diary. He told me I need not worry since it would not be published for fifty years after his death, a decision he subsequently altered, rightly or wrongly I find it hard to say. He thus wrote very frankly, quite often about me. Our values were clearly different. But when his strong sociable instinct brought people who actually mattered to his table—the Prime Minister being treated *en prince*, the Duff Coopers aflame against Munich, General Smuts expounding Holism, Harry Hopkins acting as Roosevelt's go-between in our finest hour—an extra dimension was given to politics which one could find neither in the House nor in the Office. Chips also had a useful nose for gossip, and a great sense of friendship.

What the Indians would call the great 'Sahib-dil' of the Foreign Office was Sir Alexander Cadogan. He too kept a diary which will provide the most intimate record of these fateful years. His ancestor had served Marlborough as Chief of Staff. Alec was himself a first-class Chief of Staff, employing his Rolls-Royce brain to keep the Office boat steady, to avoid collisions with No. 10 and Horace Wilson, to serve his Ministerial master loyally, and to 'bring up' and 'bring out' those like me whom he must often have found lacking in experience of foreign affairs. I remember one evening at about eight o'clock when we were at last leaving the Office, Alec and I walked down the huge stairway behind the Secretary of State and a man dressed in check tweeds. Alec whispered to me, 'The Private Office say he comes from Yorkshire and has ideas on foreign policy. We shall have to work very hard tomorrow to counteract this latest stuff.' The truth is that Edward Halifax's mind was always open to the last comer; but, after hearing new ideas, he would commune with himself, with his Maker, and with Alec—so plenty of time usually elapsed before he took a decision. Lord Birkenhead gives an excellent picture of this strange and imposing figure—half unworldly saint, half cunning politician—in his monumental *Life*.[1] The biographer agrees with Wheeler-Bennett about Munich and that is fair enough, but I doubt whether sufficient credit has yet been given to Halifax for leading the Cabinet swiftly but steadily in 1939 towards an inevitable declaration of war.

On 16th March, 1939, the day after Czechoslovakia fell to pieces and Hitler occupied Prague, I lunched at No. 10 with Neville Chamberlain and Edward Halifax. The Prime Minister said with resignation, but with our solemn approval, 'I have decided that I cannot trust the Nazi leaders again.' Next day he made a speech to the Birmingham Unionist Association which I described to his P.P.S., Alec Douglas-Home, as being more like an oration by the younger Pitt. Halifax said later that it was he who had insisted on the need for this fighting speech as the prelude to a revolution in foreign policy. I am sure that this was true. Shortly after Easter I wrote in my diary: 'Whence comes the present drive away from the policy of appeasement? The Foreign Office is certainly surprised and gratified by the energy with which this has been prosecuted. I have decided that the determination comes from Halifax himself. Sometimes he has moved the Cabinet by the use of what appeared at first sight to be rumours. For instance, the Berlin correspondent of the *News Chronicle* was used to impress the Cabinet with the possibility of the invasion of Poland. But whatever the methods it is clear that Halifax is determined to set up a force counter to Germany and that he is going ahead single-mindedly.' Oliver Harvey's feelings at the time are shown by this extract from his diaries:[2]

'February 17th: . . . I feel H. now sees his way much more clearly. . . . He is almost unrecognisable from the H. of a year ago. He says bluntly "no more Munich for me"; and I am sure

[1] *Halifax, The Life of Lord Halifax*, by the Earl of Birkenhead (Hamish Hamilton).
[2] *The Diplomatic Diaries of Oliver Harvey, 1937–1940*, edited by John Harvey (Collins).

he is convinced that now we are stronger we must stand firm. He felt in September that we were not strong enough to risk fighting unless it was absolutely vital to us and that the Czech issue was not vital, but he always spoke of our being "between two horrible alternatives" and never saw anything to be proud of in the result. He won't allow us to get caught again like that.'

A few weeks later I wrote: 'Edward's method may be described as holding out in front of him long antennae which feel every movement of the nation and touch every kind of person. He thus regularly sees Winston Churchill, Anthony Eden and the Labour leaders. He walks from his home with junior M.P.s and sees discreetly other figures outside the Office. He is therefore well informed of every aspect of a question. Being in the Lords he takes a detached view. His main difference with the P.M. is that he believes in broadening the base of the government and bringing back Eden and Churchill into the Cabinet.' Halifax had, indeed, been urging this course ever since Munich.

I found the Prime Minister temperamentally incapable of forming a nationally based administration. By nature and by intention his approach to political problems was the exact opposite of Baldwin's. Whenever I thought of this approach I always found myself comparing it to a 'ton of bricks'. Talking to him day after day about statements and answers in the House, I got to realize that, if one phrase or one word were out of place, an order would be given, the builder's lorry would be tipped, and if one didn't watch out the ton of bricks would descend on one's own head. Shortly after I took office I described his attitude in less metaphorical prose to my parents, who were in India: 'He frequently redrafts in pencil with very little hesitation and very little crossing out. He does not like vague and polite phrases but wishes to go straight at the Opposition and express exactly what he means. The traditional soothing of Members by such phrases as "the honourable and gallant gentleman will be aware" is usually erased. There is no doubt, however, about his loyalty to his friends and his courage.' In the Commons itself, where I used to sit next to him, he could not conceal his impatience with the Labour and Liberal leaders. He would fidget and fume expletives in a manner which brought to my mind the famous physical eccentricities of Dr. Johnson. Nor was I ever wholly convinced that the revolution which had taken place in Edward's mind was reflected in Neville's. On the Good Friday of 1939, which Mussolini chose for the invasion of Albania, I hurried up from the country and at once called at No. 10 for instructions. I was led into a small room upstairs, overlooking the garden, which the Prime Minister used as a study. The window was partly open, showing a table for bird food suspended outside. Neville seemed irritated at my intrusion and surprised that I was perturbed. He said, 'I feel sure Mussolini has not decided to go against us.' When I started to talk about the general threat to the Balkans, he dismissed me with the words, 'Don't be silly. Go home to bed', and continued to feed the birds. At least he did not tell me, as he had once advised Anthony Eden, to take an aspirin.

All the same, the alliance with Poland—followed after the Albanian episode by guarantees to Roumania, Greece and Turkey—proved a decisive event. We had called Hitler's bluff. And he was not bluffing. But neither were we. In all the weeks before the German armies drove into Poland I saw in the Foreign Office, and particularly in the upright mind of Alec Cadogan, an absolute inhibition against pressing the Poles to negotiate and noted in my diary that this was a result of the shame engendered by Munich. From 25th August onwards I was closely involved with Halifax and Cadogan in most of the discussions at No. 10 and helped where I could with drafting the various statements made in Parliament, the instructions to Ambassadors and the messages to the dictators. I was in the Cabinet room at eleven o'clock on 3rd September when our ultimatum to Germany expired. Ten minutes later the Prime Minister told me to inform the Service Departments that they might consider themselves at war. I went into the adjoining room and telephoned Gladwyn Jebb, who by arrangement was to be the link. This was the action which set the war in motion.

CHAPTER FIVE

WILLINGLY TO SCHOOL

T HE PRIME MINISTER's broadcast on the outbreak of war
was pathetically moving, but scarcely a tocsin ringing to
arms. However, none of us was obliged to comment on
the spur of the moment; for he had hardly asked his colleagues
how we liked it, when the air was rent by a terrible wailing
which no wartime Londoner will ever forget. 'That is an air-
raid warning', announced Chamberlain quite calmly. We all
laughed, and someone said, 'It would be funny if it were.' He
repeated several times, like a school-teacher dinning a lesson
into a class of late developers, 'That is an air-raid warning.' Then
Mrs. Chamberlain appeared in the doorway with a large basket
containing books, thermos flasks, gas-masks and other aids to
waiting, and everybody began to make their way to the War
room through the basement of No. 10. I found myself alone in
the Cabinet room. A few people were scurrying across Horse
Guards to try to take shelter. I decided that I had better die in
the Foreign Office and so walked slowly across Downing Street,
which was by then deserted. Members of the Office had assembled in the basement; and we sat on the floor, there being no
furniture. An officious warden told me that he did not antici-
pate the immediate use of gas. Neither, of course, did he antici-
pate that, without any intervening aerial bombardment, the
sirens would soon be sounding the all-clear. That phase which
was later to be called the phoney war (and by some humorists
the 'bore war') had started with a phoney alarm.

It was no part of Hitler's initial strategy to provoke Britain, or
even France: he hoped that, once Poland had been defeated,
they would call the war off. In so far as the Allied governments
had an initial strategy, they regarded economic blockade as the
main weapon, accompanied by an unhurried building up of

military resources which would eventually provide the *coup de grâce*. Both were wrong. The catalogue of catastrophes which began with the subjugation of Poland and ended with the fall of France was indeed punctuated by insidious suggestions—from the Germans, from the neutrals, and from defeatists at home— that we should sue for a negotiated peace. But to the best of my knowledge and belief no one in the British Government, and more emphatically no one with responsibility in the Foreign Office, ever encouraged the view that we would depart from the path of honour. Thus, after the defeat of Poland, I recall saying of a not intrinsically unreasonable peace formula suggested by Harold Nicolson and recorded in his diary, 'I am afraid that that sounds rather like appeasement. The Prime Minister is much more bellicose than that.' And I certainly do not recall giving the amusing Swedish Minister, Björn Prytz, on the day France capitulated, grounds for supposing that any of us had become less bellicose. Mr. Prytz, who was not a professional diplomat, later attributed to my interview with him a significance which was disputed not only by me but also by Sir Alexander Cadogan.[1] Winston wrote a letter to Halifax dated 26th June, 1940, accusing me of defeatism. Halifax replied as follows on 27th June:

'I had been into the matter of Butler's conversation with the Swedish Minister with Butler before I got your letter last night. He has since given me a full note of what passed between him and the Swedish Minister, and I have discussed the matter fully with him. I am satisfied that there is no divergence of view, and that the explanation is partly to be found in the last paragraph but one of telegram No. 534 Dipp of June 23rd that we sent to Sweden, after we had explored the matter further with the Swedish Minister here. I should be very sorry if you felt any doubt either about Butler's discretion or his complete loyalty to Government policy, of both of which I am completely satisfied.'

This followed up the official telegram referred to in the preceding paragraph from the Secretary of State to our Minister in

[1] Cadogan said to me that if he had thought it important he would have put it all in his Diary.

Stockholm, dated 23rd June, which included denials by the Swedish Minister in London that a construction could be placed on his language which could imply defeatism on my part. This was accompanied by an expression of surprise that the Swedish Minister for Foreign Affairs should have taken the matter so seriously. The Swedish Minister in London concluded by saying that he supposed that certain interested parties in Sweden had mixed themselves up with this affair in an attempt to cause mischief. I certainly went no further in responding to any neutral soundings than the official line at the time, which was that peace could not be considered prior to the complete withdrawal of German troops from all conquered territories. This was common sense, not bravado.

But if Hitler had misjudged our resolution, we had equally misjudged his strength. Of this misjudgement, Narvik was the first painful and humiliating proof. The proposal to mine the Leads, within whose safety Swedish iron ore was being transported by German ships from the Norwegian port of Narvik, was originally conceived of as a strengthening of our economic blockade. In all the various forms in which it was exhaustively considered, I was against it, and for three main reasons. First, because territorial waters were equivalent in law to national territory and our invasion of them would outrage neutral opinion. Secondly, because we should risk involving Scandinavia in war before she was ready, and thereby reduce her possible future value to us in the struggle. Thirdly, because it would dissipate our war effort. 'I dislike action for action's sake,' I concluded in a memorandum to Halifax and Cadogan, setting out these objections, 'but if we want activity let us help Finland to a greater extent. This would be a better alternative to an expedition, which may have unforeseen results and may rank in history with Walcheren and the Dardanelles. However brilliant a mind may have conceived it, let us remember that Jellicoe and the War Cabinet resisted the same Narvik temptation last time'. This was written on 11th January, 1940. On 3rd April, Winston Churchill, as First Lord of the Admiralty, finally prevailed on the War Cabinet to authorize the mining of Norwegian waters —together with the occupation of Norwegian coastal towns, including Narvik, if the Germans reacted—on 8th April. This

1939
DER SECRETARY OF
TE FOR FOREIGN
AFFAIRS

William Gordon Davis

WITH MR. MAISKY
AT GENEVA

1942. PRESIDENT OF
THE BOARD OF EDU-
CATION

Cartoon By E. H. Shepard,
Punch December 1943

THE BUTLER'S DREAM

"It came out of my head."

was the same day the Germans had chosen for their full-scale occupation of Denmark and Norway, and the British were taken completely by surprise. Our counter-strokes failed due to inadequate forces and lack of air cover, and in this first clash of war between German and Allied armies, the Allies were in effect routed.

It will always be one of the ironies of history that the man who stood most exposed to blame for this defeat, similar to several others in his career, became Prime Minister as a result of it. Churchill himself wrote in his history of the war that it was a marvel he survived. It was also a marvellous stroke of good fortune for the country that he should now have emerged as the hero and leader. A genuinely National government drawn from men of all parties had become urgently necessary. Chamberlain remained incapable of forming one. At the outbreak of war he had invited both the Labour and Liberal oppositions to enter the government, and had received from them a brusque and unsurprising refusal. Eight months later their attitude to him was even more hostile. On the evening of 8th May, while the Commons debate on the Norwegian campaign was still raging, Hugh Dalton came to see me. He told me that the Labour party would enter a government under Halifax, but not under Chamberlain or in the company of Simon, the Chancellor. This, he said, was the view he and his friends hoped I would pass on to my chief. I cross-questioned him as to whether the Labour leaders would join under Chamberlain if he pruned his team first. Dalton replied, 'No, we have too many grudges against Neville.' He added that there was no choice but Halifax: Churchill must 'stick to the war' and Anderson, the Home Secretary, had not been sufficiently 'built up'. After the debate, in which 33 Conservatives voted against the government and double that number abstained, I saw Herbert Morrison who said that the idea of Labour joining the government was 'coming along well'. But he made it clear that the conditions were the same as Dalton had outlined.

I was myself much influenced by my proximity to Edward Halifax to support his claims. His name had been canvassed for more than a year as the possible head of a government of national unity. He was acceptable to his own as well as to the opposition parties, and was clearly preferred by Neville Chamberlain who, in the event of resignation, would be called on to tender advice to the King. The Prime Minister's P.P.S., Alec Douglas-Home, who with his native shrewdness was one of the first to see how badly things would go for Chamberlain, had come to my room at the Foreign Office immediately before the debate on Norway; he urged me to talk to Halifax and persuade him to become Prime Minister. This was easier said than done. I duly passed on the encouraging messages from the Labour leaders, and on the morning of 9th May waited for Halifax in his room to hear an account of his conversations with the Prime Minister. He returned from this with, in his own phrase, 'a bad stomach-ache'. Chamberlain had pressed him strongly to accept the succession; Halifax had put all the arguments he could think of against himself. He told me he felt that he could do the job. He also felt that Churchill needed a restraining influence. Could that restraint be better exercised as Prime Minister or as a Minister in Churchill's government? Even if he chose the former rôle, Churchill's qualities and experience would surely mean that he would be 'running the war anyway', and Halifax's own position in the Lords would speedily turn him into a sort of honorary Prime Minister. This would be an impossible situation. I did not seek to contradict these arguments. I saw their force; I also saw that, in truth, Edward did not really want the Premiership, was indeed bent on self-abnegation.

· A further meeting was due to take place at 4.30 that afternoon between Neville, Winston and Edward. As the bearer of a message, I happened to be in the Cabinet room when the three men came in accompanied by David Margesson, the Chief Whip. Winston immediately said to me in good spirit, 'There is no place for you here. Your turn will come later. You had better go.' I obeyed with alacrity. I had little doubt what the outcome would be so far as he was concerned; I should have been less than human if I had not doubted the consequences for my own immediate future. Over the Whitsun holiday, however, some curious reassurances came my way. These I imparted to Edward Halifax at the first opportunity. 'The appointments are now in the hands of Max Beaverbrook and Brendan Bracken', I told him. 'I have heard from a woman who went out last night with

Beaverbrook, after he had dined with Winston, that she understood they thought "young Butler has brains and had better be left where he is". I have also heard from an American who breakfasted with Bracken that he too considered I was "all right".' Halifax was greatly entertained when I asked him what Stanley Baldwin, with his obsessional distaste for the right-wing press, would have thought of these sources of patronage.

Shortly afterwards I was sent for by the new Prime Minister who was sitting in the Cabinet room, his face flushed, his eyes gleaming, trying to light the remains of a very wet, half-bitten-through cigar with the aid of a bunsen burner. He came to the point at once: 'I wish you to go on with your delicate manner of answering parliamentary questions without giving anything away.' I said, 'Thank you very much. We have disagreed a great deal in the past; now I shall do my best to serve you.' He bowed very formally. We discussed whether, like his predecessor, he wished me to bring Foreign Office parliamentary questions to him, and he indicated that he would be too busy with other things. He showed me the message he was sending next day to Mussolini ('Down the ages above all other calls comes the cry that the joint heirs of Latin and Christian civilization must not be ranged against one another in mortal strife'), which I noted would rank with some of the great expressions of history. Finally, I was given insights into the reasons for my reappointment which could not have been obtained at second hand from his entourage. He said, 'Although we have had disagreements, you once asked me to your private residence.' 'That was not very remarkable,' I pointed out. 'No,' he replied, 'but it shows goodwill.' Then, when I was half-way to the door, he called out, 'Halifax asked for you. He seems to get on well with you.'

I stayed with Halifax, in the subordinate role of Under-Secretary, until the turn of this historic year when he was dispatched to Washington. He did not want to go a bit, and I was very sorry to lose him, but he fulfilled his time at the Foreign Office by becoming an exceptional Ambassador. One of the last memories I have of working with Halifax and Churchill was when we were invited to march up and down in the garden of No. 10 while Winston was rehearsing his speech 'We shall fight on the beaches'. There we were, the lanky Edward, the stocky Winston and myself. As Winston declaimed, he turned to us and said, 'Would you fight in the streets and on the hills?' Pacific as we were we warmly agreed, saying 'Yes, certainly, Winston', and then continued to march up and down with him.

I went on serving at the Foreign Office under Anthony Eden for a further six months until, in the summer of 1941, I was given my opportunity to harness to the educational system the wartime urge for social reform and greater equality. This change was much to my liking. The Foreign Office provided absorbing avocations in the centre of affairs; but sensational diplomacy cannot precede military triumphs and, except over the skies of Britain, these were not yet within our reach. When Churchill decided to close the Burma Road, China's life-line, he opted to rely on me to defend the unwelcome and unpopular decision in the Commons. He said to Halifax, 'I intend to put young Butler over the sticks.' My speech was made easier because the session was secret and, unfussed by publicity, I was able to quote several of our dispatches, especially to Washington, and to paraphrase replies. 'Bobbety' Salisbury, as he now is, sent me a note when it was all over which said, 'Warmest congratulations on a great parliamentary performance.' But in the eleventh month of the war there was no glory to be found in defending what appeared, and was assumed, to be the appeasement of Japan. During the winter I had a chance, in the course of a long talk with Harry Hopkins, Roosevelt's personal representative, to express our belief that the Americans were behindhand in their understanding of Japanese ambitions in the South Seas. I developed this with some emphasis, and Hopkins said that, though this was not the official view, he personally thought that the U.S. would react immediately to any Japanese advance in the Far East. He then asked anxiously whether we really wanted America in the war. I said, yes; a great democracy could not really get to work until it was up against it. But Hopkins replied that this observation was too general and that we must wait and see how much could be done under Lend-Lease. The Americans were even harder to draw out in public than in private, and our nightmare that the Japanese might attack British bases in Asia without provoking the U.S. into war persisted until Pearl Harbour.

Like every other inhabitant of London, I accustomed myself to the ritual existence and constant peril of the Blitz. Many of the Diplomatic Corps had taken houses in the country, so that business luncheons were substituted for dinners and no appointment was asked for after 4 p.m. I was bombed out of my father-in-law's home in North Audley Street, where we slept in a cellar while the guns grunted and barked, and out of my own home on the terrible night when the House of Commons and our church in Smith Square were both burned into devastation. While 3 Smith Square was being partially repaired, Chips Channon welcomed me to Belgrave Square where, despite the bombing, we dined under the heavy glass chandeliers, and with the Meissen china. I still went regularly to Stanstead for weekends. In the spring 'Gil' Winant, the American Ambassador, came down to stay with us, feeling very strained, but as usual full of confidence in our future. Despite his great difficulty in expressing himself, it was impossible to be with Winant and not to feel his genius. He forecast to me that England would go socialist after the war: I knew no one else whose instinct was then so sure. He also said that I ought to take over the Board of Education 'when the present man goes'. I asked him whether he had got this idea from Brendan Bracken; but he said, 'No, I thought it out for myself. This is where you can influence the future of England.'

I was strongly drawn to Winant's idea, while still doubting whether it had been entirely self-generated. And it was not long afterwards that the ubiquitous Brendan Bracken informed me that the Prime Minister's friends desired to 'make a complete break with the past and the Munich period', and that he thought Herwald Ramsbotham would shortly retire, leaving a vacancy for me at Education. This prophecy loomed large in my mind as I drove down for the night to see my old chief, Stanley Baldwin, who was staying with the Davidsons just outside Berkhamsted. It was June and the summer was vainly trying to emerge. S.B. was sitting in the porch rather like an old villager outside his cottage. He stood up for a while when we arrived, but then said he felt his arthritis too much and we all sat down and talked before dinner. His first agonized question was, 'Did any of you foresee the collapse of France?' I had been told that he had been suffering from very serious depression, and so I took as optimistic a view of the situation as I could. During dinner I noted that S.B. had lost none of his old habits. He sniffed the knives and forks and curled up his eyes and clicked his fingers in exactly the way he used to do. But his conversation had declined in vigour, point and quality. At 9 p.m., this being a typical British household, there was a rush to hear the news. S.B. pulled out an old turnip watch and asked if he really need participate in this ritual. Joan Davidson gave way and the women went off to hear the B.B.C. We then talked for more than an hour, and the theme to which S.B. continually returned was that his military advisers had told him Germany would not be fully prepared until 1942; he had therefore felt that by starting rearmament when he did, in 1935, he was just in time. I tried to steer him away from this controversial quicksand towards the Conservative part in post-war reconstruction. Long afterwards I was sent the following extract from a letter Baldwin wrote Halifax on 17th June, 1941: 'Rab Butler came for the night. I hadn't seen him since the war began and I was delighted with our talk. He has come on tremendously and I think has in him the makings of something really good.'

On 5th July I was asked to dine with the Edens in their new flat above the Foreign Office. The Churchills and Max Beaverbrook were there. Surprisingly, Baldwin was the starting point of the conversation. Winston said he was very sorry for him since he had a sense of history, so I naturally described my visit to Berkhamsted. Beaverbrook argued that Baldwin had no right to blame his military advisers; he alone was to blame. I said something about Baldwin's difficulties with the League of Nations Union and his services over the abdication. My first remark was brushed aside by Anthony Eden who observed that S.B. had never given enough support to the League of Nations Union. My second red rag caused Winston to say to Max: 'We were together over the abdication and you said we had been beaten by the fundamental moral sense of the British people.' Clemmie Churchill broke in, 'Of course you were wrong. We have the right man on the throne', to which Winston replied,

'One is often wrong in public life. At any rate my stockbroker, who met the Duke of Windsor in Barbados, says he does not believe that the Americans will come into the war. That has upset me. Let us change the subject.' But Max, who was now getting warmed up, was most loath to change the subject. He declared that his objective during the abdication crisis had been to get rid of Baldwin, but he had been thwarted by the ability of Margesson. Winston said angrily that *his* objective had been to save the King.

Clarissa Eden, in a valiant effort to get away from this treacherous ground, teased her uncle by avowing that she had three favourites: Edward VIII, Leopold of Belgium and Lindbergh. At this the Prime Minister pretended to splutter with rage, but was eventually led on to the subject of the German invasion of Russia. I had been with Anthony Eden in his room overlooking the pelicans when the news of this invasion came through and he had remarked very modestly, 'If it could be said that by my diplomacy I had arranged this, my name would be made for ever as Foreign Secretary.' Churchill, deeply depressed by Wavell's conduct of affairs in the Middle East ('I do not understand his intellect. It may be my own fault, but I always feel as if in the presence of the chairman of a golf club'), sounded an altogether more sombre note. 'What can we do to show the Russians we are in earnest?' he asked. 'Remember that on my breast are the medals of the Dardanelles, Antwerp, Dakar and Greece, and I cannot support any more adventures or expeditions like that. I do not believe our generals could manage a major raid. They have not got beyond Crécy and Dettingen.' I said innocently, 'What about General Wolfe at Quebec?' and he snapped back that he had had long experience in the Seven Years War. Max then leaned forward and, showing his good influence as a friend, besought Winston not to be pessimistic: 'You have saved us in the early summer and you will do so again.' Before we broke up Winston said, 'I have been pessimistic partly on purpose, but I really feel that the Russian campaign is the turning point of the war.' We all congratulated him on the broadcast in which he had pledged unreserved solidarity with Russia against Hitler. I had not time to add that Baldwin had described Churchill to me as our greatest war leader.

Ten days later, the Prime Minister sent for me. He saw me after his afternoon nap and was purring like a tiger. He began, 'You have been in the House fifteen years and it is time you were promoted.' I objected gently that I had been there only twelve years but he waved this aside. 'You have been in the government for the best part of that time and I now want you to go to the Board of Education. I think that you can leave your mark there. You will be independent. Besides,' he continued, with rising fervour, 'you will be in the war. You will move poor children from here to here', and he lifted up and evacuated imaginary children from one side of his blotting pad to the other; 'this will be very difficult'. He went on: 'I am too old now to think you can improve people's natures. Everyone has to learn to defend himself. I should not object if you could introduce a note of patriotism into the schools.' And then, with a grin, recalling our conversation the previous week, 'Tell the children that Wolfe won Quebec.' I said that I would like to influence what was taught in schools but that this was always frowned upon. Here he looked very earnest and commented, 'Of course not by instruction or order but by suggestion.' I then said that I had always looked forward to going to the Board of Education if I were given the chance. He appeared ever so slightly surprised at this, showing that he felt that in wartime a central job, such as the one I was leaving, is the most important. But he looked genuinely pleased that I had shown so much satisfaction and seemed to think the appointment entirely suitable. He concluded the interview by saying, 'Come and see me to discuss things—not details, but the broad lines.'

When I saw the King to receive the seals of office he at once directed the conversation away from education and towards the Foreign Office. He asked whether I had had someone with me to make records of conversations with the Soviet Ambassador, Maisky. I said, 'No, I dictated them immediately he had left the room.' He was very intrigued by the 'watch-dog' who used to accompany Maisky and I told him that I had once asked where he came from and had been given the improbable answer 'Moscow'. I said this showed they were all snobs as the man had a bright yellow face and was clearly Mongolian. At this the King laughed. He then asked whether I thought the young Conser-

vatives and Labour would keep working together. I said I hoped
so, particularly organized Labour. The King made some dis-
paraging remarks about Church House, which was being used
for parliamentary business, and questioned me minutely about
the accommodation. He thought the peers had behaved well in
letting the Commons have the House of Lords. It was a difficult
place to talk in and he said his father insisted on having very
large type for the King's Speech so that he could hold it three
feet away. He said he always tripped up over some of the words
but did not like to alter the type at present. Then he bade me
goodbye and wished me luck at the Board of Education, adding
'I suppose you want to go there.'

Yes, I wanted to go there. The time was ripe. The crisis of
modern war is a crucial test of national values and way of life.
Amid the suffering and the sacrifice the weaknesses of society
are revealed and there begins a period of self-examination, self-
criticism and movement for reform. It is remarkable how in
England educational planning and advance have coincided
with wars. In the earlier years of the twentieth century the Boer
War and the First World War had both provided an impulse.
Alas, many of the proposals of the Fisher Act of 1918 were killed
by the economic blizzard which was to freeze the educational
pattern for most of the inter-war years. Grammar schools,
which had emerged as part of the public provision of education
when the century was young and which were the acknowledged
route to the professions, were restricted to a small minority of
children. The vast majority spent the nine years of their education in elementary schools, which still suffered from the blight
of poverty and inferiority associated with the traditions of the
past. Thus, through sheer lack of opportunity, much human
potential was wasted. Already in 1926 the Hadow Report on the
Education of the Adolescent had recommended reorganization
of schools with the provision of separate post-primary schools
for the senior (11+) age groups. The Board of Education had
encouraged reorganization—in practice the building of new
senior elementary schools—but among local authorities progress had varied and in many areas the old all-age elementary
school persisted, indeed was not finally obliterated for another
forty years. The Hadow Report had also recommended that the

school-leaving age should be raised to 15—an increase called for by the need to make post-primary education a course with sufficient length to be meaningful. The Education Act of 1936 gave partial effect to this by laying down that, *as from 1st September 1939*, all children were to remain at school until the age of 15 unless they obtained work which the local education authority approved as beneficial. On that day, however, German troops invaded Poland, the evacuation of school children began, and the raising of the leaving age was indefinitely postponed.

War brought the building of schools and education itself to a halt in many areas. The evacuation of school children threw the educational system into serious disorder, and thoughts of re-form were put aside. There were considerable doubts whether the structure itself could be held together. In January 1940 some half a million children were getting no schooling at all. Ener-getic action by the Board of Education gradually restored the position. But the revelations of evacuation administered a severe shock to the national conscience; for they brought to light the conditions of those unfortunate children of the 'sub-merged tenth' who would also rank among the citizens of the future. It was realized with deepening awareness that the 'two nations' still existed in England a century after Disraeli had used the phrase. The challenge of the times provided a stimulus for rethinking the purposes of society and planning the recon-struction of the social system of which education formed an integral part. Realization of a full democracy—an order of society free from the injustices and anomalies of the pre-war period—was the ideal. Educational problems were thus seen as an essential part of the social problem and the urgent need for educational reform was increasingly realized. The first active move came before the end of 1940, and from the Churches. The Archbishops of Canterbury and York, the Roman Catholic Archbishop of Westminster and the Moderator of the Free Church Federal Council wrote a letter to *The Times* on 21st December. In this, under the heading 'Foundations of Peace', they urged that extreme inequality of wealth and possessions should be abolished; that every child, regardless of race or class, should have equal opportunities of education, suitable for development of his *particular* capacities; that the family unit should be safeguarded, and that a sense of divine vocation should be restored to man's daily work.

A scheme for putting some of the aspirations of the time into practice was drawn up by officials of the Board of Education and issued in June 1941. From the colour of its cover, this became known as the 'Green Book'. Its object was to serve as a basis of preliminary talks with all the bodies associated in the educational service. The document was therefore marked 'highly confidential'; but, in Lester Smith's splendid phrase, 'it was distributed in such a blaze of secrecy that it achieved an unusual degree of publicity'. In answer to one of the first parliamentary questions I received on arriving at the Board, I promised to make public a summary of its contents. Though many of the Green Book's proposals, notably those to do with the knotty problem of the Church schools, did not survive exposure, its production did stimulate thinking about educational reform and inspired a spate of booklets on the subject, each in its own distinctive colour. Thus the National Union of Teachers produced a book in a more sombre and less vernal shade of green, the Association of Directors and Secretaries an orange book. (But it was many years before a Black Book was to appear.) With the Parliamentary Secretary, Chuter Ede, I gave the fullest consideration to this response, interviewing deputations and touring the country. Chuter Ede was a Labour man and a Nonconformist, many years my senior in age and experience. I pleased him at our first meeting by offering for his perusal any document that passed through my Private Office, whether personal or public, political or otherwise. In the end a convention grew up between us that we did not bother about each other's purely party correspondence. I was very lucky to have this consistently loyal and wise friend as my chief lieutenant. I was no less fortunate to be served by a quite outstanding group of civil servants: the brilliant Sir Maurice Holmes, Permanent Secretary, derisive of many of the persons and fatuities that came our way, yet acute in ideals and practice; Sir Robert Wood, who did much of our drafting; S. H. Wood, who kept us on the progressive path; the traditionalist, G. G. Williams; William Cleary, with his great reservoir of experience; and the young Neville Heaton, who was the secretary of so many of our committees and who, in my opinion, was of the calibre to be Permanent Secretary himself Sylvia Goodfellow was my private secretary and worked her way passionately through a mass of paper. Her contribution was important and deserves special mention.

With such a team, it was natural to find intense activity and infectious enthusiasm when I arrived at the Board. Shortly after assuming office I told the House of Commons that it was necessary to reform the law relating to education, and a few weeks later I sent the Prime Minister a letter stressing the need to adapt the educational system to present social requirements. I instanced the need for industrial and technical training and for a settlement with the Churches about their schools and about religious instruction in schools. This was on 12th September, 1941. The next day the Prime Minister replied as follows:

'It would be the greatest mistake to raise the 1902 controversy during the war, and I certainly cannot contemplate a new Education Bill. I think it would also be a great mistake to stir up the public schools question at the present time. No one can possibly tell what the financial and economic state of the country will be when the war is over. Your main task at present is to get the schools working as well as possible under all the difficulties of air attack, evacuation, etc. If you can add to this industrial and technical training, enabling men not required for the Army to take their places promptly in munitions industry or radio work, this would be most useful. We cannot have any party politics in wartime, and both your second and third points raise these in a most acute and dangerous form. Meanwhile you have a good scope as an administrator.'[1]

Sir Maurice Holmes took the Prime Minister's Minute as a veto on education reform and wrote me a philosophic letter:

'R. S. Wood and I have discussed the P.M.'s Minute to you. I do not think we need be unduly cast down. It seems to me axiomatic that a major measure of educational reform will be demanded in quarters which will make the demand irresis-

[1] Crown copyright © reserved. Reproduced by permission.

tible, and the question then is not whether but when such reform will be brought about.

'And there are, I feel, some advantages in having more time than ever your revised programme contemplated for reaching the greatest common measure of agreement on the more contentious issues, so that from this point of view the P.M.'s frigid reception of your proposals has its brighter side.

'However, if educational legislation is to be shelved till the war is over, we shall then be able to think more clearly in terms of bricks and mortar than is possible while the war is in progress, and so form reasonably sound estimates of the dates when this and that measure of reform can become operative. The delay is of course disappointing, particularly to those of us who, like myself, cannot hope to accompany you into the Promised Land, but that you will lead the Children of Israel there, I do not doubt.'

Churchill's Minute was quite definite and Holmes's letter disappointingly compliant. But, having viewed the milk and honey from the top of Pisgah, I was damned if I was going to die in the land of Moab. Basing myself on long experience with Churchill over the India Bill, I decided to disregard what he said and go straight ahead. I knew that if I spared him the religious controversies and party political struggles of 1902 and side-tracked the public schools issue, I could win him over. I intended to have an Education Bill, and three years after receiving his Minute I had placed such a Bill on the Statute Book. And, as will be seen, I received on its passing a warm telegram of congratulation from him. This was typical of the man.

My first step was to push forward into the light the proposals made in the Green Book. On 23rd October, 1941, I made public a summary of its main contents. These were of unequal merit and practicality. On its 'lay' side, the Green Book stressed the need for a system of free secondary education for all as outlined in the Spens Report of 1938. This was imperative. On the other hand, the religious solution proposed in the Green Book, had I ever considered accepting it, would have led to a head-on collision with the Free Churches. This was because the Green Book proposed the abrogation in the secondary schools of the ban on denominational religious instruction imposed by the Cowper-Temple clause of the Act of 1870. This would have meant that such instruction could have been given in secondary schools provided by local education authorities ('provided schools') as well as in Church secondary schools ('non-provided schools'). During the winter of 1941–2 I worked on my own plans for educational reform and presented the lay aspects of these to the Conference of the National Union of Teachers on 9th April, 1942, with the warm support of Chuter Ede who had been himself a teacher. The Union's President described the proposals as 'the most progressive ever outlined by a President of the Board of Education'. I said that the aim should be elementary education up to 11 and secondary education for all over that age. Educationally after the war Britain had to be one nation, not two. So there must be an education system providing a 'training suited to talents' of every individual. This would have to be combined with more expert training for industry, with a revivified system of apprenticeship, and with a practical form of continued education, later to be called County Colleges. I did not, however, go any further on the religious side than to call for a final settlement of the 'Dual System' of provided and non-provided schools. Since this issue was a particularly thorny one, I was to spend more time in trying to reach the settlement than on anything else.

For most of the nineteenth century, schools had been provided not by local authorities, but by voluntary bodies who raised money by public subscription and financed the building and running of schools. From 1833 the State had assisted these bodies with grants of money which increased in amount as time went on. The most important of the voluntary bodies was the Church of England's National Society. At the end of the nineteenth century it had nearly 12,000 schools in England and Wales and was responsible for educating nearly two million of the country's children. Of the other voluntary bodies that of the Roman Catholic Church was the most important. Altogether the voluntary or Church schools educated two and a half million children. At the same time, however, far fewer schools, provided by the local education authorities, were educating two and a quarter million children. Many of the Church schools were small, with a wide age-range of pupils, a limited number of teachers (sometimes, in villages, only one) and, very often, antiquated and ill-equipped buildings. Yet any attempt to increase central government help meant greater expenditure, which was resisted by the Treasury, and any proposal to assist Church schools from the rates aroused a furious and bitter opposition. A main reason for this was that Church schools gave the religious instruction of the Church to which they belonged, while local authority schools gave religious instruction unconnected with the formulary or beliefs of any particular Church. There were relatively few Nonconformist schools and in many areas, particularly in the villages, the Church of England school was the only school. These were known as 'single-school' areas. Nonconformists naturally resented sending their children to a school which taught the catechism of the Church of England, especially when the local parson took part both in the control of the school and in the religious instruction. There were political implications too—the Tory alliance of squire and parson in the village drew the village school and its master within their orbit as lesser satellites.

In preparing myself to deal with the religious question, I looked back to the precedents of the 1902 Education Act and read what historians had had to say. Elie Halévy's immortal *History of England* and Jacques Bainville's smaller history were both illuminating. These two French observers remain, in my opinion, the best commentators on those English affairs. They bring out the political composition of the English countryside most clearly, the strength of the combination of landlord and parson in retaining the Tory influence on country seats. Halévy described the school situation of 1902 as: 'State schools favoured by the Free Churches and free schools favoured by the State Church.' The 1902 Act, by making local education authorities responsible for paying for elementary education in Church schools as well as in their own, aroused a fierce religious dispute. The cry went up of 'Rome on the rates', and some Welsh authorities refused to pay for the education in Church schools in their area. Halévy comments, 'To read the Liberal newspapers of the day you would imagine that the Cecils were preparing to revive the policy of Laud if not of Strafford and that in every village a Nonconformist Hampden was about to rise against their persecution.' Winston Churchill remembered very vividly the battles over the Education Act of 1902 and the serious damage it did the Conservative party. When the Liberals took over in 1905 their efforts to settle this question met with no success; three Bills put forward by successive Presidents of the Board of Education failed. The first of these, Birrell's Bill of 1906, was not unlike my final settlement. I was anxious not only to achieve a solution to this problem, but in doing so not to do damage to the interests I represented.

Though religious tensions had lessened since the 1900s, the problem of the Church schools was becoming more serious. The Church of England had built hardly any schools since the 1914–18 war and had been giving them up at the average rate of 76 a year. Far too many were appallingly old and out of date. The Hadow reorganization, which involved the introduction of separate schools for the primary and post-primary pupils, meant new buildings. The Church of England particularly had great difficulty in responding to this new need, and its voluntary schools were largely unreorganized by the time war broke out. Many of them, particularly those in rural areas, were too small to be efficient. Educational progress would not be possible unless the problem of the Church schools could be solved. The radical solution of abolishing the Church schools and of putting all schools equally under local authorities was urged by such bodies as the T.U.C., the National Union of Teachers and the Free Churches. The N.U.T. were concerned that the rights of school managers to appoint their own teachers meant that thousands of posts were open only to teachers of a particular denomination. The N.U.T. stated in 1942 that 'the only fully satisfactory solution would be the achievement of a national unified system of education by means of the transfer of all non-provided schools, whether included at present in the elementary or secondary system, to the control of the local education authority'. The Nonconformists also wanted the Dual System to go, since they particularly resented the Anglican monopoly of schools in over 4,000 rural areas—schools which, to quote Halévy once more, were 'built with the squire's money and taught the parson's catechism'. The Free Churches, while strongly in favour of Christian teaching in the schools by qualified teachers, regarded undenominational religious instruction as essential and the Cowper-Temple clause of the 1870 Act as a Charter of their rights.

An important development which met the wishes of the Nonconformists and of many Anglicans was the 'agreed syllabus'. In Cambridgeshire in 1924 a committee of Anglicans, Free Churchmen and teachers had met and had drawn up a syllabus of religious instruction for use in the county's schools. By 1942 the Cambridgeshire syllabus was in use by over 100 local education authorities. Because of this, many Anglican managers were willing to hand over their schools to the local authorities in return for Christian teaching on these lines. The Prime Minister, I soon discovered, was fascinated by the idea of the agreed syllabus. He called it the 'County Council Creed' and on one occasion 'Zoroastrianism'. He asked me whether I intended to start a new State religion. I replied that the Roman legionaries in North Africa may have fallen for Zoroaster but that I was more orthodox.

There was a division of opinion in the Church of England between those who felt a truly Christian atmosphere and teaching could come about only in Church schools, and those who thought the 'agreed' syllabus was sufficient. On the question of the Dual System, many Anglicans wanted denominational schools put on the same financial basis as provided schools. Behind these Anglicans were many members of the Conservative party. The Roman Catholics, though not co-operating with the other Churches, disliked the agreed syllabus (Cardinal Hinsley called it 'disembodied Christianity' and the Tablet 'a synthetic article') and wanted to retain their own schools. When it came to negotiation they were not prepared to compromise. They argued that they had to pay rates and taxes for the upkeep of the local authority schools which their consciences would not let them use. Since 1870 they had spent millions of pounds in preserving their schools and they were determined that they would not be lost now. Thus Dr. Downey, Archbishop of Liverpool, said on 31st May, 1942, 'We shall continue to struggle for denominational schools even though we have to fight alone' and Cardinal Hinsley wrote in a letter to

The Times on 31st November, 1942: 'No equal opportunity will exist for a minority who are saddled with extra and crushing financial burdens because of their definite religious convictions and because they cannot accept a syllabus of religious instruction agreeable to many.' Churchill cut this out, and sent it to me with a curt covering note saying, 'There, you are fixed.'

In spite of all the difficulties it seemed a suitable moment, during a National government and with a loyal collaborator from the Labour party working with me, to attempt a solution of these political problems. Not long after I reached the Board, I had had to receive a massive deputation of Church leaders; but the absence of the Roman Catholics made it essential for me to say as little as possible at this stage, though I provided some innocent diversion and surprise by asking Cosmo Gordon Lang, the Archbishop of Canterbury, to conclude the interview with prayer. To begin with, discussions about the future of the Church schools centred on the plan outlined in the Green Book—very exquisitely drawn and much in favour of the Anglicans. In the spring of 1942 an alternative plan, largely the work of Chuter Ede, and known as the 'white memorandum', was privately circulated by the Board. Both plans broke down: that in the Green Book on the issue of denominational religious teaching in the future secondary modern schools; that in the white memorandum because Anglicans opposed compulsory transfer of their schools to the local education authorities in single-school areas. Wolmer, later Lord Selborne, in particular was most anxious that I should not stand by the white memorandum plan, saying that it had no chance of acceptance by the Anglicans. We accordingly set about drafting another plan, which would attempt to satisfy the Free Churches in that their children could feel, in most places, that they were entering a school which was not conducted in the atmosphere of the Church of England alone, but which would attempt to satisfy the Anglicans by a continuation of some doctrinal teaching and would not involve any change in the ownership of the premises.

The solution I reached after much patience and experimentation was to make an offer of two alternatives. Thus a Church school could choose either to be 'controlled' or 'aided'. If 'controlled', the local education authority became responsible for all the expenses of the school, and for the appointment of all but a limited number of teachers; the religious instruction was, for the most part, to be in accordance with an agreed syllabus; and a majority of the managers or governors were appointed by public bodies. If 'aided', the local education authority was responsible for the teachers' salaries and the running expenses of the school; but the managers were responsible for any alterations and improvements needed to bring the school up to standard (for which they would receive a 50 per cent grant from the Exchequer), and they retained the right to appoint and dismiss teachers and to control the religious instruction; the Church had a majority on the managing body. 'Controlled' status met the needs of the Free Churches and the Low Church Anglicans. Sir Maurice Holmes was always adamant that to extend State help to one community without extending it to all denominations was impossible. The Roman Catholics felt that the 50 per cent grant was not enough. But we knew that if it were raised, and if many Anglican schools were involved, this would only continue the Dual System of Church–local authority schools under slightly different terms. For the plan to succeed Anglican schools would have to opt for controlled status in large numbers. This insistence was a key to the whole success of the plan. I thought that the aided status was perfectly fair to both Anglicans and Roman Catholics since they were going to get so much additional help from public funds, while retaining their rights with regard to teachers and religious instruction.

This was the solution of the problem which I hoped the various parties concerned would accept. But difficult negotiations lay ahead, with the Church of England and with the Roman Catholics. As I have indicated, the Roman Catholics still wanted to act independently. There was no question of an alliance between them and the Church of England. I had to deal with each body separately yet achieve a solution which would satisfy all parties concerned. In these negotiations the leading personalities were clearly of the greatest importance. I have had considerable experience of dealing with religious bodies: Moslems and Hindus in India, when Sam Hoare drafted the Communal Settlement which Ramsay MacDonald

approved; and again when I had to help Malcolm MacDonald
with the Palestine dispute between Arabs and Jews. There is little
hope of agreement with prominent religious leaders, particularly of a minority, and what hope there is lies in getting hold of
them personally and assuring them of the sincerity and sympathy of one's approach. The Free Churches knew quite well
that my uncle, George Adam Smith, was one of them, having
been himself Moderator of the Free Church of Scotland. As for
the Anglicans, I was fortunate in having to deal with Archbishop
Temple (who succeeded Lang in April 1942) and with the then
Bishop of London, Fisher, who played an important part in
helping me set up the Fleming Committee to deal with the
public schools question and proved a most effective ally in
getting my Bill through the Lords.

Temple was physically obese, but intellectually and spiritu-
ally a first-class athlete (as his *Mens Creatrix* shows) and a very
good advertisement for Oxford. We have few bishops today who
could hold a candle to him. I disagreed with his rather amateur
attack on the 'profit motive', but would far rather see the Church
tilting at windmills in the City than sitting in lawn sleeves and
self-satisfaction in the Upper House. The Church of England is
really fighting for its life today and Temple led the fight at a
critical point. There had, indeed, been some doubt about his
preferment in Conservative circles where his political tendencies were suspect. But I remember that Garbett, who later
succeeded him at York, was entirely in favour of it; and I
myself was never in doubt that he would help owing to his
devotion to the cause of education and his special knowledge of
these matters developing from his chairmanship of the Workers'
Educational Association.

The occasion when the Archbishop was tipped over to support a plan on my lines was one hot morning in the Conference
Room at Kingsway, its windows blitzed out and covered with
cardboard, no air in the room, in the summer of 1942. On that
occasion I described to him and those few with him—including
the Dean of St. Albans and the Bishop of Oxford, two zealots
indeed, and Mr. Hussey, secretary of the National Society—the
condition of the Church schools, the number of them on the
Black List, and the small extent of reorganization. He was

moved by the figures and said he had not realized what a bad state the Church schools were in. Of the 10,553 voluntary schools, 9,683 were over 40 years old. On the Black List were 543 voluntary schools out of a total of 731. I noted at the time that 'these statistics visibly impressed his Grace, who said he would have to do his best to wean his flock from their distaste at the challenged threat to their schools'. Ever after that date he adhered to his part of the understanding. He told me he had decided that the majority of the Church schools would opt for the controlled status and therefore depend on the agreed religious syllabus. He would rather compound for 'stoical ethicism', which is how he described the religious syllabus teaching, than attempt the impossible, namely for all the Church schools to undertake denominational teaching. How important Temple thought the religious syllabus to be, it is hard to say. In Dean Iremonger's Life, he is quoted as saying that the raising of the school age was the most essential element of the Bill: 'I am putting this very crudely, but I believe that our Lord is much more interested in raising the school leaving age to 16 than in acquiring an agreed religious syllabus.' This at any rate shows that Temple was so keen on the provisions of the Act itself that he was determined not to allow a religious quarrel to hold up educational advance.

Another very important figure in the whole negotiation was Sir Robert Martin, the prominent layman in the Church Assembly and the National Society. Taking advantage of a visit to Leicester, I had gone to stay a night with Martin in the early part of the year and had sat with him at 'The Brand' until a late hour. He had told me that he thought if I could grant the Church up to 75 per cent of their expenses, they would be very satisfied. I was obliged to point out to him that I would not be able to go as high as this and, having heard what I had to say about the plan, he very gallantly gave it the National Society's backing in speeches at the Church Assembly, where he said: 'The Society had come to the conclusion that where the amenities of non-provided schools could not fulfil their legal obligations in regard to repairs, alterations and improvements, there must clearly be a wide measure of public control. This could be met by an arrangement whereby its obligations as well as the appointment of teachers could pass to the local education authority, subject to the appointment of reserve teachers to such an extent as might be necessary for providing denominational teaching as set out in the agreed syllabus.'

This revolution in policy aroused the wrath of the non-compromisers, but they were reminded by Dr. Temple of the figures of black-list schools which I had given him. To bring these schools up to a reasonable standard would take another ten or fifteen years. The Assembly decided to approve and support the policy outlined in the National Society's report. This decision set up a landmark in the history of English education and cleared the way for the resultant compromise in the 1944 Act.

It was at this juncture that Brendan Bracken called to see me with an arresting idea. He had no definite mission, he said, but wanted to sound me out on Churchill's behalf as to whether I would or could go out to India as Viceroy. He little realized what a momentous question he had posed. All my adult life this had been my greatest ambition. Now I might be given the charge to realize it. But in what circumstances? I asked for time in which to consider. Clearly I realized how very difficult it would be with Winston and me once more disagreeing on Indian affairs—I thinking in terms of early independence and he of holding Congress quiet during the war. The soldierly qualities of Archie Wavell, who got the job better suited the Prime Minister's purpose; they did not include that imaginative spark later to express itself in the brilliant attachment between the Mountbattens, Gandhi and Nehru and to culminate in India's 'tryst with destiny'. I thought of all this when Clem Attlee sent for me late in 1946 and asked if I approved of Dickie Mountbatten's being the last Viceroy under the Crown. I concurred as the member of the Conservative Opposition whom he had chosen to consult, and regard Dickie's achievement as fantastic. I should have had a different mandate, so believe Winston would in any event have preferred Wavell to me. Brendan agreed a week later with my diagnosis. I think he also respected my view, confirmed after consultation with Sir Maurice Holmes, that I could not desert the religious negotiations or the Education Bill.

I now revert to the fact that with the Roman Catholics one of the chief problems was that there was no special leader; those at the summit were very old and it was difficult to establish any personal contact. I have already indicated that they were not co-operating with the other Churches, and from the public pronouncements of leaders like Dr. Downey and Cardinal Hinsley, it was evident that it would not be easy to come to a settlement. Their absence from the deputation of 1941 had made an impression on my mind which was subsequently confirmed. There was difficulty in negotiating with an individual bishop without that bishop repudiating responsibility for the others. After I had started talking to Cardinal Hinsley and had driven out to his home in the country to do so, I became aware that his powers showed clear signs of decline. He seemed unable fully to understand the benefits of the plan—in particular, the revival of the provisions of the 1936 Act, which enabled capital grants of up to 75 per cent to be paid by local education authorities for new Church secondary schools needed for reorganization. This did not mean that one was not impressed by his sincerity. His influence was carried on by Bishop Myers, the Vicar-Capitular of Westminster, and it is wrong to say that had Cardinal Hinsley lived he would have obtained a more easy settlement, though the dignity of those with whom one had to deal could never equal his. I was advised that Dr. Downey was a man ambitious not only for celestial, but also terrestrial renown. He spoke quite fairly in private but appeared, as an Irishman, to enjoy a public fight. Unfortunately he chose the period in which I was involved in negotiations to reduce his weight by some nine stones! This rendered his health precarious, with the result that, for the critical period of the summer of 1943, he retired from Liverpool to Ireland, where he was no doubt encouraged in his militancy by his non-co-operation.

I also negotiated with Archbishop Amigo of Southwark and the apostolic delegate Monsignor Godfrey. I visited the former on 24th November, 1942, and my records state that 'after much sounding of the bell, a sad looking, rather blue-faced Chaplain let me in and we climbed a massive palace stair to the first floor where the Archbishop was sitting, fully robed, in a small room overlooking the ruins of Southwark Cathedral. His window was wide open on his left hand so that he could at once take in the

tragic picture of the ruins and inhale the chilly morning air.'
The Archbishop asked immediately we had sat down what
I had come to see him for. I obliged by informing him; but
it was not an auspicious beginning. He said that a 50 per cent
grant was not sufficient and that he saw no chance of agreement with politicians. He said that if I had belonged to his
community he would have suggested that we should pray. I
said that I would be very ready to do so since I was also a
churchman.

This interview indicated the nature of the head-on collision
with the Roman Catholic Church. When the White Paper on
Educational Reconstruction—the blue-print for the Education
Bill—was published, the Roman Catholics attacked the pro-
posals and Cardinal Hinsley said that in negotiating with the
President of the Board of Education they had 'at no stage agreed
to the financial conditions now made public'. Thereafter, in
December 1943, I was invited, together with Chuter Ede and
Maurice Holmes, to meet the Northern Roman Catholic
Bishops. Near Durham we came to the imposing parterres of
Ushaw College. We were greeted by the Bishop of Hexham, in
full robes, and taken almost at once into the evening meal,
which, in the tradition of the younger Pitt, was served at about
6 o'clock. There was a large *gigot* and tolerable quantities of a
red wine. Immediately this feast was over we were taken to see
the Chapel, and a magnificent ivory figure was taken down
from the High Altar for our benefit. We were all filled with a
certain awe, which was no doubt intentionally administered.
Chuter Ede told me he thought he was going to faint. So we
came to our conference with the Bishops, at the start of which I
tried to explain that against the background of difficulties in
1902, the important thing was to handle this problem so as to
remove bitterness and deal with the great majority of the Church
schools, amounting to some 10,000. I sketched the growth of aid
to voluntary schools by a process of geometrical progression
from the settlement of 1870 to the present day. I said that, if the
Catholics were patient and accepted this settlement, they could
in my view (which has been proved correct by events) hope for
more within another generation. If, on the other hand, they
placed themselves athwart the stream of national progress,

they would be doing their cause so much harm, especially in some districts, that it might never recover.

I was perhaps misled by the great understanding apparently shown of this speech by all the bishops present, and by the personal conversation of many of them. The Bishop of Salford, for example, said that he desired his followers to suffer and pay as part of their faith. Bishop Flynn of Lancaster told Maurice Holmes that he could work the scheme. Archbishop Downey told Chuter Ede and myself that it would enable him to get over all his troubles in Liverpool. But, in the event, none of them attempted to control their own supporters, believing that their anxieties justified them in encouraging a fuss. Still, it must have been quite a good speech; for Maurice Holmes passed me a note which said, 'Your utterance was at once so human and so statesmanlike that it nearly brought tears into the eyes of a very hardened administrator.'

CHAPTER SIX

THE EDUCATION ACT

THE WELSHMAN who was Prime Minister when H. A. L. Fisher gave birth to the Act of 1918 had been brought up in the atmosphere of educational and religious problems, the intriguing qualities of which always appealed to him. In Winston Churchill I had a very different sort of leader. His sagacious mind realized that the issues I have described in the preceding chapter could lead to domestic trouble. Therefore he wished to keep them, and me, quiet. He could be very quelling. I recall comparing notes with one of his political staff who asked me, in a heart-rending manner, 'Have you ever felt when talking to Winston that words rise in your throat and then give a gurgle before they pass out completely?' He added, 'I was driving with him in the car last night and said, "It is very dark," to which I received the immediate reply, "It always is at night."' It certainly was difficult to conduct a conversation with Churchill on a subject which did not engage his interest, and his interest in education was slight, intermittent, and decidedly idiosyncratic. Over dinner one night during the autumn of 1941, he claimed that thirty-five years earlier Campbell-Bannerman had told him, 'You are the brightest and best of our Under-Secretaries— you always shine in debate. I should like to offer you the Presidency of the Board of Education. However, I do not think you are suitable for smacking children's bottoms and blowing their noses.' Then, turning to me, he said, 'Things are very different now; you have a fine job. You must make all the young boys Cadets. Call them Gentlemen Cadets if you like—I shall call them powder monkeys. They will relieve the pressure on gun sites. There is a war task for you.' Twelve months later he gave all his senior colleagues a pre-Session lunch at Admiralty House ('The worms have got into the structure of No. 10; the floors could not bear so weighty a burden as the Cabinet') and came up to me beforehand to say, 'I like the good stern stuff your people have written about education. What is important is to go into the question of population—we must keep that up.'

I did not think that my principal task at the Board of Education was to man the Home Guard or to raise the birth rate. But the only reference to educational reform I was able to persuade Churchill to include in the King's Speech was to the factual effect that discussions were proceeding. Even this was secured after considerable initial hesitation—and quite deliberately no specific mention was made of a Bill. This was how matters stood publicly in March 1943 when I was invited to spend the night at Chequers. I drove down with 'the Prof', as everyone called Lord Cherwell, that sharp-witted, sharp-tongued, pertinacious, and more than slightly conspiratorial character who had long been Churchill's closest friend and confidant. He told me that the Prime Minister would be wanting to talk about education, especially in the context of a speech on 'the home front' which he contemplated making. The Prof hoped that I would encourage him to make the speech, though some of the wording needed attention. Apparently the Minister of Agriculture, 'Rob' Hudson, had been down earlier in the week and had made a poor impression on the Prof. His manner was bad, he did not pay enough attention to vegetables, he had made a mess of eggs, and—a particularly heinous sin—most of his statistics were wrong. I thought this criticism rather undeserved and put in as good a word as I could for my colleague and friend—only to be told that the financial statistics at the end of my own paper on educational progress, then before a Cabinet committee, were incomprehensible. We spent much of the journey from Whitehall to Princes Risborough discussing what now seems the extremely academic thesis that a continuing fall in the school population (which did not, as it happens, take place) would still involve the country in additional expenses, since the slack (which did not, in the event, appear) would be taken up by reducing classes to the proper level (which, a quarter of a century later, we still had not done). Neither of us was prophetic enough to see the future 'bulge' in the birth rate, even less its duration. However, the Prof was understanding about my efforts in the religious sphere, saying that I had made a good bargain with the Anglicans. We then returned to genial asperities, with a review of the work of the Scientific Advisory Committee of which I was chairman. The Prof said that it was a pity this committee had ever been appointed, that it had been called into existence only to appease the *amour propre* of the scientific establishment, and that he himself did not think it worth a moment of his worry. It seemed, however, to be worth more than a moment of our journey.

We arrived soon after half-past seven and were ushered into the vast sham hall, which Baker built in 1929 and of which it is not possible to think very much. It was simply crowded with pictures, purchased by Arthur Lee, and presumably measured to fit the different spaces—which, I noted, they did exactly, right up to the ceiling. I was inspecting an enormous one of a lion caught in a net when there was a lion-like noise on the stairs and the Prime Minister appeared in his siren suit, asking stridently whether I had observed the mouse with whose aid the poor brute was attempting to escape. Then, as though immediately infected by Lord Cherwell's presence, he said *sotto voce*, 'You are to tell nobody you are here. Nobody knows, do they? And you must not inform your officials. Anything I want from you must be kept very private. I shall not talk now.' He ambled off to do some work in what I quickly discovered to be the Private Secretaries' room, since in a few moments a swarm of Private Secretaries emerged hurriedly from it, carrying books, correspondence, files and other *impedimenta* to the other side of the house. By a little cross-examination of them all under the stairs, I learned that they were off to the room specially allotted to the Prime Minister, because whenever he decided on impulse to take over their room, he complained so much of the rustle of papers that they were obliged to move the whole of their gear to his. We went up to change. Dinner had been ordered for a punctual half-past eight. But shortly before it was announced, the Prime Minister settled down to a game of Corinthian bagatelle. The board was eventually found to be uneven, so we all adjusted it; and the arithmetic proved difficult, because the incorrect balance of the board had caused him to produce an unnaturally large score. So it was some time before we started our meal—rather to the distraction of Clemmie Churchill, who was worn out by having written a speech which would occupy six minutes at Nottingham, but which had taken her six hours to compose, and which her husband corrected several times during the course of the evening.

Dinner had not been going long when the P.M. turned sharply to me and said, 'What do you think about India?' It was the previous spring when the unfortunate Stafford Cripps had been dispatched to the sub-continent, armed with what Gandhi called 'post-dated cheques upon a bankrupt Empire'. Risible stories had reached us of other conciliatory gestures. 'Did he really take off his shoes and breeches and squat on the floor?' inquired Churchill incredulously. 'Not his breeches,' I replied, 'but the rest is right.' 'How awful!' he exclaimed, and then launched into a most terrible attack on the 'baboos', saying that they were gross, dirty and corrupt. 'I should now like to clear out of India. Our army is going to be kept there only to prevent one section of the population mauling and murdering the other. The answer is Pakhistan'—the word (so spelt) that was coming into use to describe the division of the British Raj into Moslem and Hindu components. 'Indian unity is the thing for which the Raj has always stood,' I objected, to which he retorted, 'Well, if our poor troops have to be kept in a sweltering, syphilitic climate and lice-infested barracks for the sake of your precious unity, I'd rather see them have a good civil war.' 'Winston!' chided Clemmie, 'you don't mean what you're saying.' 'No,' he admitted, 'but when I see my opponents glaring at me, I always have to draw them out by exaggerated statements.'

'What I really feel about the central government,' he went on, 'is that we might sit on top of a tripos—Pakhistan, Princely India and the Hindus.' I said that this was a bit better and reminded him that both my uncle and my father had had to deal with Gandhi, and that the former had sent a case of champagne to Motilal Nehru when he was in jail at Lucknow. 'A shocking waste,' grunted the P.M. 'I can barely get any champagne today.' He described an offer which he had turned down, from a lady in the north of England who wished to sell him champagne at 78s. a bottle: 'She thought she was doing me a favour.'

Then he became most affable, wagging his finger at me as he said, 'We shall make an Imperialist of you yet. But let there be no mistake: in India we shall be bound by the Americans, if by nobody else, to all the promises we have given. The whole future of the Indian Ocean and of Asia will prove extremely distracting to British statesmen.' He added as an afterthought that it was a pity Madame Chiang Kai-shek appeared to be so influenced by the news and views she got from Jawaharlal Nehru. 'However,' he said, 'all is offly-toofly; they are in love with one another'—whereat he was again rebuked by Clemmie, and Commander Thompson (whom he called his 'Flag Commander') took the opportunity to tell him that later in the evening there would be a film on the love affairs of Czarist Russia. 'I shall be interested in that, Tommy,' he allowed,' but great matters of state should not be governed by these considerations.'

When dinner was over everyone was sent away except the Prof and me, and the Prime Minister produced his draft speech from which he proceeded to recite at great length and with exaggerated gusto. He asked me whether I thought that, after his recent illness, he lacked force or vigour. I said definitely not. There was a portion about the need for refreshing the House of Commons as soon as Hitler was defeated, at which time it would be necessary to put before the country a four-year plan, involving such subjects as agriculture and education. What he said about agriculture appeared to me to have too much insistence on cheap food to please the farmers or the Minister. Then he read four pages on education, which were in a flowing style and derived from Disraeli's view that a nation rules either by force or by tradition. His theme was that we must adhere to our traditions, but that we must move from the class basis of our politics, economics and education to a national standard. There were some sharp words about idle people whether at the top or the bottom, some very pungent remarks about the old school tie (the time for which, he said, was past), and a definite assertion that the school-leaving age must be raised to 16. He remarked that his daughter Mary had told him he must say 16, 'because it had been promised', and that he agreed with her as this would keep people off the labour market where 'blind-alley occupations' started so fair and often ended so foul. I said that I agreed with Mary too, but that perhaps I had better have a good look at the wording later on. His first reaction was that I mustn't 'go messing about'. But then he handed me the entire speech and said, 'You shall have the whole night—sitting up, correcting it, revising it in pencil—and will speak to me in the morning.' The Prof looked very disturbed that I should have the only copy of the precious document in my hands, and hurried after me to my room whispering, 'Don't leave it on your dressing-table.' 'No,' I reassured him, 'I propose to lock it up.' He watched glumly as I did so.

We were then summoned to the cinema which had been set up in the long gallery. The garrison of soldiers had sent a contingent, as also had the A.T.S. who did the waiting. We sat in immense armchairs in the front row, equipped with gout stools and a gigantic box of cigars. The Prime Minister wore a quilted dressing-gown and a rug over his knees, and punctuated the show with complaints (the digest of the news was far too short for him) and comments ('In 1909 I was asked to a glittering function at the Winter Palace with my cousin, the Duke of Marlborough, but was unable to go') which at times drowned the sound-track. The main film ended with the murder of a nineteenth-century Russian ruler just before he was to be married to a princess who, from her French training, had inculcated him with radical ideas. In the last scene the Chief Minister announces to the bereaved princess, 'The new Czar has declared null and void the draft Constitution which His Majesty was about to promulgate'; she replies, 'Poor Russia.' At this Churchill rose abruptly and said in a grave voice, 'That's a very open question, whether we ought to have a Constitution or not. I think we had better not discuss it in front of the servants. Let us depart.'

As we went out I noticed Lord Cherwell muttering in the Prime Minister's ear, and suddenly Churchill turned on me with great vehemence and declared, 'You can't have the whole speech. Why did I give it to you? I wish to work on it during the night. You shall have your own portion. Give me my speech.' I obediently went to fetch it, and he tore out the four pages on education, handed them back to me and bustled off with the rest to his bedroom. By this time it was nearly one o'clock in the morning, but I sat up for a considerable period rewriting. In particular, I added a piece on religion and its place in the schools, modified the reference to the school-leaving age by saying that it must be progressively prolonged, inserted a few lines on further education and part-time release from industry (using the Prime Minister's own words about blind-alley occupations), and substituted for the rather rude remarks about the old school tie a statement about the need for every type of school and every type of tie.

I was up and about well before nine next morning, and was rather shaken to be told that it wasn't certain whether the P.M. would actually want to see me. However, at a quarter to eleven my presence was demanded and I found him in bed, smoking a Corona, with a black cat curled up on his feet. He began aggressively by claiming that the cat did more for the war effort than I did, since it provided him with a hot-water bottle and saved fuel and power. Didn't I agree? I said not really, but that it was a very beautiful cat. This seemed to please him. He then asked me if I had done anything overnight or whether I had been lulled to sleep. So I produced my handiwork which was critically surveyed. He did not agree at all with my wording about religion, but allowed that there were people in the country who would have noticed its omission. I observed mildly that there were quite a lot. The P.M. said he would rather express the idea in his own way, if I would allow him to; whereupon he began to expatiate on the subject of freedom of conscience, toleration, consideration of the other man's point of view, and the kindly character of our country—into which pattern the schools must fit themselves. At this moment a rather flustered Private Secretary burst in to say that there was a Private Notice question down for that afternoon from Aneurin Bevan; would he like to take it, or should the War Office? 'Pray do not look so nervous and hotted up,' replied the P.M. 'You have no experience of public affairs. I shall have to take the question, of course. But it is very sad, very sad indeed, when I was just in the middle of my majestic speech.' The Private Secretary fled and the Prime Minister cheered up. He had been in politics, he explained to me, since 1899. At 68 he felt very vigorous, full of push and grip.

REE GENERATIONS AT CAMBRIDGE. THE
THOR WITH HIS FATHER, SIR MONTAGU
TLER (MASTER OF PEMBROKE COLLEGE) AND
HIS SON, RICHARD

SYDNEY BUTLER WHO DIED
IN 1954

WITH SYDNEY AND THE CHILDREN

Barratts Photo Pr

1954   CHANCELLOR OF THE EXCHEQUER

Anyway, that was how he felt every morning. Lloyd George had made terrible mistakes at the end of the last war. He ought not to have shown his hunger for power and he should have had no personal fund. He, Churchill, would show that he didn't mind whether he had power or not: the result would be that power would come to him, and he would go on after the war, as he had so much more political experience than other people. In any case, he really didn't mind one way or the other. It was a lovely day, and would I like to hear the rest of his speech read to me?

I said that I should be glad to hear the early part again, and this he then declaimed. There were the awkward pieces about leaving decisions on policy until after the war; when added to his hints on refreshing the House of Commons as soon as the Nazis were beaten, they made a bad political impact. So I suggested it might be better not to give the impression that a coupon election was in sight, still less that he proposed to leave reform untouched. However, what was required were not so much snippets of policy as a grand design. He said he thought these observations quite sensible and made a note of them. Then we came to what for me was the crucial part of our conversation. 'I advise you', he declared, 'not to come out too much on education immediately, because they will only drag you down in the present political atmosphere. I admired what you said about not bringing out snippets of policy. You will have to make a great statement when the time comes—a State Paper or a speech, a great speech.' So I said I was drafting a Bill, with the aid of my colleagues. To this he paid no attention at all. I repeated, in a louder voice, 'I am drafting an Education Bill.' Without raising his head from the papers before him on the counterpane, he said simply that I must show him my plans when they were ready and that he was sure they would be very interesting. I gladly left it at that, and we turned to the other and detailed amendments I had made to his speech, all of which he accepted quite calmly, saying he thought they were improvements. I asked him whether he wanted to thank the teachers for their part in the war effort, but he dismissed this with a jocular reference to the long and boring list of acknowledgments in theatre programmes, 'Wigs by Clarkson. No.' However, when the speech had been broadcast—and I naturally arranged with the Prof and the Private Secretaries to vet it, so that it would contain nothing precluding the consideration of my educational plans that summer—he minuted a brief acknowledgment to me from No. 10: 'Thank you so much for your help.'

The sequel to my visit to Chequers was that in April I sent a memorandum on educational reconstruction to the Cabinet, in July I published the White Paper, decorated by a quotation from Disraeli ('Upon the education of the people of this country the fate of this country depends'), and in January 1944 I moved the Second Reading of the Education Bill in the House of Commons. The original idea was that the Bill and the White Paper should come out together. But the Bill proved so complicated to draft that it was decided to issue the White Paper separately and references in it to what the Bill 'provides' were changed to what it 'would provide'. This was accepted as a thoroughly democratic way of proceeding. It also proved extremely advantageous from a tactical point of view. For the reception of the White Paper made it plain to my Ministerial colleagues that, whilst there might well be controversy over certain sections of the Bill, and particularly over the religious settlement, it would have the minimum of disruptive effect upon the Coalition character of the government. The *Times Educational Supplement* said of the White Paper, 'The ingenious and intricate compromise—product of many months of patient and unwearying negotiations on the part of the President of the Board of Education—which is proposed as a solution for the inveterate problem of dual control, though it commands the agreement and one would imagine the respect of all the moderates may yet not satisfy the intransigents or the extremists on either side. Yet he will be a rash and irresponsible man who is prepared to attack the settlement now proposed without offering to put in its place another which will command an equal degree of consent and will be equally well conceived to promote the success of the plan as a whole.' There were indeed strong attacks on the arrangements outlined for the voluntary schools, notably from the Roman Catholic community. But despite the anxiety raised by this opposition, indeed largely because of it, there was a desire on the part both of government and back-benchers to get this matter well out of the way before an election.

Another decisive argument in favour of an early Bill was that no other Minister on the home front had been able to bring his plans to fruition. Sir Granville Ram, the Parliamentary Counsel, who with Sam (now Mr. Justice) Cooke was responsible for the drafting of the Bill, told me only ten days before it was issued that he had nothing else whatever on the stocks—not even a keel laid down. Thus, for example, the whole problem of how to implement the Beveridge Report on social security and allied services was still at the stage of drawings, and not under construction. This was due to the fact that most of the issues of post-war reconstruction impinged directly and immediately on the pocket, and appeared in one way or another to touch the sensitive political area of economic planning and control. It may seem strange that the enormous capital and current commitments which the full implementation of the Education Bill would entail were not considered an insuperable barrier to progress. But I was very careful at all stages to say, what was indeed the case, that their full implementation would take at least a generation. This was naturally a great comfort to Sir Kingsley Wood and Sir John Anderson, the two Chancellors with whom I had successively to deal, and they and their Treasury officials were therefore reasonable and helpful over finance. I was also encouraged by the Whips' Office, then under the direction of James Stuart, for whom the beauty of the Bill was that it would keep the parliamentary troops thoroughly occupied; providing endless opportunity for debate, without any fear of breaking up the government. Its provisions were broadly acceptable to moderate and progressive Conservative opinion and consistently supported by Labour men, both those inside the government (notably Ernest Bevin) and those 'in opposition' (notably our former colleague Arthur Greenwood). *The Times* noted that, in a two days' debate on the White Paper, 'not a single voice was raised in favour of holding up or whittling down any one of the proposals for educational advance'. For all these reasons I was able to carry on with my hands strengthened.

I began my Second Reading speech by observing that a schoolmaster friend had explained to me how, if it were too academic, it would be set by schools as a subject for prize essays. This was my excuse for getting down to the practical details of the Bill without too much philosophizing. For it was a long Bill—122 clauses and eight schedules—and to make a précis of it would take at least as long as to play a football match. I proposed, with this image in mind, to divide the speech into two halves—playing the first half 'with the wind', that is to say dealing with proposals about which everyone was pretty happy, and the second half 'against the wind', that is to say dealing with issues that might prove, or had already proved, contentious. In the first half I described the revised powers and influence of the central authority (soon to be renamed the Ministry of Education), the setting up of advisory councils for England and Wales with a wider scope than the old Consultative Committee, and most important of all, the replacement of the elementary code, with its emphasis on the three R's, by a continuous process of education conducted in successive stages and suited to the three A's, 'the age, ability, and aptitude', of each child. For children below the age of five the aim was a sufficient supply of nursery schools. The period of compulsory school attendance, and hence of free schooling, would be extended from 14 to 15 without exemptions and with provision for its subsequent extension to 16 as soon as circumstances permitted. And this period would be divided into two stages—primary education up to about 11, and secondary education for all, 'of diversified types but of equal standing', thereafter. When the period of full-time schooling ended, it was proposed that young people should continue under educational influences up to 18 years of age, either by staying on at secondary school or by attending county colleges. Throughout all these stages the benefits of full medical and dental inspection and treatment would be available, and special schools would be provided for children suffering from physical or mental disability. Opportunities for technical and adult education would also be increased.

I had just got to the second part of my speech, in which I anticipated playing against the wind, when Mgr. Griffin, the newly appointed Archbishop of Westminster who had been enthroned the day before, was ushered into the Distinguished Strangers' Gallery. There, with the sun illuminating his bright red hair and his pectoral cross, he sat looking directly down on me as I outlined the provisions of the religious settlement and replied to those who had criticized its compromises. 'I would ask those who feel deeply,' I said, 'to dismiss from their minds the wholly unwarrantable views that the Government desire either to tear away Church schools from unwilling managers or to force them inhumanely out of business. The best way I can reassure them is by quoting a verse from the hymn:

> "Ye fearful saints, fresh courage take,
> The clouds ye so much dread
> Are big with mercy, and shall break
> In blessings on your head."'

The unexpected, gratifying and witty sequel was the delivery to me next morning of a large parcel, containing not a bomb but a set of Abbot Butler's *Lives of the Saints*, the classic Roman Catholic work on hagiography. Indeed, I must in fairness say that, though the Roman Catholic interest never accepted the financial basis laid down for voluntary school building, the religious clauses aroused far less acrimony and a much greater sense of responsibility in the House of Commons than past experience had suggested was likely.

The other two issues on which controversy was expected were the future of independent educational provision, and most particularly the public schools, and the proposed abolition of what the Act of 1902 had called 'Part III authorities', those responsible for the oversight of elementary education only. A system had been written into the Bill for improving sub-standard independent schools and for closing those that were inefficient or inadequately equipped. But the central political issue—whether, and if so how, public schools might be more closely associated with or integrated into the general educational system—had been remitted for study by a committee under the chairmanship of Lord Fleming. I had been advised that Fleming was a distinguished Scottish judge who could be relied upon to provide impartiality; I had not been prepared for the limitations of his views or for the humourlessness with which he gave them rein. The sensationally ingenuous report produced in 1944, in common with its successor a quarter of a century later, tended only to confirm the view of my old Corpus mentor, Sir Will Spens, that there was no practical solution to the problem of public schools, since they were *sui generis*. Certainly it had little influence on the course of events. But, though Labour members breathed a certain amount of ritual fire and fury about social exclusiveness and privilege, the appointment of the Fleming Committee had temporarily removed the fuse. Or, in a railway metaphor, the first-class carriage had been shunted on to an immense siding.

The abolition of the Part III authorities was, mercifully, provided for in a schedule to the Bill. What would have happened if this issue had been fought out at an earlier stage is anybody's guess. The proceedings in committee were very slow to begin with—it took eight days to get through the first 27 clauses—though later a voluntary time-table was evolved and things went more rapidly until the fateful night when the government were defeated on clause 82 on the question of equal pay for women teachers. Many sensational accounts have been given of this incident. It arose because of the clear resolve of the Tory Reform group, led by Quintin Hogg to whom I had quite fruitlessly appealed for a modicum of uncharacteristic restraint, to vote with the Labour rebels against the government. Owing to their jubilant and overweening attitude, I did not feel it right to adopt an appeasing line, particularly as they had for some time been creating difficulties for my other colleagues in the government. We should have escaped defeat if only one of the less sprightly Ministers, like Sir John Anderson, who had been working in their offices in Whitehall, had proved more fleet of foot. But they arrived in the Chamber out of breath and too late to prevent our being beaten by the margin of a single vote. After the event I was sorry to have shown a measure of irritation; but I did take it rather hard that major political issues with which I had been dealing for so many months should have led to no trouble, whereas a matter (implicitly affecting the entire Civil Service) which could not conceivably have been settled within the context of an Education Bill should have resulted in a government defeat due to the irresponsibility of a small minority in my own party.

However, the current gossip about my telling the Prime Minister I was in an impossible position and appealing to him for support, had no basis whatever in fact. Having returned home to dinner with my P.P.S., I was asked to go along with the Chief Whip to see the Prime Minister at about a quarter to ten. We found Churchill in a very resolute and jovial mood. He said that he warmly supported my language, which he had heard on the 9 o'clock news; he was sorry that the issue should have been that of equal pay, but it was not the issue that mattered so much as the opportunity to rub the rebels' noses in their mess. He had long been waiting for this opportunity; the by-elections had been going against him, and the House seemed to be utterly unaware that there was a war on and that we had severe struggles ahead. Now the Lord had delivered the enemy into his hands, and he reminded me of the strategy of the Battle of Dunbar ('Both sides confidently appealed to Jehovah; and the Most High, finding so little to choose between them in faith and zeal, allowed purely military factors to prevail'). Happily, he had the big battalions, and it would be valuable to secure a vote of confidence before the Second Front opened. So clause 82 as amended must be expunged from the Bill and the original, unamended, clause put back as a matter of confidence. He dictated on the spot the statement to this effect which he made in the House next day. It had the cordial backing of all the other members of government who had been badgered by the Tory Reformers from time to time. Anthony Eden, then Leader of the House, was particularly firm in his support, while Ernest Bevin went so far as to say that, if my position were to be in any way prejudiced, he would leave the government. These were indeed cheering reactions. It is when one gets into a scrape that it is easiest to count one's friends.

On the night before the confidence debate Churchill prepared a splendid piece of oratory which he invited me to read. It highlighted the magnificence of the British Constitution, compared it in somewhat doubtful terms with the written Constitutions of Russia and the United States, and depicted Prime Ministers riding upon the sea of Parliament as our battleships do upon the waves. Polite and even gracious noises followed about my handling of the Bill; almost everyone was in agreement with it and with the manner in which it had been piloted through Parliament. But, he went on to say, to insert the massive and far-reaching issue of equal pay into its provisions was like placing an elephant in a perambulator. (In the original text, he had referred to my Bill as a milk cart, but, seeing that I was not over-pleased by this description, changed it to what he called 'a less clattering vehicle'.) Unfortunately, the Chair's ruling prevented this speech from being delivered; so the House was sadly de-prived and the P.M. sulked visibly on the Treasury bench. In the vote that followed the government had an overwhelming majority, and we continued, without further distractions of a similar magnitude, to pass the Bill through the Commons. Indeed the equal-pay fracas paid a handsome dividend. For there-after no member proved so bold as to press an amendment which was unacceptable to the government if there was any prospect of its being carried. This made it very much easier to deal with the potentially controversial abolition of the Part III authorities which, as I have already mentioned, had been rele-gated by the unwitting prescience of Sir Granville Ram to the tail end of the Bill.

In the House of Lords the Bill was in the capable charge of Lord Selborne (whom Churchill incurably persisted in address-ing by his previous title of Wolmer). 'Their Lordships', he wrote to me at a time when, having carelessly fallen from a tree in my father's Cambridge garden, I was incapacitated with a broken rib, 'are a very formidable assembly comprising four ex-Presidents of the Board of Education and three ex-Lord Chancellors, and a million Bishops, to say nothing of ardent spirits of varying eloquence and wisdom.' Their ardour was somewhat quenched when they had to call off a vote because they simply did not know how to divide in the temporary quarters they were then occupying in Church House. But in any case the proceedings proved less exciting, certainly less troublesome, in the Lords than in the Commons. By August the Bill was law, and I received the following telegram:

'Pray accept my congratulations. You have added a notable Act to the Statute Book and won a lasting place in the history of British education. Winston S. Churchill.'

I cabled him back:

'Very many thanks for your generous telegram which much

encourages me on the inauguration of the reformed system of education. R. A. Butler.'

The Act of 1944, in common with its predecessors of 1870, 1902 and 1918, affords a classic example of what Dicey called 'our inveterate prejudice for fragmentary and gradual legislation'. It did not, as some would have wished, sweep the board clean of existing institutions in order to start afresh. On the contrary, it established a financial framework within which schools provided by the local education authorities and schools provided by the Churches could continue to live side by side. The more generous assistance which it made available to the voluntary bodies enabled the physical reorganization of schools into primary and secondary to proceed, albeit slowly. It was therefore possible for the Act to cut right out of the educational vocabulary the word 'elementary', to which the stigma of an inferior kind of schooling for children of the poorer classes had continued to cling. Henceforth every child would have a right to free secondary education and in order that these secondary courses should become a full reality, they were to last for at least four and eventually five years. It was, however, equally important to ensure that a stigma of inferiority did not attach itself to those secondary institutions—and they were bound now to be the preponderant majority—which lacked the facilities and academic prestige of the grammar schools. Conditions in each of the different types of school, grammar, modern and technical, would therefore have to be made broadly equivalent: indeed, as my 1943 White Paper stated, 'It would be wrong to suppose that they will necessarily remain separate and apart. Different types may be combined in one building or on one site.' This forecast the comprehensive idea. Even so, equality of opportunity would remain something of an empty phrase if children entered the period of compulsory schooling from conditions of family deprivation, or left it to pursue what Churchill called blind-alley occupations. Accordingly, the Act made provision, on the one hand, for a major expansion of maintained and grant-aided nursery schools and, on the other hand, for compulsory part-time education up to the age of 18.

It will, I think, be generally conceded that many of the opportunities for progress offered by the Act of 1944 have been profitably seized. Succeeding decades have brought great quantitative growth and much qualitative improvement to education. But although, by the late 1960s, a series of reports from the Central Advisory Committee and other bodies was thought to be carrying the system near to the threshold of a further massive redefinition, not all the promises of the original Act had yet been fulfilled. The provision of adequate nursery facilities for children of pre-school age remained patently inadequate. Day release from industry for part-time further education was still voluntary, not mandatory, and affected less than half the under-18s. Though a gratifying increase had taken place in the numbers staying on at school beyond 15, the compulsory school-leaving age had been unchanged since 1947 when Ellen Wilkinson bravely implemented the first stage of my plan, against the advice of countless Jeremiahs. The future of the grammar schools had been turned into a political football through the obsessive insistence of the Labour Party on a doctrinal rather than an empirical approach to composite or comprehensive schemes of secondary organization. Most important of all, in the long run, the perfunctory and uninspired nature of the religious instruction provided in all too many local authority and controlled schools had begun, in the opinion of people well qualified to judge, to imperil the Christian basis of our society. These faults of omission and commission are not intended to constitute a roster of despair: rather they are a challenge to us to take another look at the agreed syllabuses and ask whether they are really good enough for adolescents; to take another look at the wide variety of secondary experiments so that knowledgeable advice and not dictation can be given to education authorities; to take another look at the proportion of our national wealth spent on education, in the realization that the more we develop a full secondary education for all—which was the main theme of the Act of 1944—the greater inevitably is the thirst and the need for higher education.

The crippling qualities of expense were much in the minds of my Coalition colleagues when they came to consider the further and wider problems of post-war reconstruction. 'We cannot initiate the legislation now or commit ourselves to the expenditure involved', was Churchill's initial reaction to the Beveridge Report. But, as with my plans for educational reform, a certain modification of view was produced by time and pressure. In November 1943 Lord Woolton, then still a non-party man who had won a large reputation as Minister of Food, became Minister of Reconstruction with a seat in the War Cabinet. A Reconstruction Committee was established under his chairmanship, with Sir John Anderson as its most influential member, Attlee, Bevin and Morrison as regular attenders from the Labour side, and 'Bobbety' Cranborne, Oliver Lyttelton, the Prof and I as the principal Conservatives. It framed a town and country planning measure and laid the foundations of the post-war housing policy. It discussed and approved White Papers setting out the principles for a national health service and for post-war schemes of pensions, sickness and unemployment benefits, and workmen's compensation. It worked on the historic document which committed all parties to 'the maintenance of a high and stable level of employment after the war'. It was even tempted by Herbert Morrison early in 1945 to pledge itself to a public corporation structure for the electricity industry. The notes I made about these meetings at the time record that 'Morrison's cleverness increases every day', that 'electricity is the worst ground to fight upon' where nationalization was concerned, but that after a discussion between Conservative Ministers, enlivened rather than swayed by the vehemence of Max Beaverbrook, 'it was decided that we should attempt not to get involved in decisions about State ownership prior to the election'. My notes add: 'The fact is that the Committee has done a good deal of useful work in framing the future social and political structure of the country. The importance of its work can never be over-estimated. It will be seen that the work is of a type suitable to a National government.' Indeed, the Labour government which was swept to power in the summer of that year had, in the fields of social reform and reconstruction, only to complete the work which the Coalition had begun and in some cases to bring forward Bills already drafted.

CHAPTER SEVEN

THE CHARTERS

THE OVERWHELMING electoral defeat of 1945 shook the Conservative party out of its lethargy and impelled it to re-think its philosophy and re-form its ranks with a thoroughness unmatched for a century. To this extent Clemmie Churchill's now famous remark about 'a blessing in disguise', though it did little enough to console her husband at the time, proved prophetic. Power is the first goal of party politics, the *sine qua non* of political effectiveness. But thirty years of almost uninterrupted power, such as we had exercised either alone or in coalition, must be regarded as unnatural in a properly functioning democracy. Such democracy does not necessarily require, like a tennis match, the regular alternation of service and defence; on the contrary, it is frequently strengthened by a lengthy continuity of experience in administration. But just as its post-war periods of office have mellowed and matured the Labour party, educating it out of many callower socialistic assumptions, so the Conservatives, when thrown into opposition, were provided with a healthy opportunity and a compelling motive for bringing both their policies and their characteristic modes of expression up to date. The adaptations and adjustments of both sides were, on a long-term view, of benefit to the country.

These, of course, are retrospective reflections. In the early months of 1945 I could be excused for not viewing the electoral prospect with an equal philosophic detachment. Like Churchill himself, but unlike most of his influential colleagues, I was very strongly in favour of maintaining an all-party National government. The Coalition had not, in my view, outlived its usefulness, and I thought we should stay together at least until the Japanese had been defeated and preferably until the social reforms upon which we were in general agreement had been passed. This seemed best in the national interest; in the party's interest it seemed imperative. Our organization up and down the country was in a parlous condition, much harder hit than that of our opponents by the absence of agents and organizers on war service. Our policy, on which David Maxwell Fyfe and I had been working sporadically since 1941 at the head of the Post-War Problems Committee, was as yet inadequate for the basis of a party appeal and had been insufficiently, if at all, disseminated in the constituencies. At a meeting of the principal Conservative members of the Coalition, which was presided over by Churchill in the Cabinet room. I therefore argued that the Conservatives were not ready for an election in 1945 and that, if one were held, the result would be disastrous. Beaverbrook came up to me afterwards and said, 'Young man, if you speak to the Prime Minister like that, you will not be offered a job in the next Conservative government.' I replied, 'That doesn't really affect me; for if we have an early election, there is not going to be a Conservative government.'

Churchill bore me no grudge for the warning. He was himself in great perplexity, even agony, of mind—'deeply distressed', in his own words, 'at the prospect of sinking from a national to a party leader'. Unfortunately, the great man was seldom able to do things by halves, and the sinking was therefore altogether deeper than it needed to be. His first election broadcast, with its rollicking polemic against Socialism which, he said, could not be established without a 'Gestapo', was by common consent a strategic blunder. In my diary I reflected that, as La Bruyère had said of Corneille, *'parfois on s'étonne qu'il aît pu tomber de si haut'*. The following evening, in company with Beaverbrook, Oliver Lyttelton and James Stuart, I dined with him and listened to Attlee's sober but stinging answer ('The voice we heard last night was that of Mr. Churchill, but the mind was that of Lord Beaverbrook'). Beaverbrook rushed from the table to the telephone to call *Daily Express* experts in various cities, who reported that Attlee's broadcast had been a failure. But I do not think Churchill was much comforted by this intelligence. He had been deeply affected by the rancour of what he had heard. 'In the past, when I was with the Liberals,' he said moodily, 'those in politics used to slang each other every day; but then they would dine together at night and drink champagne.' 'That is exactly the trouble now,' I commented. 'Your opponents do not live the same life. They suffer from a considerable feeling of inferiority. You cannot depict them in a sinister light without their taking personal offence.'

Among those who took most offence was Ernest Bevin. I succeeded him at the Ministry of Labour during the brief months of the Caretaker government, and got the extremely sharp edge of his tongue when calling upon him at his request. 'I'm fed up with Winston. We ought to have kept the Coalition going much longer. It's bad enough him calling a khaki election which he thinks we'll lose. But to be insulted in this brutal manner over the radio is the last straw'—and more, in more colourful language, to the same effect. According to Bevin's biographer, what he said to me about continuing the Coalition may not have represented his settled view. But it was difficult for me to disagree with him. 'I'm sorry you feel upset,' I said quite sincerely. He replied, 'Oh! I feel as light as a feather; but I'm bloody well not going to show you round the department.' Then he rang the bell for his Private Secretary, growled, 'Fetch me my 'at,' and stamped out. Later, as Foreign Secretary, he was to be more gracious to me.

The Churchill-Attlee exchange was a pivotal event in the history of the election and set its tone; but it did not, I believe, affect the final verdict. It was sad that the work done by the Post-War Problems Committee played so little part in the formulation of our Conservative campaign, and that the conduct of the election swept away much of the idealism which we wanted to instil and which emerged only in the 1945–51 period in opposition. It would have been better if affirmation of post-war policies had not taken a poor third place to the concentrated exploitation of Churchill's personality and a negative attack on the Labour Party. But the election would probably have been lost in any case. When I said in my own broadcast that one important thing I had learnt in my last job, as Minister of Education, was that progress could best be achieved by the patient fitting of different points of view into an agreed plan rather than by turning everything upside down, I was—to an extent of which at the time I was unaware—on a completely different wave-length from millions of voters who, six years later, were to help us back into office. They wanted, or at least they thought they wanted, a great deal turned upside down. The forces' vote, in particular, had been virtually won over by the left-wing influence of the Army Bureau of Current Affairs. Socialism provided them with a vision and a doctrine to which we had no authoritative answer or articulated alternative.

ASCOT HAT

"LOR, SURELY MA ISN'T GOING TO WEAR THAT OLD FRIGHT AGAIN."

Herbert Morrison knew this and had taken advantage of his position on the home front to roll out pamphlets and speeches which gave a very firm impression of leading to the left. He recorded in his autobiography that I carefully examined what he had done for the Labour Party prior to and during the 1945 election and told my staff that I wanted to do the same for the Conservative party. This information was correct. Surveying the wreckage in the summer of 1945, which I had been almost alone in predicting, I resolved to do whatever lay within my power to ensure that we did not go into another election with the propaganda victory already lost.

The then Chief Whip, James Stuart, writing to me on 5th August, said, 'I do not forget that you were against fighting when we did—however, it is done and with dire results!... My present feeling is not so much one of depression as of waking up bewildered in a world completely strange to me. I feel that my entrails have been pulled right out of me.' The early atmosphere in the House of Commons, which I remember vividly, was certainly very strange and hardly reassuring. On their first arrival at Westminster the Socialists were self-confident, arrogant and aloof. They were the ruling class now and nothing would move them for twenty years. They laughed at 'old' Churchill and smiled compassionately on the Opposition. Red ties abounded and there was little fraternization.

But this mood was both understandable and impermanent. The triumph of the Labour party was, and was naturally felt to be, historic—the consummation of more than half a century's devoted work and passionate service to which every branch of the movement had contributed. However, the movement had had the wit to choose a large proportion of middle-class candidates wherever the constituency bodies of Labour had not secured the option. The result was that there sat on the government side of the new Parliament a large proportion of men, of varying degrees of property and education, who were still on the rise and had little desire to subvert existing institutions: a moderate affluence was, in their view, respectable and their main (and legitimate) targets were the remaining extremes. There was also in the lower ranks a considerable number of ex-Civil Servants and brain workers from the party offices; these, too, adopted a constructive rather than iconoclastic attitude. Through regular association with our party members in committee, and under the influence of an occasional shared bottle of South African wine, there was a gradual softening of personal relationships. Indeed, since the days of Baldwin, whose own contribution in this respect was inestimable, real bitterness of feeling between men on either side of the House of Commons has been the fortunate exception, never the rule. This has been as true with Labour's 'sons of toil' as with Socialism's intellectuals—perhaps truer. David Kirkwood, for example, talked to me one day in the lobby about the threatening attitude of Russia and said, 'If it comes to another fight we'll surely all come in together. You fellows would serve with the Labour Prime Minister as we did with Churchill.'

There is no doubt that the continuity of foreign policy—
which caused one Labour man to remark of Ernest Bevin,
'Hasn't Anthony Eden grown fat?'—blunted the blood-letting
edge of party warfare during much of the Attlee government's
tenure. Bevin was among several prominent Labour politicians
who in the 1945 election had promised that Anglo-Russian
relations would be better with a left-wing British Government:
'Left can speak to left in comradeship and confidence', he had
claimed. In office he proved a man big enough to eat his own
unguarded words, and will rank high in history as one of the
chief organizers of Western resistance against the advance of
revolutionary Communism from the East. Particularly in the
latter part of the 1945–50 Parliament I spoke with some fre-
quency on foreign affairs against Bevin—or, rather, with Bevin;
for, not only was our private relationship friendly, but on the
major public issues arising from the 'cold war' there was rarely
much between us save a difference of emphasis or detail. I
remember his taking me into the Smoking Room one evening
and saying, "Ave a beer, Rab, I'm worried about the A-rabs.'

On domestic and imperial topics as well it was often my lot,
as it is certainly my nature, to wield a pruning knife rather than
an axe, to offer constructive comment in preference to blood
and thunder. I had, of course, been a member of the Coalition committee which had worked on the Beveridge plans and
therefore found it an agreeable and a rewarding experience to
lead for the Opposition on the great Insurance Bill. Similarly,
my pre-war work at the India Office gave me, as I saw it, both a
right and a duty to speak, not altogether without anxiety, but
wholly ungrudgingly, about the grant of independence to
India and Pakistan in 1947. These parliamentary episodes had
their importance in aligning the Conservative party with the
more positive secular trends of the post-war period—the
creation of a Welfare State and the development of Empire into
Commonwealth.

The government was vulnerable principally on the economic front. I leave it to the cool voice of history to apportion the
blame for its failures between bad judgement and bad luck; it
certainly had a lot of both. But the failures themselves became
increasingly self-evident and self-confessed. 'At the end of the

war', said Stafford Cripps on the day he devalued the pound, 'we all thought that this post-war period was going to be easier than it has, in fact, turned out to be, in the economic sphere; and we have been trying to deal with it ever since by a series of temporary expedients which have led to a series of crises as each expedient became exhausted.' Even for a public man of the utmost piety and probity this was an unusually ample white sheet in which to choose to envelop himself and his colleagues. Yet despite the inexorable rise in the cost of living, increasing burdens of direct and indirect taxation, intensification of physical controls, restrictions and rationing, a quite early disenchantment with the results of nationalization and, above all, the series of recurring economic and financial crises to which devaluation did not put an end, the government's stock in the country remained obstinately high. It did not lose a single seat in a parliamentary by-election, and two general elections were needed before it was dislodged from power. The explanation for this lay partly in the strong personal character and cohesion of the Labour Ministers, undermined only at a late date by the loss through ill-health of Bevin and Cripps, and ultimately by the Bevanite schism. But this strength was re-inforced by the magnitude and difficulty of our own Conservative predicament—our need to convince a broad spectrum of the electorate, whose minds were scarred by inter-war memories and myths, that we had an alternative policy to Socialism which was viable, efficient and humane, which would release and reward enterprise and initiative but without abandoning social justice or reverting to mass unemployment. Until the progressive features of our thought had been fully exposed to public view, no one (to adapt Charles II's epigrammatic cynicism) was going to kill Attlee in order to make Churchill king.

It was by no means easy to persuade Churchill of this. Defeat had not shaken his personal prestige: he had taken it with impressive dignity and a characteristic stoutness of heart. When he first walked into the Chamber at the beginning of the new Parliament the Conservative ranks stood as one man and sang in a deafening roar 'For he's a jolly good fellow'. In active politics as in the hunting pack, the strongest wolf will retain leadership while his fangs are still firmly bedded in his jaw. It became clear after endless armchair exchanges that Churchill was fitter than for several years and was prepared to fight. But the constructive part of his mind always dwelt more naturally on the international scene than on bread-and-butter politics. The themes of Anglo-American partnership and European unity, which he first developed in great speeches at Fulton and Strasbourg, were of enduring importance. They represented a fitting contribution from a leader of his world fame and stature and gave him welcome release from the confinements of domestic Opposition. On the home front he preferred to employ his formidable powers of exposition and debate to combat what he called 'positive folly' rather than to propound what I was merely the first of an increasing number of his colleagues to tell him was necessary, namely positive policy. This preference of Churchill's was partly temperamental. But it stemmed also from his historical sense—a wish not to appear as 'an old man in a hurry', peddling nostrums in order to regain power, and a fear of 'giving a hostage to fortune' by promising now what could not be performed later. Honourable as these considerations were, an apter historical analogy outweighed them. Quintin Hogg put this most pithily when he wrote to me at the time to say that what the Conservative party needed was a new Tamworth Manifesto. That was exactly my view. As in the days of Peel, the Conservatives must be seen to have accommodated themselves to a social revolution.

In some detail and after much deliberation, I tried to indicate guidelines of future policy in a speech in March 1946 to the party's first post-war conference on political education. My starting point, naturally enough, was the fundamental reason we found ourselves out of office: 'I do not believe that at the last election many independent electors without party affiliation voted for doctrinaire Socialism. I believe that many were misled because a positive alternative was not put before them with sufficient fervour.' This positive alternative must recognize that circumstances were changing, rapidly and fascinatingly, and that we could no longer 'sit in entrenched positions or rely on holding old-fashioned fortresses'. I called for a total reorganization of the social structure on which our party rested, an acceptance of redistributive taxation to reduce the extremes of poverty and wealth, and repudiation of *laissez-faire* economics in favour of a system in which the State acted as 'a trustee for the interests of the community and a balancing force between different interests'. Elaborating this last point, I envisaged codes of behaviour for industry, with sanctions as a last resort, which would expose anti-social monopolistic and restrictive practices, lay down standards of quality for the consumer, and above all create a spirit of partnership between management and workers as 'the real link between political and economic democracy'.

This foray was almost certainly ahead of the party in the country and quite certainly anathema to its right wing. The *Observer* was kind enough to say that, if my line of thought were taken up and developed, Conservative prospects would be much brighter; but the *Manchester Guardian* paid me a more ambiguous compliment in remarking that 'if what he foretells comes about, the majority of the present Labour parliamentary party would be on his side'. In 1943 the pioneering work of the Post-War Problems Committee had already roused hostility among the die-hards and one of the most forthright and intelligent of them, Sir Herbert Williams, had expressed fear that under cover of war the Conservatives were being led to accept 'pink Socialism'. It was a good phrase, and it stuck. Politically, it was something I always had to take account of in manœuvring for acceptance of our post-war policies. Intellectually, however, it did not trouble me in the least. I had derived from Bolingbroke an assurance that the majesty of the State might be used in the interests of the many, from Burke a belief in seeking patterns of improvement by balancing diverse interests, and from Disraeli an insistence that the two nations must become one. If my brand of Conservatism was unorthodox, I was committing heresy in remarkably good company. In fact, Conservative principles adapted to the needs of the post-war world meant that we should aim for a 'humanized capitalism', of the kind which my father-in-law, Samuel Courtauld, had written about in *Ideas and Industry*. The jibe that our *Industrial Charter* tried to 'amalgamate the Tory party with the Y.M.C.A.' was not only funnier than 'pink Socialism'; it was perceptibly closer to the mark. For what basically we were saying is that, untouched by morality and idealism, economics is an arid pursuit, just as politics is an unprofitable one.

Churchill eventually described the *Industrial Charter* as 'a broad statement of policy, to which those who are opposed to the spread of rigid Socialism can now rally'. If, in common with its successors, it was indeed 'broad' rather than detailed, vague where it might have been specific, and restrained instead of following the simple, connected line I wanted, this was largely because he himself would not have tolerated the binding of the Leader before the party was back in power. 'When an Opposition spells out its policy in detail,' he lectured me, 'the Government becomes the Opposition and attacks the Opposition which becomes the Government. So, having failed to win the sweets of office, it fails equally to enjoy the benefits of being out of office.' There is rather more truth and tactic in this than I was always happy to allow at the time. However, the 1946 party conference at Blackpool had overwhelmingly demanded some reformulation of our policy, and Churchill moved to meet this demand soon after by appointing a special Industrial Policy Committee. It consisted of five members of the Shadow Cabinet —Oliver Stanley, Oliver Lyttelton,[1] Harold Macmillan, David Maxwell Fyfe[2] and myself—and, from the back benches, David Eccles, Derick Heathcoat-Amory, Sir Peter Bennett and Colonel Jim Hutchinson. I was made chairman of this strong, knowledgeable group—rather to my surprise, since the two Olivers at least were technically senior to me. But the appointment must have seemed logical to Churchill because so much of the spade-work had already been started on my initiative and was proceeding under my formal chairmanship or general control. Within months of our electoral defeat the Post-War Problems Committee had been reconstituted as the Advisory Committee on Policy and Political Education, and the principal agencies concerned respectively, but in reinforcement of one another, with its two spheres of interest—the Conservative Research Department and the Conservative Political Centre—had been created or revivified. Together, they equipped the Party with what I later called a 'thinking machine', which helped us to wrest from the Left much of the middle ground in the battle of ideas.

[1] Lord Chandos.   [2] The late Lord Kilmuir.

The Conservative Political Centre, though sometimes accused of occupying an ivory tower, began life in a semi-basement office at 11 Wilton Street, a house which subsequently achieved notoriety as the scene of a shooting affray between two Latin American diplomats. It owed its birth, or rebirth, to Sir Robert Topping who, first as Principal Agent and then as General Director, had built up formidable power in the party, to whose exercise he brought a venturesome, unorthodox mind. I had been fortunate enough to win his liking and approval, and he had personally picked me both as chairman of the central committee which in the immediate pre-war period ran the education work of the Central Office, and, later, as chairman of the Post-War Problems Committee. We shared a determination to reconstruct the educational wing of the party after the 1945 defeat, and, basing ourselves on pre-war experiences, created the C.P.C. with a sort of dominion status in its relation to the Central Office.

The first Director of the C.P.C. and its leading light was Cuthbert ('Cub') Alport, my junior by ten years and the contemporary and close friend of my only brother, Jock. At the outbreak of war my brother, who was in the Home Office, found a loophole in the regulations preventing a civil servant from being called up. His chiefs, Sir John Anderson and Sir George Gaiter, tried hard to stop him. Like so many of his friends, he was killed almost immediately while serving as a bomber navigator. Jock was a great loss since he had a very strong and direct character. Nobody with him was left in any doubt of what he felt on any subject. I recognize his characteristics in my own sons and in his family; that is how life goes on. This tragedy was my first link with Cub. Afterwards we became firm friends. Collaboration between us was always easy and I admired his strong feelings about the need for a new expression of party faith. He never claimed the intellectual distinction of those I was recruiting into the Research Department, but he certainly had the necessary qualities of imagination and drive, together with assiduity and a dogged sense, which he retains, of sticking to the last. Our purpose was not merely to develop political education methods and to influence public opinion indirectly by reasoned instruction within the party, but to create a kind of Conservative Fabian

Society which would act as a mouthpiece for our best modern thought and attract that section of the post-war generation who required an intellectual basis for their political faith.

My personal contribution to the breaking of new ground was the concept of the Two-Way Movement of Ideas. I felt that if the party was to have confidence in the policy of its leaders, its rank-and-file members must be able to share in the task of hammering out that policy. By the time of the Llandudno conference in 1948, I was able to say that the days had gone by when policy was brought down from Mount Sinai on tablets of stone and the faithful were often blinded by the light which they saw. Instead, many scores of discussion groups up and down the country, including those of the Young Conservatives, were receiving well-written pamphlets and briefing materials from the C.P.C., debating and answering the questions these raised, and enjoying the knowledge that the study and collation of their reports had already proved a helpful factor in the shaping of the new Conservatism. The organization of these innovatory methods was worked out with the aid of a talented team of young education officers who had joined the C.P.C. and with the advice of the area education committees which Cub Alport had started up throughout the country. In addition to discussion groups, their range of activities soon included lectures, brains trusts, surveys and investigations, correspondence courses, conferences and residential schools.

At times, it may be that we set our sights rather too high. Of the C.P.C. bookshops which were planned to cover the whole of England and Wales, only the original London branch in Victoria Street was long to survive. Similarly, when we jumped at Lord Swinton's offer to take over part of his castle in Yorkshire so that keen party members could sit at the feet of the leaders of modern Conservatism, we called it our 'College of the North' in the (unrealized) hope that a College of the South would later replace the pre-war Bonar Law College at Ashridge. Swinton, however, under the zealous direction of my old Cambridge friend Reginald Northam, who had both the charisma and the volcanic eloquence of a minor prophet, became a sort of Tory Mecca—perhaps all the more romantically attractive to southerners for being so far from home and quite far even from a convenient railhead. This residential college, the weekend 'schools' organized at holiday resorts and spas and, above all, the annual C.P.C. Summer School in university cities, began to attract considerable attention to our political education movement. They helped to generate real critical and objective interest, particularly among people of university age or background, and the party gained prestige from the publicity given to large meetings which were conducted in an adult and sympathetic manner and avoided crude political indoctrination.

Northam's tenure at Swinton College was a very long one. When he died, still in harness, he was to be succeeded as Principal by David Clarke who twenty years earlier had devoted his attention to building up our post-war Parliamentary Secretariat and the Research Department to which it was formally linked in 1948. A memorandum of mine, prepared for one of the last meetings of the Post-War Problems Committee, reflected my views on the form and function of our future research organization.

'No party Research Department can possibly possess the resources for extensive original work. What it can and must do is to keep a systematic watch on other people's ideas, analyse them, sift the good from the unsound, warn the policy-makers of the party against the latter (however attractively dressed up), and think out means of weaving the former into the texture of a programme.

'This kind of research work, if it is to be of any use, must always be directed towards the building up of material that might form part of a future Election programme. When an Election approaches the leaders of the party must decide, on political grounds, which bits they wish to use. But the business of the Research Department is to make sure that the bits are there, and that (at any rate from the administrative and economic standpoints) they are sound and will not come to pieces in the hand. That is why a second-rate staff, however large, is useless. The staff may have to be small, but it must be first-rate in reliability and thoroughness. . . .

'All this will indicate the tasks awaiting a Research Department, as I see them. In the sifting of ideas there are four criteria:

1. Is it in harmony with Conservative philosophy?
2. Is it in practical form?
3. Will it be acceptable, or can it be rendered acceptable, to the party?
4. Does it meet a real want?'

The choice of the right team was therefore my first concern. I was looking for people with great intelligence and constructive minds, essentially alert and preferably young. But they did not have to be made from the same mould. Individual flair, imagination and even idiosyncrasy were to be encouraged, provided all concerned remained loyal to the party and did not go into rebellion on a major issue. Because we followed the middle way we were at times attacked from our left as well as from our right; but one of the abiding assets of the Conservative party is its flexibility—it can absorb wide discrepancy of views among its members and still remain a coherent and unified entity. The Research Department quickly established an *esprit de corps*. This was due in large measure to the leadership of David Clarke who combined intellectual distinction with a tough integrity and strength of character. He was in need of these qualities for dealing both with the politicians and with his staff. The politicians worried him most; for he was constantly at the receiving end of their attentions, as drafter-in-chief of our documents and lord-in-waiting at the Shadow Cabinet. When particularly exasperated by them he would retire for long periods into the cloakroom where he effected a catharsis of his emotions by puffing at his pipe and alternately praying and cursing gently. This therapy could not work for ever, and before the 1951 election he opted for a job with a more academic and administrative flavour. It was a serious wrench, since he had been extremely good at upholding the pride and efficiency of the Department and at handling its staff, all of whom were able and most of whom could be difficult.

The earliest members of the Research Department included Michael Fraser and Peter Goldman. These two were soon to establish a long-lived working partnership based on an empathy which ensured that, whatever crisis arose, they never flapped simultaneously. Michael Fraser, the best adjutant the party has ever had and the most loyal friend, succeeded David Clarke as Director of the Research Department before eventually rising to the Deputy Chairmanship at Central Office. Peter Goldman, whose loss to the party would later be as important as the resignation of any Cabinet Minister, was originally recruited by me into the Department while still an undergraduate at Cambridge, where he started collecting his Firsts. Senior to them, but birds of passage, were the brilliant men straight from the Services who were thirsting to get into the House of Commons. This thirst might have meant that there would be no peace or rest in the Department because people were either wanting to move or about to move from the back room into the front. In fact, the opposite was true. Those with such ambitions were able to give of their best in study, knowing at the same time that they had a career opening up before them. All this applied particularly to Reggie Maudling, Enoch Powell and Iain Macleod.

It was Oliver Stanley who observed during this period that the party had become all Eton and Magdalene—pronounced Eden and Maudling—because the latter was preparing, with flair, the domestic parts of the former's speeches. Even in those days Reggie had close contacts in the City, which were useful to the party since he was responsible for writing economic briefs for the front bench. Clearly they were also agreeable: he would arrive from lunch fortified for the afternoon and smoking a fragrant cigar. He gave at the Research Department the impression of being much more at ease and of not straining himself to the same extent as the others. This is a feature he carried into later life, and in a way it was a pity, because people were to think that he was too easygoing, perhaps even insouciant. In fact he was extremely industrious: able to take jobs in his stride and master them with dispatch. But he struck an attitude that was deceptive to those who knew him less well, and I feel it did not do him justice.

There was nothing languid or easygoing about Enoch Powell. A former Fellow of Trinity, Cambridge, and Professor of Greek in Australia, he was probably the most intellectually formidable of the men who have passed through the Research Department. He took an interest in almost every subject, and on almost every subject he had strong and pungently expressed views. Only some of these were eccentric. I remember that on one occasion he brought me a paper in which he argued that with ten divisions we could reconquer India. At his request I submitted the paper to Churchill, who seemed distressed and asked me if I thought Powell was 'all right'. I said I was sure he was, but explained that he was very determined in these matters. I was then fetched to Hyde Park Gate where Churchill shook his head sadly a great deal and said that it was too late for him to invade India and that, in any event, ten divisions would not be enough. This particular hobby-horse was heard of no more. But there have been several since, for Powell has an inventive mind. He has also a warm heart and I think it a thousand pities that he ever made his first notable speech on immigration, when the Tiber was to run with blood. This led him on to an incurable rift with his own party leaders which has been made wider by the variety of causes of schism which he espouses. Powell could be a most valuable lieutenant instead of a lost assailant, and this is a pity.

Iain Macleod was in charge of social policy when he was in the Research Department, but as a politician he was potentially the best all-rounder of the three. His tragically foreshortened career will long provide inspiration. Gifted with a phenomenal memory and an enviable mastery of the written and spoken word, he drafted policy documents with precision and elegance and was never at a loss for a fact or an argument. His natural ability as a bridge player, which was sometimes exercised during spare time at the Department, gave him a perhaps undeserved reputation for cool calculation. He was the most unabashedly ambitious member of the staff and the prospect of a parliamentary seat weighed heavily on him. The Research Department was, and still is, wise to benefit from the by-products of such ambition, but since the 1945–50 period the candidatures have tended to space out more.

The Research Department was typically overworked. It provided official secretaries for every parliamentary committee of the party except the '1922'. It prepared briefs on issues coming before Parliament. It helped leading front-bench spokesmen with the drafting of their speeches. It kept M.P.s, candidates, accredited speakers and key party workers supplied with information and guidance on current politics, and even permitted itself to receive and placate deputations. It wrote, especially in the early days, many of the best pamphlets published by the C.P.C., and continuously aided all departments of the Central Office by vetting and sometimes rewriting their own effusions. This immersion in the detail and hurly-burly of day-to-day politics could well have detracted from the Department's most important function, which was the undertaking of long-term research coupled with constructive assistance in reformulating party policy. In fact, though I myself look back with a longing nostalgia to the first couple of years before the research functions, under David Clarke's direction, were formally married to the servicing functions, which were presided over by Anthony Eden's nominee Henry Hopkinson,[1] and the library and information services under the experienced Percy Cohen; the complex amalgam worked well. Policy cannot be made in a vacuum and it was intellectually (if not physically) healthy for the officer specializing in a particular subject or group of subjects to be closely in touch with the currents of thought and feeling in the House and in the constituencies. The burden was heavy and the hours worked often preposterously long, but all of us were buoyed up by the excitement of the period and the sure knowledge that what we were doing could be the basis of any future success of the Conservative party.

I enjoyed the period so much that I had little time to worry about personal ambition, though I clearly saw that a fine opportunity had been given me to render service to the party. A prominent journalist who came to see me at the Department asked, 'Why the hell do you slave away all the time here, when most of the others are managing to do jobs in the City?' I replied, 'It is because I am passionately interested.' This was the literal truth. My working day typically began over breakfast when urgent mail would be discussed with my supremely efficient secretarial assistant Pat McCraken; each morning would be spent at the Research Department dealing with policy

[1] Lord Colyton.

and other problems, and most afternoons and evenings too unless I was speaking in the House or in the country. After a brief sojourn at Wilton Street, the Department had moved back into its old home where between 1930 and 1939 it was used as Neville Chamberlain's private brains trust. The more desirable accommodation provided tempting views of Birdcage Walk and the Park; I was well content to be consigned to a sunless, Hansard-bedecked office, overlooking the parked cars of Old Queen Street, but of an imposing length, conducive to thoughtful pacing and convenient for the holding of formal meetings. Around its battered mahogany conference table, the Industrial Policy Committee had most of its meetings in the long winter of 1946–7. David Clarke served as secretary to this Committee, with Maudling and Fraser as his principal aides.

The Committee had been chosen with skill and worked both harmoniously and at a steady pace. When the *Industrial Charter* was eventually published I received a generously appreciative letter from Oliver Lyttelton who reminded me of the saying, '*Il n'y a que le calme qui règne sur les âmes.*' It is true that we were a calm body; perhaps this helped to produce from some of the brightest members of the Committee the kind of constructive contributions they made. Lyttelton himself was the head of a big business and as such brought useful practical experience to bear. He comforted us greatly by saying that he hoped he could carry the philosophy of the 'Workers' Charter' within his own industry. Derry Amory,[1] an employer in a West Country textile firm and closer to the Liberal school of thought than any of us, was less sure that the schemes could be generally applied, but believed ardently that the psychological value of putting forward the Workers' Charter outweighed such reservations. The presence in our midst of Bennett, a powerful, sensible businessman from Birmingham, and Hutchinson, admired by all for his high-mindedness and wartime gallantry, helped us with the right of the party: they gave invaluable support when later we were pushing the Charter through the party conference and were being accused of having produced a rather 'pink' document.

Neither David Maxwell Fyfe nor Harold Macmillan was a

[1] Lord Amory.

stranger to the accusation of being pink. David, though an essentially orthodox character, had had the task, which he managed admirably, of soothing the right-wing rebels when they were up in arms against the progressive work of the Post-War Problems Committee. He may have been living proof that Carlyle was wrong to define genius as a transcendent capacity for taking trouble; but he did have a most astounding appetite for and application to paper work, which he often carried to bed with him—to the discomfort of his wife who complained to me good-humouredly of the difficulties of sleeping with drafts of the *Industrial Charter* littering the eiderdown. He was not only painstaking over every last detail but immensely loyal, and I never knew him spiky or difficult except in parts of his memoirs. Macmillan, of course, had been reared in a very tough school of politics. Permanently influenced by the unemployment and suffering in his constituency in the North-East, Macmillan had revolted against the Montagu Norman banking school and against the Conservative front bench, whose Whip he at one time refused. The fact that he had spent much of his early life as a rebel while I was a member of the despised and declining 'establishment' underlines a difference of temperament between us. It also may lie at the root of our future relationship. But in political philosophy we were not far apart. I admired, for the most part, the economic doctrines of *The Middle Way* which he still espoused and a great deal of the intellectual background of the *Industrial Charter* was due to him. Along with David Eccles, whose thrusting mind was particularly reflected in the economic and financial sections of the Charter, he affected its positive content more than my other helpers on the Committee.

Though Oliver Stanley's contribution was less obviously constructive, I have no hesitation in singling him out as the most capable of us all. He had the acutest brain on the Conservative front bench, the keenest lance I have ever known in opposition, and a flowing pen which could draft several pages of immaculate foolscap in the same time that most men would take to write a decent paragraph. Had he lived, I rather doubt if he would have made a good Prime Minister, or even a good Chancellor, for in office he too frequently exhibited an almost physical incapacity for making up his mind. But he was a joyous master of the arts of opposition, more consistently entertaining even than Churchill, and a far more sensitive and flexible tactician. Without his insistent influence, which was happily seconded by Anthony Eden, the Industrial Policy Committee might never have been set up, and his critical wit not only enlivened our sessions but saved us from many a mishap or mistake.

As the Charter neared completion in the early months of 1947, we had to take a number of important hurdles. Oliver Stanley, Oliver Lyttelton, Harold Macmillan, David Fyfe and I divided up the country between us and, accompanied by other members of the Committee and one of its secretariat, held private discussions with selected groups of Conservative businessmen, managers and trade unionists in industrial centres. At the same time, the reactions of prominent members of the '1922' were ascertained by Oliver Poole,[1] whose extraordinary skill and energy were already to the fore and whom I employed with absolute confidence as 'contact man' with the parliamentary party. The penultimate draft, which took account of these soundings, was then discussed, adjusted and approved by the Shadow Cabinet under Anthony Eden's chairmanship and submitted to Churchill. Silence ensued. Though Churchill was to tell the party conference in October that the Charter 'was officially approved by me at what we call a Consultative Committee, six months ago', his ultimate imprimatur was not so much obtained as divined. At a dinner party for his senior colleagues at the Savoy, he placed me on his right hand, plied me with cognac, and said several agreeable and no disagreeable things about my work. Emboldened by this prodigality, I gave instructions that the Charter should be published on 12th May, though none of us at the time was one hundred per cent certain whether it was to be regarded as 'official' or even whether it had received the Leader's detailed scrutiny. It was not well designed to captivate his attention.

Rarely in the field of political pamphleteering can a document so radical in effect have been written with such flatness of language or blandness of tone. This was not wholly unintentional. We were out-Peeling Peel in giving the Party a painless

[1] Lord Poole.

but permanent face-lift: the more unflamboyant the changes, the less likely were the features to sag again. Our first purpose was to counter the charge and the fear that we were the party of industrial go-as-you-please and devil-take-the-hindmost, that full employment and the Welfare State were not safe in our hands. We therefore took our cue less from our historic philosophy, though that would indeed have been relevant, than from the existing complexity of modern industry and Britain's position as a debtor country which made reversion to *laissez-faire* impossible. 'In economic matters the government has very important functions', we insisted in the accents of Keynesianism. 'Foremost among these are its general powers to collect and distribute information to an extent beyond that of any private undertaking, its duties to take decisions on the scale of national expenditure and taxation, its power to control monetary policy and to guide overseas trade. It has responsibilities for stimulating industrial efficiency, in particular by assisting research and making the results more readily available to small firms. But perhaps its greatest duty is to ensure that such main priorities as the maintenance of employment and our well-developed social services are fulfilled before subsidiary objectives are sought and that the tasks set are not beyond the capacity of the resources available.' The Charter was, therefore, first and foremost an assurance that, in the interests of efficiency, full employment and social security, modern Conservatism would maintain strong central guidance over the operation of the economy.

Our second purpose was to present a recognizable alternative to the reigning orthodoxies of Socialism—not to put the clock back, but to reclaim a prominent role for individual initiative and private enterprise in the mixed and managed economy. It has been argued that the Charter was largely concerned with economic problems that were to be irrelevant in the 'fifties and that we did not therefore act upon it at all obviously when we got back into power. In so far as it was dealing with the current crisis and stress through which the country was passing there is, of course, some truth in the criticism that the emphases of the Charter were quickly dated. Yet, if it is read with this qualification in mind, what stands out very plainly is the extent to which we foresaw and foreshadowed the characteristically Conservative measures of the post-1951 period, with many of which I was myself to be associated as Chancellor—the improvement of incentives through reduced taxation, the encouragement of a high level of personal savings, the steady and orderly reduction of physical controls, the overhauling of the top-heavy administrative machine and the shrinking of the Civil Service, the reopening of commodity markets, the sharpening of competition by bringing what we called 'the floodlight of publicity' to bear upon restrictive practices, and the empirical approach to denationalization. All these are to be found in the Charter; and, if they were not the ingredients which gave it its most distinctive flavour, this was because an assertion of freedom may be taken for granted in the Conservative faith, whereas our imperative need was to establish what was then very far from being taken for granted: the Conservative intention to reconcile individual effort with a proper measure of central planning and direction and, no less important, to 'point to a way of life designed to free private endeavour from the taint of selfishness or self-interest'.

This brings me to our third purpose which was, quite simply, to make a new approach to the adjustment of human relations within industry. We offered to the worker a charter of rights giving assurance of steady employment, incentive to test his ability to the utmost, and status as an individual personality. Though we were persuaded that such a charter could not be made the subject of an Act of Parliament, since 'the conditions of industrial life are too varied to be brought within the cramping grip of legislation', there were certain aspects—contracts of service and equal pay for equal work, for example—where we considered that a statutory sanction either was or might eventually be required. But what chiefly concerned the Industrial Policy Committee was the need to strengthen by example and precept the channels of communication and co-operation between management and workers. Very often major labour difficulties had been avoided by the interest and enthusiasm of top company executives, who had broken away from the idea of industry being divided into two sides and helped to promote a new spirit of involvement and satisfaction through joint consultation, works committees, and co-partnership schemes. I was, and still am, an advocate of co-partnership, since I believe the sharing of profits to be the ideal expression of an identity of interest; but this has never been widely successful in industry because it was suspected by trade unions that political parties were trying to foist it on to them as a substitute for pay rises and other fringe benefits. All we felt able to say on the subject in our Workers' Charter was, 'We believe that such schemes in suitable forms according to circumstance are highly beneficial provided that the employees want them.' This was not a lot to show after much toil, but idealism has always to be tempered by hard fact.

On 11th May, 1947, I presided at a press conference in London at which the *Industrial Charter* was unveiled and interpreted. Every national newspaper (with the exception of the Labour *Herald*) together with most of the weeklies paid it the compliment of a leader. The reception ranged from enthusiastic eulogy to lukewarm condescension, but open hostility was predictably confined to the far right and the far left. The Beaverbrook press attacked the Charter as a compromise which the British people would never support ('If the Left fails, they will turn to the Right, but never half-Right'), while *Tribune* foretold that 'before the year is out the Butler Charter will split the Tory party as it has not been divided for half a century'. These predictions were not well based. Between May and October, when the party conference was due to be held at Brighton, the Charter was expounded and defended in the press and on the platform by Anthony Eden in his capacity as Deputy Leader, by all the members of the Industrial Policy Committee, and by scores of M.P.s and prospective candidates who were determined that the last excuse for labelling the Conservative party as reactionary should be destroyed. At Brighton it was destroyed. There, after a telling intervention by Reggie Maudling, I had the pleasure of summing up on an amended resolution 'welcoming the *Industrial Charter* as a clear statement of the general principles of Conservative economic policy' and of seeing this passed with only three dissenting votes in an assembly of nearly four thousand. My wife and I were summoned to Churchill's hotel suite. 'Well, old cock, you have definitely won through,' he said; 'I wish now to toast your victory.' Pol Roger was produced and I realized then what the psalmist meant when he sang, 'My cup runneth over.'

The way was now clear for us to press on with the restatement of Conservative policy on a broad front. Resolutions had been passed at the Brighton conference calling for 'the immediate production of a Charter for British farms', 'a policy for furthering the Empire's economic and political unity', and 'a policy for Wales to the fulfilment of which Welsh people might look forward with real hope'. Within the next two years these policy statements were duly produced as the *Agricultural Charter*, *Imperial Policy* and *Conservative Policy for Wales and Monmouthshire*, and in the same period *Scottish Control of Scottish Affairs* and a 'women's charter' entitled *A True Balance* were also published. The Research Department was again deeply involved. Michael Fraser dealt with agriculture, Enoch Powell wrote the Welsh document almost single-handed, and Iain Macleod acted as secretary to the committee of Scottish M.P.s and peers who were anxious to meet the challenge of the Covenant with practical proposals for devolution. None of these statements was attended by the political excitements of the *Industrial Charter* or can be said to have achieved a comparable impact. But they had a cumulative effect in robbing the Labour party of its favourite parrot-cry, namely that the Conservatives had no policy.

Unfortunately, the Central Office publicity machine was insufficiently active in helping to support the new image which the Charters were creating. The Chairman of the party, Lord Woolton, who had had the benefit of building on the work of his predecessor Ralph Assheton,[1] was one of the principal restorers of Conservatism during this period—financially, administratively and, perhaps above all, psychologically. He was at his best at party conferences where his very appearance, accompanied by his most comforting wife, had a calming effect on the lieges. But Woolton's activities stopped short before the reformulation of Conservative philosophy or policy. Our relationship, which was never personally close, was constitutionally peculiar, because after 1948 the Research Department was supposed to be under his general administrative control but I, as its Chairman, was responsible to the Leader of the party

[1] Lord Clitheroe.

alone. Against a background of some tension, I was prompted in March 1949 to write a constructive memorandum to Woolton:

> 'In the war years, we kept the illusion going that the Conservative party was alive by issuing documents from the Post-War Problems Committee, of which I was Chairman and David Maxwell Fyfe Vice-Chairman.
>
> 'This was succeeded by the Advisory Committee on Policy and Political Education, which reports to the National Union. We have built up a nation-wide system of education discussion groups, bookshops and members—all run by the C.P.C.
>
> 'We have published endless books and booklets, and with the aid of my colleagues and the reorganised Research Department have issued general reports, including the Industrial and Agricultural Charters. The Leader gave the strictest injunctions that no detailed policy was to be published, hence the general form and conception of the Charters. . . .
>
> 'I have never been satisfied by the progress made. . . . Nevertheless I have been agreeably surprised by the real success—however you look at it—of the Industrial Charter. This has placed the party on the fairway of modern economic and political thought. I regard the Agricultural Charter as having less psychological importance, though it has "pegged" the agricultural situation, and prevented it slipping away to Tom Williams [Labour Minister of Agriculture].
>
> 'Despite a limited satisfaction, I must register our intense disappointment that the Charters have been followed up by inadequate publicizing and propaganda. No concerted attempt has been made by the party to follow them up. As a result it has become fashionable and indeed an amiable pastime to smile at "Charters".
>
> 'We now find, as a result of losing a by-election [Hammersmith South], that Policy in clear and simple terms is imperative. Indeed, Private Members have volunteered the view that we should consider our attitude towards unemployment and the housing question.

'What remains to be effected?

(a) a proper link up with the Private Members so that they can both "give" and "know" more.

(b) a gearing up of our propaganda and its close backing of our policy activities.

'(a) can, I think, be achieved quite easily by making the Advisory Committee on Policy and Political Education more representative—or rather causing those who at present represent interests, such as the Private Members, women and Young Conservatives to attend. It would also help if the Executive of the 1922 Committee were acquainted with the present policy-making "set-up".

'(b) Unless this, i.e. linking up of propaganda, is effected, I do not think justice can be done or seem to be done to our policy or our policy making. . . .'

These suggestions did not fall on stony ground. Within a matter of months the Maxwell Fyfe Report on the Party Organization recommended that the Advisory Committee on Policy and Political Education should be reconstituted. The new Advisory Committee on Policy ceased to be responsible for the work of the C.P.C., a loss which I personally regretted, but it became more broadly representative of the party, a course which, contrary to subsequent academic assumptions and speculations, it will be seen that I was myself strongly advocating. In addition, and more important, the publicity machine at Central Office greatly improved in the last two years of opposition and helped to make a success of the policy statements produced in advance of the 1950 and 1951 elections. *The Right Road for Britain*, approved by the London party conference in 1949, covered the whole field of policy at home and abroad. It was the most comprehensive of the Charters, whose main proposals it incorporated, and the first to be proof-corrected by the Churchill pen and dignified by a Churchillian foreword. Churchill himself launched the publication in a powerful speech to a meeting of many thousands of people at Wolverhampton, and I was very moved by the magnanimity of his opening words in which he said, 'Great pains and care have been bestowed on this work by many of my colleagues in the Opposition, and by none more than Mr. Butler, who has rendered distinguished service, not only to his party, but to his country.'

The Manifesto for the 1950 election—which was so self-evidently based on *The Right Road for Britain* that we called it *This is the Road*—was the subject of several sessions with Churchill. I recall arriving at Chartwell with the latest draft one mid-afternoon to find him, needless to say, asleep. But we started work full strong at the dinner table, and at 4 a.m. he raised his eyes from the task and said, 'It must be nearly 11, we must think of moving.' He brought the whole weight of his mind to bear upon the paragraphs prepared, shredding to bits every discrepancy, ellipsis or muddled metaphor. For instance, paragraph 40 of our original draft ran:

'We shall drastically reorganize the structure of the Coal Industry and the Railways as public undertakings. By decentralizing their activities we shall give greater responsibility to the men on the spot and create again local loyalties and enthusiasm.'

'You cannot use the same argument for coal and for railways,' he pointed out. 'A railway is in perpetual motion. By what contortion of the inner eye can those running it be visualized as "on the spot"?' But his reminiscences were as entertaining as his corrections of style. He warned me never in policy statements to postulate premises into single lines or to generalize on vital issues; reminding me how in 1905 Lord Spencer had tacked on to a disparate thought 'Nor must we forget Ireland', thus bringing down devastating and irremediable ruin on his head. When we got on to the social services, he said Edward Grey had told him that Gladstone believed there were no politics in social reform because 'the old Liberalism which had torn the shackles from the slaves was petering out'. I could not forbear from inquiring whether it was Gladstone, Grey or Churchill who had forgotten that Wilberforce was a Tory. 'A Liberal Tory,' he replied, 'like me.'

A real difficulty about finishing the Manifesto arose from the Liberal Tory's determination to write the English of it himself. This issue was actually resolved at a luncheon party a week later attended by Anthony Eden and Brendan Bracken. I said that if Winston wrote part and I wrote part of the contrast would be so awful that the public would make fun of the effort. He said that he supposed I wished to replace him as Leader of the party. There was no need to answer this, fortunately, since he had to go out to a telephone call. When he eventually returned he was singing quite a different tune and said that I was to produce a completely revised version 'without style and without paragraphs' by lunch-time next day. This was achieved thanks to the infinite flexibility and resourcefulness of the Research Department. Thus we produced our policy of enterprise without selfishness. The party had come a long way since 1945.

CHAPTER EIGHT

'UNE IDÉE EN MARCHE'

THE PHYSICAL decomposition of the Labour government preceded its political extinction by many months. In the general election of February 1950 its parliamentary majority was reduced to only eight, and by the spring of the following year the Treasury bench had been ravaged by sickness and rent by schism. Bevin, alas, was dead and Cripps dying; Attlee was in hospital, Morrison in *terra incognita*, Bevan in the cave of Adullam, and Wilson in there with him. The rising star of the movement was now Hugh Gaitskell, who could bring to the Exchequer the best professional qualifications of any Chancellor in this century. But 1950–1 was an unlucky fiscal year to reach this high office—a year when the outbreak of war in Korea imposed a wholly new set of strains on the economy, including massive expenditures on rearmament, very sharply rising prices and a drastic reversal of the favourable trend in the terms of trade. Though the government clung tenaciously to power, its sorrows came 'not single spies, but in battalions', and clearly its days were numbered.

In these circumstances, I felt it prudent once again to restate Conservative party policy; but quite unnecessary to 'rethink' it, and most unwise to add to it any commitment that might complicate the economic difficulties we should have to overcome. *Britain Strong and Free*, drafted in the Research Department under the detailed direction of Selwyn Lloyd whom I had recruited as my principal lieutenant, differed in manner from the Charters that preceded it. It was much less urbane and much better written. But in matter it contained only two additional items of importance: a promise to build 300,000 houses a year and a proposal to introduce an Excess Profits Levy during the period of rearmament. I had serious doubts about the wisdom of both additions. The first had its origin in a famous wave of hysteria which swept the party conference at Blackpool in the autumn of 1950. Lord Woolton, who was sitting beside me as the figure began to be picked up by representatives with the mounting excitement one customarily associates with an auction, whispered, 'Could we build 300,000?' I replied, 'The question is should we? And the answer is: it will make it that much more difficult to restore the economy. But if you want to know if it's technically feasible, ask David Clarke.' So the Director of the Research Department was consulted behind the scenes and opined (correctly) that the thing could be done, and Lord Woolton stepped forward to the front of the platform to declare in beaming surrender, 'This is magnificent.' And so, in a sense, it was. Both the promise and the achievement were magnificent politically; economically, however, they placed a severe inflationary strain upon our resources which contributed to the difficulties of 1954–5.

The Excess Profits Levy, by contrast, was invented by Churchill himself. Somewhere at the back of his mind was the memory that when rearmament had got going in the 1930s special measures had been proposed to offset any profiteering. What he did not remember was that this so-called 'national defence contribution' had been greeted with a Stock Exchange slump, a torrent of protest in the Commons, and devastating criticism by Keynes who dubbed it 'a tax on enterprise, growth and youth'. And even had he remembered, no one could quarrel with the argument that there was now a United States prototype, and no one was disposed to question his motive of showing that Conservatism favoured profits fairly earned, but set its face against profits fortuitously come by. This argument particularly appealed to Anthony Eden. But it was very much an eleventh-hour argument. Attlee had announced the forthcoming general election on 19th September, 1951. Britain Strong and Free was published on 3rd October. In the intervening fortnight the presses had to be stopped twice: on the first occasion, to insert into a document originally intended for the party conference some suitable references to the election campaign; on the second occasion, to squeeze in ten explanatory lines about an Excess Profits Levy. 'In framing the details of our plan', said the concluding sentence, which I dictated over the telephone to the Research Department, 'we shall be guided by past experience and by study of the American system.' I hoped that this would reduce our intellectual vulnerability during the election, and afterwards give some room for manœuvre to Oliver Lyttelton, the obvious candidate for the Chancellorship in a Conservative Government.

It was many years later that I learned from the *Chandos Memoirs* precisely how Oliver eventually accepted the Colonial Office. I was interviewed, as he was, in the Prime Minister's bedroom at Hyde Park Gate where Churchill lay watching his Gallup Poll lead disappear in the booths, leaving the Conservatives with a slim majority of 16. On the coverlet was a sheet of writing paper with a short list of names and offices set out in very large type. He handed it to me gravely and silently. Chancellor of the Exchequer: R. A. Butler. 'I have thought much about this offer,' he said, 'and in the end Anthony and I agreed that you would be best at handling the Commons. In this crisis of our island life, when the cottage homes could so easily be engulfed in penury and want, we must not allow class or party feeling to be needlessly inflamed. For that reason also, you will have to show our goodwill by putting the Excess Profits Levy into force. It is no great matter that you are not an economist. I wasn't either. And in any case I am going to appoint the best economist since Jesus Christ to help you.' I asked who this might be, and he replied 'Arthur Salter.' Arthur, a nice man with a record of progressive thought but very many years my senior, was accordingly provided with a high-ranking ministerial title and for thirteen months wrote me numberless minutes in green ink, with which I did not always agree. It would have been good had I succeeded in taking the reliable Selwyn Lloyd with me to the Treasury. But when I telephoned him within minutes of being appointed Chancellor and invited him to join me as Financial Secretary, he explained that Anthony Eden had just asked him to be Minister of State at the Foreign Office.

I started my Treasury life by responding to an invitation to meet Edward Bridges and William Armstrong at the Athenaeum Club. The first was head of the Treasury and, in those days, of the Civil Service; the second, destined to head the Civil Service himself in later years, was to be my Private Secretary. We sat at a table in the window and ate what remained of the Club food after the bishops had had their run; for we were somewhat late, and the bishops attack the sideboards early. Both my singularly able advisers stressed the critical state of the economy and promised me a memorandum within a few days. Their story was of blood draining from the system and a collapse greater than had been foretold in 1931. I returned home in sombre anticipation of what was to be dished up to me, but already comforted by the personalities with whom I was to work. Besides them I had the two stalwarts of Treasury Chambers, Bernard Gilbert and Herbert Brittain; on the overseas side, Leslie Rowan and Dennis Rickett. I had also Edmund Compton, the first Ombudsman; and many others of rare talent in the Inland Revenue and Customs. Robert Hall, the chief economic adviser, was our strong, silent man who came to have more and more influence. But I depended on Edwin Plowden, as head of the economic planning staff, to interpret and give practical edge to the advice generated by the less voluble and extrovert Hall, to act as *vulgarisateur* or publicist for his ideas. Plowden was to become my faithful watchdog-in-chief, and his departure for industry in 1953 undoubtedly weakened my position and that of the British economy. But meanwhile all these Treasury knights and knights-to-be stood in purposive array on my chess-board ready to move against our economic problems—as only such pieces are permitted to move—in more than one direction simultaneously.

The first move was to cut imports, and cut them good and hard. On current trends and policies our foreign payments deficit was running at between £500 million and £600 million a year. So in November 1951 I knocked £350 million off external expenditure and followed this up with £150 million more in January and another £100 million in March. Our balance of payments position justified these exceptional actions, but we were acutely aware that import cuts limited expansion, carried the danger of reprisals, and could not for both these reasons be regarded as more than temporary. One evening in the autumn of 1952 Churchill sent for me and said, 'I am very worried about my poor friend Daladier losing his seat in the French Chamber.

You really must attend to the matter.' I asked what this could possibly have to do with me, and he explained, 'His district exports glacé cherries, which you have brutally stopped coming into this country.' It was not entirely in the light of this touching story that I repented, but by slow degrees the restrictions were relaxed and we began to work actively to bring about a freer system of trade and payments, and thus give to our exporters wider opportunities. I was the last to use such import controls and must testify to their efficiency.

The second move was to return to the pre-war use of a flexible monetary policy in order to regulate demand and restrain inflation. Cheap money, so long the ark of the covenant, had proved to be the very opposite of what the post-war situation demanded. In November I made a token increase in Bank rate from 2 to $2\frac{1}{2}$ per cent, and in March braved the opprobrium of my political opponents by going to 4 per cent. This sharp rise was announced in the Budget—an unusual course which left the country, and the foreigner, in no doubt that I was prepared to make a thoroughgoing use of monetary as well as fiscal policy in controlling the economy. But the Budget may well have helped to stem the outward flow of short-term capital as much by what it did not do as by what it did. The Commonwealth Finance Ministers' conference which had met in London in January under my chairmanship had declared the ultimate goal of the sterling area to be the convertibility of the pound. Since then rumours had been rife that I wished at the time of the Budget to make the pound convertible to non-residents at a floating rate of exchange. These rumours were well founded. But they inevitably weakened the reserves, and when the Budget was seen to contain no proposals to this end the reserves were correspondingly strengthened.

That was the short-term result. In the long-term, however, I believe that the decision not to free the pound was a fundamental mistake. The absence of a floating exchange rate robbed successive Chancellors of an external regulator for the balance of payments corresponding to the internal regulator provided principally by Bank rate. If such a regulator had existed, and a floating rate been accepted, Conservatives would have been saved some of the uncertainties and indignities of 'stop-go' economics and Socialists the traumatic experience of a second formal devaluation. This is not being clever after the event. I was well advised at the time—by the Governor of the Bank of England, by most of our Treasury team, and by financially experienced back-benchers in my party. But among ministerial colleagues I could count Oliver Lyttelton alone as a consistent supporter. Lord Birkenhead, in *The Prof in Two Worlds*, made much of Lord Cherwell's activities in countering these 'Robot' proposals, to give them their incongruous code name, and Lord Salter, in *Slave of the Lamp*, claimed his own meed of credit. But neither the Prof's private detective agency in economics, fascinating as it was to the Prime Minister, nor Salter's stream of sea-green memoranda would have sufficed to carry the day if the senior members of the government had been of a different turn of mind.

In February 1952 I received a letter from Lord Swinton in which he described Robot as a dangerous gamble. Of all the men who have not been Prime Minister in England I always regarded Philip Swinton as having the endowments most suitable to an occupant of No. 10—prodigious memory, driving energy, whimsical resource, a certain asperity attractive to those who know how to answer back, and very great experience. He was a Minister at the Board of Trade at an early age under Lloyd George and in middle life was responsible for the Spitfires which won us the Battle of Britain. When I was appointed Chancellor I asked Churchill to let him help me with the economy on the materials side, and he later became Chancellor of the Duchy. Now he advised me that the currency gap could not be bridged nor the sterling area saved 'unless and until all the countries of the Commonwealth have put in force cuts like our own, which will be and will be seen to be sufficient to restore collectively and individually the balance of payments. That and only that will give the world confidence in sterling. If that is not done your plan will not succeed. If it is done then the world may have enough confidence to make it work. Moreover if the whole Commonwealth has clearly put its house in order that makes us an insurable proposition, and that is the best way to bring in the U.S. to underwrite the policy which to my mind is the other factor indispensable to the success of the plan.' I naturally paid attention to what Philip said, and I quote him for two reasons: first to show that he did think the plan might ultimately work in conjunction with the United States; but second, to show that opposition to the plan was not confined to peripheral kibitzers —it was widely sustained. Indeed I had a very tough time with my colleagues. The Prime Minister was perplexed by the controversy, felt in his bones that it was right to free the pound, seemed impressed by the support I had as Chancellor from Oliver Lyttelton, but was persuaded not to make a dash for freedom by the marshalled arguments of Lord Cherwell and the cautious conservatism of the elder statesmen. A note from Oliver Lyttelton, passed to me across the table, summed up the situation as it appeared in February, as again when I raised the matter in June: 'This goes ill. The water looks cold to some of them. They prefer a genteel bankruptcy, *force majeure* being the plea. Yours sincerely, Micawber.'

If the pound had been set free in 1952 the word 'Butskellism' might never have been invented. It was, of course, a term compounded by *The Economist* out of Gaitskell's name and mine, and Gaitskell was known to be, indeed expressed himself as being, violently opposed to the 'disastrous turn in our policy' which the Cabinet had resisted and rejected. Despite our friendship, which became warm, we never discussed the 'doctrine' that united our names and each of us would, I think, have repudiated its underlying assumption that, though sitting on opposite sides of the House, we were really very much of a muchness. I admired him as a man of great humanity and sticking power, and was to regard his untimely death in 1963 as a real loss to the Labour party, to the country and to the tone of public life. But I shared neither his convictions, which were unquenchably Socialist, nor his temperament, which allowed emotion to run away with him rather too often, nor his training which was that of an academic economist. Both of us, it is true, spoke the language of Keynesianism. But we spoke it with different accents and with a differing emphasis. Norman Macrae of *The Economist* paid me a compliment in an article he wrote describing my work at the Treasury as representing '*la puissance d'une idée en marche*'. This *idée* could be summed up in a single word: expansion—an expansion I believed capable of achievement only if the fresh winds of freedom and opportunity were allowed to blow vigorously through the economy.

I gave official expression to this theme at the end of my first Budget speech which lasted for nearly two hours and was designed, like a symphony by Mahler, in sharply contrasting movements. The opening movement (*Feierlich und gemessen*) reviewed the deterioration in our trade reserves, which had fallen by over 40 per cent in the second half of 1951 but much less rapidly in the early months of 1952. If we had not checked the drain, I said without exaggeration, 'We here in this island would before the end of the year have found ourselves unable to secure either our daily bread or the raw materials upon which our employment and production depend. There would have been expanding areas of real want and of growing unemployment.' The second movement (*Stürmisch Bewegt*) was greeted by the Opposition with scorn and indignation, since it contained all the disagreeable parts of the Budget. These included the rise in Bank rate and further import restrictions, to which I have already referred, a number of increases in indirect taxes, among them the duty on petrol, and a £160 million cut in the food subsidies. This last announcement provoked terrible cries of 'class war' and 'Woolton'. Woolton was sitting in the Peers' gallery and while in the concentration of my speech I could not see very much, I did notice the Duke of Edinburgh leaning over to ask him what was the matter. The matter was that Woolton had given an imprudent pledge that we would not reduce the food subsidies. I was later informed that he had turned a bright red, but happily he did not find it necessary to resign in response to Attlee's intervention when I sat down. This was due to the content of my succeeding and final movement (*Heiter, bedächtig*) in which I proceeded to hand back the savings on the completely indiscriminate food subsidies, and more besides, to the neediest members of the community—the pensioners, the mothers of large families, and the smaller wage earners. Two million were relieved of paying income tax altogether. 'Restriction and austerity are not enough', I concluded. 'We want a system which offers us both more realism and more hope. These are the underlying purposes of the measures I have proposed—the deeper explanation of their character. We must now set forth braced and resolute to show the world that we shall regain our solvency and with it our national greatness.'

The Times was kind enough to insert at the end of its report, 'prolonged ministerial cheers, many members rising in their places to wave their order papers'. Winston was close to tears and said to me in a muffled voice, 'That is the Tory Democracy of my father.' Socialist criticism of the Budget followed conventional lines. But in the domestic press, and more important in the overseas markets, its reception was good. The drain on the reserves ceased during the spring. Throughout the summer they held steady. In the last quarter of 1952 they rose significantly; and by the end of the year we were able to pay interest and repay capital due to our Canadian and American creditors without default or demur. The balance of payments was in surplus in 1952 by an estimated £291 million, since revised to £259 million—a turn-round from the previous year substantially greater than the £600 million target referred to in the Budget speech. 'It would have been less than human', says one high-minded assessment of British fiscal and monetary policy during the post-war period, 'if the government had not claimed credit for this transformation.' It would also have been less than accurate.

However, I did not hide then and I do not deny now that there were events outside Britain which aided and supported the benign influence of government policy. Our economy, I pointed out in April 1953, is like our climate—'always exposed to changes in the world economic weather, which are, to a large extent, outside our control'. I added that at that point of time the international barometer still stood at 'changeable' but that we might hope to see it climb to 'fair'. Such homely metaphors, which I used very freely as Chancellor, were welcomed by the press (particularly the cartoonists) and greeted with indulgent amusement by my predecessor. Two and a half years later, when I ran into a patch of bad weather, he cheerfully pelted me with them. 'We used to be travelling in a ship through a storm', recalled Gaitskell. 'We are accustomed to climbing mountains with Mr. Butler. Sometimes we are undergoing operations in hospital. Sometimes we are convalescing . . . [but] when we tell people that "the roses have to be pruned", they do not think of themselves as the rose.' This was good political knock-about, and not hard to reply to in kind since my critic could himself be represented in metaphor as a political mouse who, confronted with a gigantic deterioration in the balance of payments, responded by cutting a sliver off the cheese ration. In speeches delivered amid the dust of parliamentary battle party politicians are characteristically and inevitably unfair to one another. But

THE BOYHOOD OF BUTLER

it is neither necessary nor seemly for them to import such slants into memoirs composed in the relative tranquillity of retirement. Gaitskell was Chancellor for only a brief period, during which the terms of trade swung violently against us: I was Chancellor for more than four years (still a record post-war) during most of which the management of the economy, though a perpetual headache, was helped by external circumstances. I hope not to be guilty of undue partisanship or self-righteousness if I claim that it was helped also by the careful maintenance of foreign confidence in our efforts and, just as important, by a consistent emphasis on giving *incentives* to work, earn and save—even in a year like 1952, when no net reliefs could be offered. Unless confidence and incentive are adopted as keynotes of policy, I would wager the whole of the gold and convertible currency reserves that no future Chancellor, whatever his political complexion, will succeed in the long run.

However, it was not until 1953 that I was able to dispense liberally what a famous predecessor would have called 'rare and refreshing fruit'. Meantime, as Conservative Central Office reports relate, the government was unpopular in the country even among its own supporters. A friendly letter from Walter Monckton, the Minister of Labour, catches a troubled, muddled mood of the moment which was soon to evaporate. 'I can't go away for this Whitsun weekend', he wrote on 30th May, 1952, 'without sending a word of affectionate respect for the manner in which you have borne and are bearing yourself. I should like to see the government rid itself of controversial regulation or other matters and call all men of goodwill of all parties to the economic rescue. But that is for more experienced minds than mine to determine. In any case we shall all loyally follow you.' Monckton was a diplomat by nature, a friend of princes, admired by women, of acute intelligence and perception, fearless in defence of his friends, high or low. But he did not like taking executive decisions; his strength lay in an ability to inject his own sweetness and light into the atmosphere. This strength was precisely what was wanted by Churchill who, with unhappy memories of the General Strike to live down, was determined to pursue a policy of industrial appeasement, even at the cost of highly inflationary wage settlements. I myself am on record as saying that a voluntary system of wage restraint was best. But I did suffer. One morning in the following year the Prime Minister sent for me and said, 'Walter and I settled the rail strike in the early hours of this morning on their terms. We did not think it necessary to keep you up.' However, despite this gaping hole in our armour, the economy improved and with it both my own standing in the government and my personal relationship with its head. In 1952 the Leader of the House, Harry Crookshank, was appointed to preside over the Cabinet in the simultaneous absence of Churchill and Eden. A year later, when both were ill, it was taken for granted that I should act as head of the government.

Winston always used to tell me 'There are no friends at the top.' In politics this observation has much truth, but it is not the whole truth. He himself had been fascinated by the rapier of F. E. Smith and the dynamism of Max Beaverbrook; Brendan Bracken and the Prof remained his constant cronies; 'Pug' Ismay he treated perhaps less as a friend than as a nanny, licensed to scold with impunity. For most members of his Cabinet he evinced an old-world gentlemanly respect. 'I like the spirit in which you conduct our affairs', he said to me after the 1953 Budget, and I record with strong emotion that however exasperated one became at times, a word of commendation from him always set one up cheerfully. Churchill's affectionate admiration for Anthony Eden was beyond doubt, but equally so was the disservice he did his successor in making him wait too long. This did not suit Anthony any more than it had suited Edward VII. The latter took it out in life and licence, the former in a controlled impatience. There is no doubt which of these is better for the nerves. Anthony and I had been on good terms since the days when I served him at the Foreign Office. Winston's niece, Clarissa, had proved a marvellous wife for him and helped to make him more approachable; so when in March 1953 we set off for New York in the *Queen Elizabeth*, wives and all, I had a hope that we might get much closer together. This did not happen, since each of us was preoccupied with the mission ahead, and whilst I did not fully realize what he hoped to get out of the new President and Secretary of State, he scarcely began to understand my economic brief.

To be perfectly fair, my economic brief was pretty unintelligible. I spent hours in my cabin with a proverbial wet towel round my head trying to put in plain language the 'collective approach to convertibility' which was its theme. I had expressed all this simply enough in England by coining the expression 'Trade not Aid', and the idea had caught on with the headline writers of the *Herald Tribune* (BOLD RAB BUTLER: BRITAIN'S TRADE NOT AID MAN: EXCHEQUER HEAD BRINGS HIS UNORTHODOX FRANK-NESS TO TALK TO US), though perhaps less so with the commentators of the *Christian Science Monitor* ('It is customary when a British delegation approaches Washington for wits to suggest that extra locks should be put upon the vaults at Fort Knox').

At the National Press Club I outlined some of our hopes. First, I pointed out that the Commonwealth included at that time nine sovereign states and fifty colonies embracing a total of 600 million people. We were inviting a larger investment of U.S. dollars in this area. Secondly, we looked for a cut in American

FEMININE SUSPICION

tariffs, an end to discrimination against foreign shipping, a modification of the controversial 'Buy American' laws, and a cessation of elaborate conditions on export credits. In a word, I asked the Americans to live up to the slogan which they had been dinning into me ever since I arrived at the Treasury, namely 'non-discrimination'. But I certainly got no change out of them. At a dinner at the White House I sat on President Eisenhower's left, Anthony being on his right, but was unable to elicit a single constructive comment. When I mentioned our desire to bring the economic links between our countries closer he gazed at me in silence. Many a Roman Emperor owed his elevation to success in the field, and Pug Ismay had told me that Ike was the great diplomat of the Allied Forces. But to me he remained an enigma. He appointed 'Lew' Douglas, whom I knew well as Ambassador to London, to 'grill' us and this process continued in committee rooms for a few fruitless days. I also talked with George Humphrey, the Secretary to the Treasury, with whom I made a warm and lasting friendship. But it was clear that the American team had been instructed to pour cold water on the collective approach to convertibility, to tell us to put our own house in order, and to raise as few hopes as possible of Congressional support for better creditor policies. Back in the House of Commons, Anthony Eden's report on his diplomatic mission had to be couched in such resounding platitudes as to call forth Opposition sallies of 'Have the marines heard this?' But my report was even less enlightening.

Compensation came in the following month when, against the background of the great improvement in Britain's affairs, I introduced the first Budget since the war to contain neither proposals for new taxes nor increases in existing ones. Because, as Lord Morley once observed, 'there is something repulsive to human nature in the simple reproduction of defunct Budgets', and because I was responsible in all for five of them, I shall resist the urge to list the multiplicity of tax reliefs I made in 1953 with the aim of encouraging investment, enterprise, effort—and cricket. They were, of course, extremely popular with everyone except the Opposition; and Churchill's description to a Glasgow audience of just how the Opposition reacted was vintage:

'From where I sat I had a fine view of the faces of our Socialist opponents, and could watch their expressions as the story unfolded. It was quite painful to see their looks of gloom and sorrow when any fact was stated which was favourable to our country and its prospects. They frowned and scowled and hung their heads until I thought that some of them were going to break into tears.

'However, we are far from being out of the wood yet, and when warnings were given by the Chancellor of the disappointments that had occurred or the dangers that lie ahead, it was wonderful to see how quickly they cheered up. Their eyes twinkled, their faces were covered with grins, not only of mirth, but of mockery . . .

'Then Mr. Butler restored the initial allowance on new equipment for our factories. . . . They did not seem to like it at all, especially as they had to support it. But worse was to come—the purchase tax was cut by a quarter.

'Then there was that awful thing about making it easier for families to keep their aged and dependent relatives. This really seems to show preference for quite old-fashioned family ties—instead of all the dreams of the Utopian State in which our Socialist friends indulge, where everyone queues up equally and is looked after more or less by the officials.

'No wonder they were upset. But the culminating point, the climax, the top notch, was hit when Mr. Butler perpetrated his most insulting and malevolent deed. He took 6d. off the income tax.

"I never take pleasure in human woe, and yet I must confess I wish you had been there with me to see the look of absolute misery and anger which swept across the crowded faces opposite.

'Sixpence off the income tax! Class favour to over 30 million people. What shocking Tory reaction! Only 9s. in the £ left for the income tax collector.

'How could anyone tell that in future years more atrocities like this might not be committed? And what about the two million people at the bottom of the income tax scale who were last year actually freed by Mr. Butler from income tax altogether?

'They were let off altogether last year, so there is no benefit at all for them this year. They just have to go on being let off altogether. What a shame!'

I had personal sorrows at this time. My mother, to whose influence I paid some tribute in the early pages of this book, was lying at the very end of her life in a house at Hunstanton. She had reached that stage which is so particularly sad for the living, where she could barely recognize me when I stole time from the Exchequer to visit her. There is a twilight between life and death when perception is dimmed and the strange contrast in terms arises that, though a twilight should blur vision and soften sorrow, this penultimate moment before passing sometimes leads to hardness of expression and apparent forgetfulness of love. To the healthy this is an understandable phenomenon but none the less hard to bear. My mother lay with a Bible beside her as a token of simple and absolute faith in after life. My father had died in the November before. With him the transition had been rapid and overnight and due to a heart attack. They had led a wonderful life together in India, in the Isle of Man and in Cambridge. They formed a happy marriage of dissimilars; my father busy, intense, conscientious and small, my mother tall, graceful and ever socially and sweetly minded. My mother wondered whether she would like the small island life of Man and made as much of a success of being Governor's Lady as she did later of being Master's wife at Pembroke. She was not enthusiastic about sherry parties for young men, but when they left they all thought she was. Meanwhile my father industriously took names and docketed them so that there was no overlap of invitations. My father's death had been a sudden shock; my mother's was a long-drawn-out pain.

I was with her when I was summoned to Chartwell because of Winston's stroke. I came by train from Hunstanton on a blazingly hot day and with a blinding headache I could not get rid of. I was given a letter from Jock Colville, dated 25th June, which ran:

'I write, very sorrowfully, to let you know quite privately that the P.M. is seriously ill and that unless some miracle occurs in the next 24 hours there can be no question of his going to Bermuda and little, I think, of his remaining in office.

'You must have noticed what befell him after the De Gasperi dinner on Tuesday. It was a sudden arterial spasm, or perhaps a clot in an artery, and he has been left with great difficulty of articulation although his brain is still absolutely clear. His left side is partly paralysed and he has lost the use of his left arm. He himself has little hope of recovery.

'His courage and philosophic resignation are beyond praise and admiration and Lady Churchill, too, is heroic.

'I have not as yet told anybody but a few of his intimate friends and among his colleagues yourself, Lord Salisbury and the Prof—though I am keeping Tommy Lascelles fully informed. Therefore although the P.M. certainly wants you to know the position, I hope you will keep the whole matter strictly private for the time being. I will let you know how things progress.'

The family and Christopher Soames were there in tears; but quite soon the mighty constitution prevailed, and I remember sitting at dinner whilst Winston with his good arm carried to his lips a beaker of brandy. However it was clear that the situation was critical and there was for some time doubt whether he would be able to return and carry on as P.M. Anthony Eden was away recuperating from serious illness, and though it was officially conveyed to me that he was the rightful deputy, I was by a tacit understanding expected to perform as the head of the government. 'Bobbety' Salisbury was asked down and invited to take charge of the Foreign Office, and we returned to London together in an ancient chauffeur-driven government car.

James Stuart, anxious that I should not join the list of invalids, wrote me a benevolent and sensible letter from the Scottish Office:

'You are now
(1) acting P.M.
(2) acting Foreign Secretary (in the Commons)
(3) Chancellor—controlling the entire financial and economic structure of this country—etc—and so on.

'But there must be a limit to the amount of work which any human frame (and brain) can tolerate for long.

'You seem well—and I hope you are—but do please remember that you mustn't break the main spring. It takes ages to mend.

'I don't like to remind you of the tragedy of Stafford Cripps, but I feel it my duty to do so.

'So good luck to you—and be careful. I am as always your well-wisher and I mean it.'

At the end of September I heard from Anthony who was in Athens at the conclusion of a yachting trip round the Greek islands. He thanked me for my help during this taxing time and added, 'I really feel well now and hope to be a passenger in the boat no longer.' By the same post I had a letter from my niece, Jane Portal, who was at Cap d'Ail with Winston as his secretary. She said, 'The P.M. has been in the depths of depression. He broods continually whether to give up or not. He was exhausted by Balmoral and the Cabinets and the journey. I sometimes feel he would be better engaged on his History of the English-Speaking Peoples which is already very remarkable. He greatly likes your messages telling him all the news and you are in high favour. He is preparing a speech for the Margate conference but wonders how long he can be on his pins to deliver it. He has painted one picture in tempera from his bedroom window.'

I went on blithely with my daily companion the economy. I was preparing for the Commonwealth Ministers' meeting at Sydney at the turn of the year. Winston got over the Conservative conference at Margate magnificently. After his speech he sent for me in the Green Room of the Hall and ordered me away for a week's change and holiday. He said, 'You have been doing too much and I am now finding my strength again.' Very few men can have got over such a paralysis in so lion-hearted a manner. I went down to Chartwell while he was still convalescing and his nurse wheeled him to look at his beloved goldfish pond. On one side of it are some stepping-stones leading to the other and, without saying anything, he started to try to negotiate these. I plunged into the water on one side and held him up while the nurse came along behind. We got him over safely and then wheeled him back to the summer-house where we sat, myself drenched, discussing English history as depicted in the Weald of Kent laid out before us. Later that same evening I returned to Treasury Chambers and Edward Bridges came in with the latest reserves figures which he waved excitedly, saying 'Look what you have done!' I felt and said quite emphatically that it was not to my personal credit, but to that of the team, who despite their Civil Service caution had supported me so wholeheartedly in the policy of incentive. However, before the end of 1953 I received the only honour I can remember from the

Daily Mirror in being chosen as the Politician of the Year. I was pleased that Cassandra would appear to have made the choice since I had a sneaking regard for this voluble Irishman. He wrote: 'The dollar gap—that freely used spectre but nevertheless ominous reality—has been to a solid extent driven a long way towards dispersal. The man has in fact stopped the rot.' Also in December, Winston told me of a less ephemeral honour, the C.H., which on his recommendation would be conferred on me in the New Year. I set out for Australia after Christmas comforted by this, but otherwise apprehensive; for my wife's health prevented her from coming with me—the first warning of the affliction which carried her away a year later. I was in Karachi on New Year's Day, but could see no mention of my name in the English papers. Ten days later I received a cable that the announcement was being made to coincide with the meeting of the Finance Ministers. This seemed a nice touch, and it was only when I got home that I discovered it was due to the simple forgetfulness of a secretary who had not forwarded the recommendation.

The 1954 Budget was described as a carry-on Budget, a standstill Budget and a dull Budget, according to who was doing the describing. It was certainly a cautious Budget. I judged that to have given widespread reliefs would only have brought inflation. But in the march to economic freedom which had been proceeding steadily since the return of the Conservative government 1954 deserved none of these adjectives. It was the year when, for the British trader and the British consumer, the war finally ended. In 1951 the law courts were crowded with about 1,700 cases each month for offences against controls. By 1954 these were down to about 80 a month. Nearly all State trade had been given back to private enterprise. Competition had been restored in the steel and road haulage industries. Most price controls were abolished. Thousands of controls on the allocation of materials and the manufacture and sale of goods were removed. Import controls had been greatly relaxed. The great commodity markets had been reopened. Above all, food rationing and other restrictions on consumption had been brought to an end. I remember taking home with me to Stanstead the plans for the derationing of meat, and being so excited that I drew the car up at a little village called Aythorpe Roding and worked away at the papers until I could administer my signature. The change in the moral climate which accompanied the return to freedom was perhaps best signalized by the virtual disappearance from our vocabulary of such expressions as 'spiv', 'snooper', 'black market' and 'under the counter'. I described the progress made in a speech at Gloucester on 10th July: 'In the past three years we have burned our identity cards, torn up our ration books, halved the number of snoopers, decimated the number of forms and said good riddance to nearly two-thirds of the remaining wartime regulations. This is the march to freedom on which we are bound. And the pace must quicken as we go forward. . . . Within the limits of law and social justice, our aim is freedom for every man and woman to live their own lives in their own way and not have their lives lived for them by an overweening State.'

By this time the reconstitution of the government was under very active discussion and it remained so until Churchill's retirement in April 1955. For more than a year the leading figures in the Conservative party had their gaze diverted from the more pressing executive problems by his long-drawn-out hesitation. As early as 11th March, 1954, I recorded the Prime Minister telling me over dinner: 'I feel like an aeroplane at the end of its flight, in the dusk, with the petrol running out, in search of a safe landing.' The only political interest he had left, he said, was in high-level conversations with the Russians. He would then be glad to retire to Hyde Park Gate to finish his *History of the English-Speaking Peoples*. I was continually brought in to witness and to help with this distressing and distract-ing transition. The first crunch came in August when, after successive visits to Chartwell, I warned Anthony, 'Winston is writing to you. He doesn't feel the world situation makes it right for him to move at present. There was little of the Russian visit talk. He rejected calmly but firmly ideas of being an Elder Statesman, or of being Lord President in a Cabinet of which he was not P.M. He acknowledged the need for a reconstituted government and wants to do this *with* you. He registered but was unmoved by my opinion that he would shock you and get opposition if he stayed on. It is all very difficult since in the interests of the party and the country we must move forward with the minimum of defections. His deep obsession with the gravity of the international situation and what seemed his determination that his mission is not yet done, are factors to which evidently we had not given sufficient weight. He had registered your wish for a year in which to consolidate, but has his own views based on precedent and history about the best way to handle successor governments.' Two days later, on 18th August, I wrote to the Prime Minister in the following terms:

> 'I value your confidence in asking me to look at your second epistle to Anthony. Since last summer at the time of your severe illness we have all accepted that Anthony is to be your successor. I have therefore a loyalty to him which you realize that I must be careful not to abuse.
>
> 'Up till my visit to you last Friday I thought you would hand over to your successor this autumn leaving him time to mobilize his forces, his programme and public opinion.
>
> 'You have now thought over the situation and have introduced a new argument, which you fortify with your experience, namely that you distrust the outlook for fag-end successor governments. This is an important argument; and no doubt in order to give it its full force, your second draft omits detailed description of the type of reconstituted government which you envisage and leaves this as well as the detailed timetable of the changeover until you have talked to Anthony. I think this is right.'

A week later the Prime Minister sent me a copy of what he called 'the final edition' of his letter to Anthony. It covered what by now was well-trodden ground. He had, he said, good reports from his doctors, did not feel unequal to his burden, and was not going to abandon his post 'at the present crisis of the world'. There followed a long disquisition on the difficulties of fag-end administrations (Rosebery after Gladstone, Balfour after Salisbury, both 'brushed aside in spite of their ability, experience and charm') and a fairly clear indication that he would soldier on until much closer to the election, thus bearing responsibility for the past and leaving his successor a fair start for the future ('the present government have not got a bad record, with Rab's and Harold's solid and memorable achievements and your own skill at the Foreign Office'). It was not so much a decision as a further postponement of decision.

I went to America in September a very troubled man. Sir Stanford Cade had operated on my wife and had confirmed that the diagnosis was cancer. He showed me his library of case-books of the disease and gave me to understand that he could offer little hope. He continued, however, to send me reports as encouraging as he reasonably could. I visited my son Adam who was A.D.C. to Vincent Massey as Governor-General of Canada. I saw how well everything was being handled there, and since they were making Adam feel at home I advised him not to return. In Washington I stayed with Roger and Alice Makins at the Embassy. They were at the height of their job and it was a comfort to be with friends.

From the meeting of the International Monetary Fund I hurried back to the party conference at Blackpool where I was to speak on the second day. There had been no time for me to prepare a speech laboriously and I therefore made one of my best. It was composed as I lay in my bedroom with a posse of collaborators sitting or standing around. Having brooded on the figures, I decided to say that we could double our standard of living in twenty-five years. In 1979 I shall consult a well-trained economist to see whether or not my forecast has come true. Certainly with more incentives it would do so. The other slogan I coined was 'Invest in Success'. This roused the conference to enthusiasm, and I was very grateful to my little group which included Michael Fraser, Peter Goldman and Chloe Otto. A good speech really ought to be made from scrappy notes. The speaker is then free to roam and range as the imagination takes him. Winston's habit of dictating every word ahead did harm to many of our younger speakers who tried to follow him. They did not realize just how much time he spent polishing his notes into his own brilliant style. Moreover, he used long-distance glasses so as to pretend not to be using his notes.

After the conference my wife's condition deteriorated rapidly and she died on my birthday, 9th December, at Stanstead. She had been fully aware of her fate and was courageous up to the end. She had made a wonderfully secure family life for us all and in the next few months I prepared a book about her for the children. We were all fortified by her determination, her resolution and her religious faith. 'I knew well that she was gathering up all her spiritual resource to face the challenge before her,' the Archbishop of Canterbury wrote to me, 'and I do pray and believe that she is now upheld in the peace and strength of God—and, indeed, I pray for you no less the same peace and strength of God to keep you in your burden of spirit.'

*

No doubt I should have been wise to have taken a longish time off for reflection, since the domestic shock was not at once fully apparent but gained increasing force during the year. However, I am satisfied that there was no shirking of duty or work and that considerable benefit accrued at any rate to the party as a result of decisions taken. I calculate that during the period between Winston's 80th birthday on 30th November and the following April when he retired I had no less than eight gargantuan dinners with him alone; the dinners being followed by libations of brandy so ample that I felt it prudent on more than one occasion to tip the liquid into the side of my shoe. The subjects discussed were always the same: his retirement and the succession, the fag-end government syndrome, a Russian Summit and, strange to relate, space travel. He was very irritated by the idea of going to the moon which he regarded as a waste of time and money. We also discussed the shape of the April Budget. I was expecting a surplus of £282 million. Winston felt that I had held back in 1954, that there was a strong case for further incentive, and that I could give away the whole surplus. My inclination was more cautious.

At the end of March Anthony and I were invited into the Cabinet room. Winston made a slip by asking me to sit on his right, but then corrected himself and beckoned to Anthony. We all gazed out over Horse Guards Parade. Then Winston said very shortly, 'I am going and Anthony will succeed me. We can discuss details later.' The ceremonial was over. We found ourselves in the passage where Anthony and I shook hands. On the day he retired I sent Winston the following letter:

'. . . It has been for me a most moving day. It was in 1945, ten years ago, that I first learned to serve you directly when we came to be in Opposition.

'After the sessions and exchanges on our policy documents at Hyde Park Gate I shall never forget the morning when you showed me the list of the new government with myself as Chancellor.

'Ever since then I have found it easier and easier to know the way in which you and your policies wanted help. I hope I have been able to rise to the occasion. At any rate for me it has been a never-to-be-forgotten experience. The *tours d'horizon* which have emerged from our morning meetings have made my mind ever so much more elastic and imaginative than before. I have learned to understand the fallibility of human nature and what is more to make generous allowance.

'I do not speak of the priceless private opportunities of colloquy or entertainment. One day I hope to paint again with you.

'Meanwhile I shall think of you enjoying the sunshine.

'We shall miss your strength and sense of direction. But we shall soon have you back and be able to exchange notes.

'I myself feel heavy and sad with the responsibility which will be bequeathed—sad when I remember your great affection for Sydney, and heavy because of the times ahead.

'But this time with you has given me at least the strength to face all things quietly.

> 'Let nothing disturb thee,
> Let nothing affright thee,
> All passeth away,
> God alone will stay,
> Patience obtaineth all things.

'This is what I, like St. Augustine, have learned.'

The outgoing Prime Minister described my decision to take 6d. off the income tax in April 1955 as a 'very Venus of Milo for probity'. He said he would like to have seen two foaming tankards of beer beside the statue of Venus, symbolic of 2*d*. off the pint. The new Prime Minister was against relief on beer or other duties on consumption, and thought I was taking a rigorous and correct line in carrying forward half my surplus. It is true that an adverse change which had come over the balance of payments in the second half of 1954 continued in the early months of 1955, and corrective measures had needed to be taken to restrain internal demand—increases in Bank rate and restrictions on hire purchase. But these measures had proved effective in strengthening sterling and I felt myself justified in relying on credit control without ruling out the possibility of a tax concession. *The Economist* of 23rd April, 1955, greeted the decision with modified rapture, but on the whole gave the Budget good marks:

> 'No one can say with any dogmatism (for the fourth dimension comes in here) that Mr. Butler's guesses will not come out right; and it is true that some of last year's judgements which were thought to be bold were justified in the event. Nevertheless, there is a distinct flavour of optimism about the calculation as a whole, especially where it relates to the rate of spending by the public. Many people would have felt happier about the general balance of the Budget if the portion of the surplus to be given away had been put rather lower. But that the right figure, in all the political and economic circumstances, lies somewhere in the middle range between giving nothing at all away and eliminating the surplus altogether hardly admits of doubt. To have given nothing would have proved Mr. Butler too much of an economist to survive in politics; to have given the lot would have shown him too much of a politician to have charge of the national economy.'

The article finally paid a personal tribute:

> 'Mr. Butler closed his speech with a brief review of the whole period of his stewardship of the Treasury, where he has now lasted longer than anyone else since the war. He was quick to acknowledge that he has enjoyed good fortune, but he can also rightly take credit for what has been achieved. More

1954 THE AUTHOR, AS
CHANCELLOR OF THE
EXCHEQUER, WITH (*above*)
MR. GEORGE HUMPHREY,
SECRETARY OF THE U.S.
TREASURY, AND (*right*) MR.
ANTHONY EDEN, THEN
FOREIGN SECRETARY,
LEAVING FOR A CABINET
MEETING

Sport and General

THE AUTHOR, NOW CHANCELLOR OF SHEFFIELD UNIVERSITY,
RECEIVING AN HONORARY DEGREE WITH (*left to right*) SIR OSBERT SITWELL,
DR. EDITH SITWELL AND MISS (LATER DAME) NINETTE DE VALOIS

progress has been made in three and a half years in restoring British public finances and in easing the burden of taxation—not to mention liberating the general economy from the stifling network of controls—than seemed at all probable when the present Parliament first met. Politics is the art of the possible, and Mr. Butler has done about as much as a Chancellor with so exiguous a majority could have done.'

The exiguous majority was substantially increased at the general election in May—the first time such a feat had been achieved for ninety years. But what with the Bank of England distracting attention back on to a floating rate at a particularly awkward moment and my advisers at the Treasury slowly waking to the full dangers of inflation, I had a very disagreeable summer. The Conservative private members, ever fickle and unsure, were not grateful for what *The Economist* had described as three and a half years' progress or for the contribution this progress had made to the election victory. But I had the following sympathetic and welcome letter from Brendan Bracken:

'You know that I am not an admirer of the government's financial policy—it's never been tough enough for my caveman's idea of public finance. But if I dislike Treasury policy, I have a long and sure-set liking for its author.

'The attitude of those who were recently acclaiming your policy and now condemn it disgusts me. How right is Swift's saying: "There is nothing in this world constant, save inconstancy."

'I wish you a safe journey to Turkey and hope that you will not be lured to madness in your congregation of currency pundits.'

By the time I got away for some shooting in August, the Treasury and the Bank between them were raising some alarm over sterling. I received a large package of papers at Swinton, and driving home at the end of the month I stopped in a byway in the Lincolnshire fens and read of all the measures which my advisers wanted. It was then in that lonely place that I first saw the necessity for an autumn Budget, which as Nicholas Davenport wrote in *The Spectator* in October was 'conceived in honesty'.

I was unable to get sufficient head of steam from the Cabinet to cut the bread subsidies and take other drastic measures instead of a Budget. The Governor was uncharacteristically critical of me but the fault was that after the successful election Ministers and, particularly, the party in the House were not in a mood for self-immolation. The first task, however, was to steady the pound, and this I did at Istanbul in September at the I.M.F. meeting. With Sir George Bolton beside me, excitedly whispering into my ears, I repeated to the domes and minarets several times the incantation that the pound was not to float but would remain within fixed margins and be steadily defended by our resources combined with stiff anti-inflationary measures. I felt that in the exigencies of the moment the Robot vision with which I began my tenure of the Treasury was clearly inappropriate. The manœuvre proved effective and Pierre Mendès-France expressed himself as filled with admiration. Though I should have preferred our team to have decided on a packet of economies instead, they gave me no alternative to an autumn Budget, dealing with purchase tax and profits tax; this aroused furious criticism from the Opposition and a personal attack on me by Hugh Gaitskell who was by then a candidate to succeed Attlee as Leader of the party. This gave me the opportunity to respond in kind and to assure Nye Bevan that, if he were still competing for the Labour leadership, he would no longer need to 'stoop to conquer'.

Gaitskell's elevation a few weeks later almost exactly synchronized with my departure from the Treasury. Anthony Eden had had ideas about reconstituting his government since May, and when I returned from Istanbul in September I was asked to Chequers and taken to sit near the wall in the garden overlooking the croquet lawn. If I had been less scrupulous about the economy I would have retired in May. I had been warned by my good friend Patrick Buchan Hepburn, the Chief Whip, that changes were afoot and had been given a clear idea of what changes I was to expect. I wrote the following when I got back to London:

'The P.M. is an artist far more able and resolute than the newspapers give him credit for. He had, he said, sedulously attempted to avoid interference with the Foreign Office, Having been there for so long he found it difficult to work with so strong a character as Harold Macmillan. No serious incidents or frictions seem to have arisen but the P.M. was riled by the situation in Cyprus and the Middle East. He was not happy about the contacts with the U.S.A. despite Harold's clever handling of Dulles. He also said that the Foreign Office was hell physically and that Harold would tire from overseas travel. Anthony said that he had never had the idea that I should go to the Foreign Office since I would be under him and that he would not like. He fancied Selwyn for the F.O. and said he would be the best subordinate. Anthony wanted the weight of the government distributed between "home" and "foreign" and would like me on the home front to lead the Commons and handle the party. He thought that I had had too many political "extras" under Winston for anyone to bear for long and that I had had long enough at the Treasury.'

From my study of English political history I knew that to be in the Cabinet without a proper department almost always renders one less powerful. This need not necessarily be so. One would have thought that the rush and grind of a big department would take away from the time free to make individual contributions to the Cabinet. Yet the fact is that the advisers in a big department, such as the Foreign Office or the Treasury, themselves provide a corpus of advice—very often on subjects outside their own—which is invaluable to a Minister. However, after a pause for thought and communion, I established a Lord Privy Seal's Office with the aid of two very devoted and diligent men: Burke Trend, now Secretary to the Cabinet, and Ian Bancroft, at the time my assistant Private Secretary, and later principal Secretary to the Chancellor. Harry Crookshank, who had previously held the post of Lord Privy Seal and was now retiring from office, came to see me at No. 11. He was a man of the utmost probity and uprightness of character, a bachelor before all bachelors, a sharp intellect, a brave soldier, an assiduous constituency member, a politician who in himself belied Winston's generalization that 'There are no friends at the top.' He was a confidant of Harold Macmillan; but his integrity was so pure that he could say to me in straight and simple terms, 'Rab, how can it be right for you to take a non-executive job, and hand over the levers of power to others?' One answer, as it turned out, was that the job did not long remain non-executive. But a second answer could be that Crookshank's warning was justified. For though later I was to sit on dizzy heights as Chairman of the party, Leader of the House and Principal Secretary of State, to snatch brands from the burning in Africa, and to be Foreign Secretary, it was never again said of me, or for that matter of the British economy either, that we had '*la puissance d'une idée en marche*'.

CHAPTER NINE

HINGE OF DESTINY

THE RESTRUCTURING of Sir Anthony Eden's government in the closing days of 1955 did not receive a favourable press. On the contrary, a series of articles began to appear assessing in decidedly unflattering and somewhat unfair terms his performance to date, and even speculating about his personal future. The sharpest of these, which was printed in the *Daily Telegraph* over the signature of Donald McLachlan, drew from the Prime Minister a pained and pungent oath, with which I expressed warm sympathy. Anthony was very susceptible to such criticism. Unfortunately, his reactions did not remain private, and accordingly neither could mine. A flurry of ill-informed excitement in the Sunday papers at the beginning of January prompted him, I think unwisely, to cause a formal denial that he intended to resign to be issued from No. 10. Since it had been alleged, to my annoyance, that he was giving way to me, I was myself pursued by the press for comment. I did my best in showing genuine astonishment at the rumours and loyalty to their victim. The personal and political strains of the past year had taken their toll and Somerset Maugham had kindly and unexpectedly lent me his villa on the Riviera to recharge my batteries. As I was about to board the aircraft, I was asked by a Press Association man: 'Mr. Butler, would you say that this is the best Prime Minister we have?' My hurried assent to this well-meant but meaningless proposition was flashed round the world; indeed it was fathered upon me. I do not think it did Anthony any good. It did not do me any good, either.

My position as Lord Privy Seal was anomalous. I had taken over, at Anthony's request, the chairmanship of what was called the Liaison Committee, a body consisting of government and party representatives which met weekly to plan the co-ordination of our publicity. For this reason perhaps, the Prime Minister paid me the compliment of expecting me, more than the Chairman of the party, to be responsible for Conservative success in the country. I was therefore at the receiving end of those innumerable telephone calls, on every day of the week and at every hour of the day, which characterized his conscientious but highly strung supervision of our affairs. At a time when there were few runs to be made on the home wicket, his lack of experience in any domestic Ministry was not a help. In foreign affairs, by contrast, his record was unequalled in modern parliamentary history and the first year of his government had certainly seen a steady decline in international tension. When the party's manifesto for the 1955 general election came to be written, it was a fact that, for the first time since the War, no actual fighting was taking place anywhere in the world. The Prime Minister understandably proposed that this should be recorded in print, and Lord Woolton and I were deputed by our cautious and hard-headed colleagues to dissuade him from this course on the grounds that the fact could well be falsified before the ink was dry on the paper. But public euphoria continued to be the order of the day and Mr. Macmillan, then Foreign Secretary, returned from the Geneva Summit with the happy comment: 'There ain't gonna be no war.' This did not turn out to be an entirely accurate prophecy nor, in his own political deportment, a lasting mood.

The Middle East was the predestined scene of the cold war for 1955 and 1956. The area was strategically and commercially vital and the Russians and their satellites were showing an increasing determination to intrude into its affairs. Britain had already demonstrated her willingness to abandon what might be interpreted as political domination—most notably by the Anglo-Egyptian Treaty of 1954 which Eden himself had negotiated as Foreign Secretary. In the face of considerable misgivings from the right wing of the Conservative party, it had been agreed to evacuate the Suez Canal zone and thus give up the military base which we had retained throughout a generation of nominal Egyptian independence. At the same time, the new Egyptian leader, Gamal Abdel Nasser, agreed to uphold the terms of the 1888 Constantinople Convention which recognized the right of the Suez Canal Company to operate the Canal until the expiry of the concession in 1968 and to 'guarantee at all times and for all powers' its free use. Nasser, however, who had helped to overturn the corrupt monarchy two years earlier and aspired to the leadership of a united Arab people, was vehemently opposed to the more positive aspects of British policy. These aimed to consolidate the Middle East against the threat of Communist penetration. We regarded the Baghdad Pact, concluded between Iraq and Turkey and acceded to in 1955 by Britain, Pakistan and Persia, as a 'northern tier' of defence for the Middle East. Nasser regarded it as a British attempt to re-establish military and political hegemony, and was successful in preventing any Arab state other than Iraq from joining. Egypt was ready enough to accept economic aid from the West, but would not consider signing any security pact as a condition of military aid. Instead a contract was signed with Czechoslovakia in September 1955 for the supply of arms and aircraft to Egypt, and Western moves to bring home the unwisdom of such a deal were met with bland assurances from Nasser that it would not be allowed to lead to Communist infiltration into Egypt. These assurances may have been naïve, but there is no reason to doubt that they were sincere. A practising Moslem and a proud Nationalist, Nasser had no love for Communism and no wish to be its agent. He was rather, in the words of Pineau, the French Foreign Minister, a *grand marchand de tapis* between East and West.

The *tapis* he was most anxious to sell was the project for a new dam high up the Nile above Aswan. In practical terms this was the latest of many schemes for improving Egyptian agriculture; in the heroic terms to which Nasser frequently had recourse it was a symbol of his country's regeneration, 'seventeen times greater than the Great Pyramid'. Russia had hinted that she would be prepared to pay for it. Eden says with complete frankness in his memoirs, 'I did not want to see Soviet influence expand in Africa, and in November 1955 we discussed the threat of this with the United States government and determined to persist.' Unfortunately this persistence did not bear fruit. In its propaganda, in its activities throughout the Middle East, and, above all, in its acceptance of arms from behind the Iron Curtain (which significantly reduced the likelihood of its being able to service massive loans from the West), Egypt appeared to be labelling itself as a hostile country. By mid-July it must have been apparent to Nasser that the Western powers were no longer interested in going ahead with the plan. 'I was surprised by the insulting attitude with which the refusal was declared,' he said later, 'not by the refusal itself.' The U.S. government, and its Secretary of State John Foster Dulles, have incurred much retrospective criticism for the abrupt insult; but the refusal itself had become the settled policy of the British government several days earlier. In common with the Lord Chancellor, Lord Kilmuir, I have no recollection of there being any discussion in the papers circulated to Ministers of what turned out to be Egypt's reprisal: namely, the nationalization of the Suez Canal Company, ostensibly as a means of financing the High Dam.

It is, of course, arguable, and has frequently been argued, that the seizure of the Suez Canal was inevitable. This foreign enterprise was the most dramatic and also the most vulnerable of the relics of Western rule which the nationalist officers' revolution in Egypt was pledged to eliminate. On the other hand, it was equally inevitable that the British government should contest such unilateral action. Britain was the largest single user of the Canal, accounting in the year before nationalization for over 28 per cent of an annually increasing tonnage passing through it. The position of the Company, in which the British government held 44 per cent of the shares, was enshrined in an international treaty which, as I have pointed out, had been reaffirmed when the Suez base agreement was signed in 1954. Moreover, the manner in which Nasser had purported to make off with this property threw doubts on his subsequent and persistent assurances that freedom of navigation would be respected in accordance with that Treaty. 'The recent behaviour of the Egyptian government', wrote Anthony Eden, summarizing the British government's conclusions at its meeting on 27th July, 1956, 'did not give us confidence that in the long term they would manage the canal with a full sense of international obligations. If they won sole control, further pressure must be expected in time, on Israel and others. We were convinced that the answer to Nasser must take account of the modern trend towards internationalism and away from nationalism. Our object must be to undo his action and to place the management of the canal firmly in international custody.'[1] I was not present at the meeting at which these conclusions were reached, but I agreed with them in every particular, both then and throughout the sensational events that ensued.

I had become ill in July as the result of a virus infection, which it took longer than hoped for my doctors, Horace Evans and Denis Williams, to cure. On 2nd August I was back among my colleagues, still feeling limp but determined to participate in the decisions that had now to be taken. My understanding was that we were not proposing a return to the *status quo ante* under which the canal had been run as an Egyptian entity under European control, but rather the internationalizing of the canal in a manner which would insulate it from the internal politics of any one country. This aim should be sought by a negotiated settlement, but if such negotiations failed then we must be ready in the last resort to use force. The British government's decisions were taken without dissent and were entirely in line with the views expressed, though not consistently held, by Mr. Dulles who had arrived in London the previous day and had told the British and French Foreign Secretaries, 'A way had to be found to make Nasser disgorge what he was attempting to swallow. . . . We must make a genuine effort to bring world opinion to favour the international operation of the canal. . . . It should be possible to create a world opinion so adverse to Nasser that he would be isolated. Then if a military operation had to be undertaken it would be more apt to succeed and have less grave repercussions than if it had been undertaken precipitately.'

I am described by Hugh Thomas in his extremely clever reconstruction, *The Suez Affair*, as acting at this meeting 'in the shadow of Disraeli rather than of Hitler'. This somewhat elliptical remark expresses an important truth. The purchase of the Khedive's interest in the Suez Canal Company in 1875 had probably been the most spectacular coup of Disraeli's career. It cut the distance from Britain to India by several weeks and some thousands of miles: this was important for trade and even more for the maintenance of Empire. Time, it is true, had reduced the

[1] *Full Circle* (Cassell).

long-range strategic value of the canal to Britain. But in 1956 it was still a vital military and commercial link, and the development of rich oil fields and the need to support a continuing military presence in the East gave the protection of the canal, through which three-quarters of the ships that passed belonged to NATO, a high priority. These considerations alone seemed to me to justify the decisions taken by the British government. But they were clearly not the only considerations in the minds of some of my colleagues. Britain had had a long and bitter experience of the one-sided denunciation of international treaties. 'The pattern', said Eden, in a broadcast on 8th August, 'is familiar to many of us, my friends: we all know this is how fascist governments behave and we all remember, only too well, what the cost can be in giving in to fascism.' Later Eden was to write, 'It is important to reduce the stature of the megalomaniacal dictator at an early stage.' This idea was certainly in his mind when he declared on 8th August, 'Our quarrel is not with Egypt—it is with Nasser.'

I listened at my home at Stanstead to this broadcast being made. I remember leaning out of the bow window into the garden and smoking one of the last cigarettes I ever had. My mood was one of deep misgiving and anxiety on hearing this analogy with fascism and this personalization of Nasser. I thought the Prime Minister had got that part of it wrong. I admired his courage, his gallantry, his wartime record and his Foreign Office achievements. He seemed thoroughly in character in standing up for British rights in the Middle East and I supported him. But it was surely unwise to use in 1956 the language that ought to have been used in 1936. The circumstances had altered. The cast had changed. Egypt's new revolutionary government was acting contrary to our interests, and probably to international law, but it represented a popular movement not an imposed tyranny. Nasser was not in politics for the good of our health, but he was no Hitler, no incarnation of evil, no megalomaniac who had to be toppled before free men could rest easy in their beds. Many able and experienced politicians, including Eden's successor and, in the early days of the crisis, the Labour leader Hugh Gaitskell, used similar language and drew similar analogies. These were deep-seated emotions affecting liberal-minded people, but they coalesced only too easily with less generous sentiments: the residues of illiberal resentment at the loss of Empire, the rise of coloured nationalism, the transfer of world leadership to the United States. It was these sentiments that made the Suez venture so popular, not least among the supporters of the embarrassed Labour party. Securing the international status of a canal is a more difficult goal to apprehend than overthrowing a greedy dictator. The two purposes are not mutually exclusive, but neither are they necessarily linked. Anthony Eden has rightly claimed that the members of his Cabinet were loyal. That many of them were muddled by this duality of purpose I have no doubt, any more than I doubt that many were perplexed by decisions taken outside the Cabinet by the 'Suez Committee'. They were not always abreast of events, but they felt that the canal must be saved. This was certainly my own position.

The attempt to negotiate a settlement was not helped by Eden's broadcast. This virtually made it impossible for Nasser to attend, as against the advice of his colleagues he had wished, the London conference of twenty-two interested countries summoned at British, French and American invitation. Instead, the conclusion of the conference agreed to by eighteen of the twenty-two—that an international board representing the maritime powers and Egypt should manage the canal—had to be taken to Nasser by a mission of five led by Sir Robert Menzies, who thus unselfishly turned himself into another 'marchand de tapis'. Unfortunately, as he afterwards complained, the rug was pulled clean out from under his feet by President Eisenhower, who chose the very moment when Menzies was warning Nasser that the alternative to acceptance could be force, to announce that the Americans would go to any length to secure a peaceful settlement. After the failure of the Menzies mission, the British and French governments determined to appeal to the Security Council of the United Nations. The Americans at once raised objection and proposed that yet another London conference should be held to design a Suez Canal Users' Association (SCUA), an international organization to deal with all the problems of canal passage. No sooner had this makeshift proposal been reluctantly agreed to by the British government, than the chances of its success were removed by the American Secretary of State who told a press conference that SCUA never had any 'teeth' in it and that there was no suggestion of fitting 'teeth' now. At this stage, the only peaceful alternative that was left, short of complete capitulation, was recourse to the Security Council. This was tried, but without success. On 13th October the celebrated 'six principles', including the principle that the operation of the Canal should be insulated from any one country's politics, were accepted, but the proposition that they should be implemented through the eighteen-nation plan was vetoed by the Soviet Union.

Governments are often accused of acting immorally because their interests happen to conflict with those of other states. Such accusations engender heat, without providing light. Both the United States and the Soviet Union were primarily concerned throughout this crisis with a vital aspect of the cold war, that is to say with winning or retaining the goodwill of the under-developed world. The simple desire of Mr. Eisenhower to be re-elected on a peace platform and the maddening twists and turns of Mr. Dulles's legalistic mind were less important than the fears of the United States that any forcible action against Egypt would incite the Arab world to regard or even call in Russia as their ally. The Soviet veto in the United Nations on 13th October was even more single-minded: it faithfully echoed, in the long-run interests of world Communism, the protest of India and other neutralist countries that Egyptian sovereignty, with which they identified their own, would be infringed by such international management of the canal as had been proposed at the London conference. But if American and Russian interests were involved in 'the third world', so also were those of Britain—and these interests, though sometimes stated in purely self-regarding terms, were not at their heart selfish. It was this thought, quite distinctive and too little regarded, to which I sought to give expression when I addressed the Conservative Political Centre meeting at the party conference in Llandudno on 11th October.

I began by acknowledging that the central fact with which we were confronted in the world was 'a deep international fissure— a divide between those who believe in two distinctly different ways of life'. Mr. Dulles had indicated at a press conference the previous week that he regarded what he called 'the colonial powers' as something of a liability in this situation. I, on the contrary, regarded the British record since the war as a positive asset. 'It is really preposterous', I said, 'that we should have to listen to lectures on Colonialism. We should not forget that whilst one hundred million people in Europe alone have, since the war, been forcibly absorbed into the Soviet bloc and system, more than five times that number have been helped to nation-hood by British governments of both parties. It is our duty to ourselves, to our friends, to the cause of freedom, and to the potential victims of Communist blandishments everywhere, to see that these facts are known, and that the lie about British "Imperialism" is not half-way round the world before the truth has got its boots on.' I went on to speak of recent political and constitutional advances in Ghana, Malaya and the Caribbean, and to our policy of extending, through the United Nations, the Colombo Pact and Commonwealth institutions, 'the helping hand to under-developed countries, which are seeking to raise their own living standards with limited resources and capital'. This brought me directly to the theme I was most anxious to proclaim, in support of the government and of the Prime Minister: 'No country in the world has shown more sympathy or given more help to the legitimate aspirations of nationalism, and not least of Arab nationalism, than has ours. But on one point we are adamant: these aspirations can only be achieved in accordance with the rule of law. If international agreements are to be broken and international assets seized with impunity, then world confidence will be shaken irreparably in all territories that rely on outside capital for their development; and the whole policy of the helping hand towards under-developed countries will be gravely and tragically prejudiced. Moreover, there are weightier considerations even than that involved in the issue. For had we abjectly decided to knuckle under to this show of predatory nationalism, what confidence then would the under-developed countries have had in *us*? What trust could our dependencies and our other friends have placed in our obliga-tions to guide and protect them? What future would we have had then as a great power and a great force for freedom and moral values in the world? The answer is "None"; for we should have abdicated from our responsibilities and our greatness alike.'

Immediately after the conference I had to fit in some meetings for the Central Office in Scotland and then, owing to the illness of Lord Salisbury, to attend the Queen at the opening of Calder Hall, the nuclear power plant in Cumberland. So it was not until 18th October that I returned to London. I went straight to No. 10 where I found the Foreign Secretary, Selwyn Lloyd, in the lobby outside the Cabinet room. He seemed moved and, gripping my arm, described how he had got back from the U.N. early on the 16th and been immediately wafted to Paris in the wake of the Prime Minister to attend a conference with Mollet and Pineau. They had discussed the ever closer line-up between Jordan, Egypt and Syria and the consequences of a pre-emptive strike by Israel, and it had been suggested that, if war broke out in the Middle East between Israel and Egypt, Britain and France would jointly intervene in the canal area to stop hostilities. Selwyn Lloyd seemed anxious about my own reaction. At that moment I was summoned into the Cabinet room. Eden had in front of him a menu card on which was some writing to which he referred. He confirmed that it was suggested with Mollet and Pineau that in the event of war between Israel and Egypt we should go in with the French to separate the combatants and occupy the canal. I asked whether a war between Israel and Jordan was not more likely. He replied that in such an event we would have to keep our word to defend Jordan against attack: the French had therefore been asked to make this clear to Israel. I was impressed by the audacity of the thinking behind this plan but concerned about the public reaction. I wondered whether an agreement with the French and the Israelis, designed to free the Suez Canal and eventually to internationalize it, would not meet our objective, but the Prime Minister indicated that things were now moving in the direction he had described and in all the circumstances I said that I would stand by him.

The Israelis attacked at dusk on 29th October. On the 30th we agreed, as decided, to send an ultimatum to both sides calling on them to withdraw. The Anglo-French military plans, which had been in preparation since the end of July, were put into operation. They involved grave delay. 'If I had had a pain in my tummy,' Winston Churchill said to me six months later, referring to the illness which was soon to strike down Anthony Eden, 'I should not have put to sea for six days.' Before our troops had even landed, a message came through that the victorious Israelis were about to cease fire. This was on 4th November and the situation was discussed by Ministers. I took the line that were the news correct, we could not possibly continue our expedition. It had not been my idea to announce that we were going in to stop hostilities, but if they had already stopped we had no justification for invasion. This argument, which was backed by Lord Salisbury, seemed to nonplus the Prime Minister. He said he must go upstairs and consider his position. If he could not have united support, the situation might arise in which someone else might have to take over from him. I employed the interval by telephoning to Mollie from the old Treasury Board Room. From the window there I could hear the roars of the crowd from Trafalgar Square where Nye Bevan was addressing an anti-Suez demonstration. When Eden returned, a message came through from the Israeli Foreign Minister, Mrs. Meir, that there was to be no cease-fire. Tension round the table was immediately relieved and it was agreed that the troops should land.

But no sooner had they landed than they were given orders to stop, within sixty miles (and perhaps forty-eight hours) of Suez. Why? Anthony Eden himself has stated the following to have been the weightiest factor: 'We had intervened to divide and, above all, to contain the conflict. The occasion for our intervention was over, the fire was out. Once the fighting had ceased, justification for further intervention ceased with it.' In other words, we were prevented from occupying the whole of the canal because of describing our expedition as aimed at 'separating the combatants', instead of internationalizing the canal— precisely the point which had troubled me on 18th October and which I had emphasized on 4th November. Other factors, however, weighed heavier in some of my colleagues' minds. Censure by the United Nations, in which most of the Commonwealth was arrayed against us, certainly had its effect upon many members of the government besides those, like Edward Boyle, who resigned. Speculation against sterling, mainly in the American market or on American account, had an even profounder effect on the Chancellor of the Exchequer, Harold Macmillan, who switched almost overnight from being the foremost protagonist of intervention to being the leading influence for disengagement—as well he might, for the loss of 279 million dollars in that November represented about 15 per cent of our total gold and dollar reserves. It was my misfortune and perhaps my miscalculation that at precisely this moment in time, when we were making up our minds to withdraw, I dined with twenty influential Conservative members of the Progress Trust, and was very open with them in speaking privately of some of the realities of the situation, particularly in relation to sterling, which no one had hitherto done. The small private room became like a hornets' nest. They all hurried off to the Carlton Club to prepare representations to the government. Whenever I moved in the weeks that followed, I felt the party knives sticking into my innocent back.

My position became even more uncomfortable and exposed with the sudden, but not unexpected, illness of the Prime Minister. I saw Horace Evans in the drawing-room of No. 10. He said that Anthony could not live on stimulants any more and that, since he was unlikely to relax at a clinic, a few weeks in Jamaica had been recommended for recuperation. It did sound the most extraordinarily remote suggestion in the middle of such unprecedented troubles. Harold Macmillan's strong character reacted in a fit of temper against Evans; he said that the Prime Minister could not possibly be withdrawn to that extent, leaving our troops in an uncertain predicament. Nevertheless the Edens went off and I was left in charge of the government, with the odious duty of withdrawing the troops, re-establishing the pound, salvaging our relations with the U.S. and the U.N., and bearing the brunt of the criticism from private members, constituency worthies and the general public for organizing a withdrawal, which was a collective responsibility.

This period as head of the government was the most difficult of my career. Not the least difficult thing was that major decisions had to be checked with Anthony in Jamaica and the only method of communication was by telegraph to the

Governor who then had to send a messenger on poor roads all
the long distance to Ian Fleming's home at Golden Eye. The
delay in waiting for replies did not help our situation. What did
help was my long-standing friendship with George Humphrey,
the American Secretary of the Treasury. Hardly had I taken
over than he rang me from his home in Georgia. He told me
that he had shut himself with the telephone in the meat safe so
as to avoid the intrusions of his family. 'Rab,' he said, 'the
President cannot help you unless you conform to the United
Nations resolution about withdrawal. If you do that, we here
will help you save the pound.' This was blackmail. But we were
in no position to argue. I gave him assurances. Then I put him
on to Harold Macmillan, my successor as Chancellor of the
Exchequer, who stood shoulder to shoulder with me in those
desperate and humiliating days. We both addressed a meeting of
the 1922 Committee early in December. The party was extremely critical. There was strong feeling that 'we should have
gone through with it'. But the Cabinet was united. 'The real
purpose of this note', wrote David Kilmuir, the Lord Chancellor, 'is to express my affectionate admiration for the way in
which you dealt with the last few weeks and a situation intoler-
able to any but the highest courage and determination. I am
quite sure that these qualities will get us out of our present
discontent.'

Anthony returned from his enforced rest on 14th December.
He at once declared his intention to carry on as Prime Minister.
Suddenly, on 8th January, he telephoned me to say that he was
going to Sandringham to tender his resignation to the Queen.
Cabinet Ministers were 'corralled' to give an immediate judge-
ment between Harold Macmillan and me as successor. Selwyn
Lloyd objected to this procedure being carried out by two peers,
Kilmuir and Salisbury. A majority of the Cabinet decided for
Harold. The Queen sent for Churchill and Salisbury. I had no
doubt what Salisbury's advice would be. I had served Churchill
for ten years and for four as his Chancellor, but he told me later
'I went for the older man.' It was clear from the representations
that had been made to the Chief Whip's office that there were
many on the back-benches who would oppose my succession;
there was no similar anti-Macmillan faction. Ted Heath was

sent to inform me of the result. As I wrote at the time, I was not surprised. I had been overwhelmed with duties as head of the government, and had made no dispositions for the emergency which occurred. Horace Evans had told me that Anthony Eden would get better, and I had relied on him going on. That night Anthony's wife sent me the following balm from Chequers:

'Dear Rab,
Just a line to say what a beastly profession I think politics are—and how greatly I admire your dignity and good humour.
Yours ever,
Clarissa.'

In the precarious situation that now confronted the government and the party, it was my duty to give the new Prime Minister loyal and sincere co-operation. I thought I could best do this at the Foreign Office, since in the aftermath of Suez so many dangerous tangles remained to be unravelled and so many ruptured friendships to be mended. However, as he pungently states in his memoirs, Macmillan 'felt one head on a charger should be enough', and was accordingly anxious not to dislodge the faithful Selwyn Lloyd. His memory plays him false in averring that I 'chose the post of Home Secretary'. But he was clearly relieved when I agreed to accept it at his hands. Dining a few nights later at the Beefsteak, I was reminded by a bright spark that Home Secretaries scarcely ever become Prime Ministers. But since the exceptions include Melbourne and Churchill, this 'rule' need depress no incumbent; nor was I ever Home Secretary *tout court*. Other jobs and dignities, including the leadership of the House, the chairmanship of the party, the conduct of Central African affairs, the oversight of European negotiations, the first Secretaryship of State, and even the Deputy Premiership, were to be added unto me for varying periods in the years that followed; and each time Macmillan went abroad—notably during his Eastern tour in 1958 and his African trip in 1960—I was automatically invited to act as head of the government. But to do him justice, the Prime Minister never gave me any impression that he wanted me to succeed him. The only time the subject was ever mentioned was late one night at Chequers when he said, 'At your age, you had better be king-maker rather than king.' This seemed strange coming from a man nearly nine years my senior, but it was of course entirely consistent with the attitude he later adopted to the succession in 1963.

"WELL, SO LONG, RAB! I'M OFF TO SEE THE FAMILY, BUT I KNOW THAT YOU'RE THE BEST BABY SITTER WE HAVE!"

Meanwhile, our relations were close and friendly, and he allowed me a completely free hand with my reforms at the Home Office—in a similar spirit of indulgent scepticism, it seemed, as Churchill had shown fifteen years earlier towards my work for education. One particular incident will serve to make this general point. It occurred in the summer of 1959 when a group of leading Ministers and party officials were gathered together in the Prime Minister's room at the House of Commons to consider a preliminary draft of our election manifesto. We had reached the passage which stated, in unexciting but I thought unexceptionable language, certain of my legislative aims for the next Parliament. 'We shall revise some of our social laws, for example those relating to betting and gaming and to clubs and licensing, which are at present full of anomalies and lead to abuse and even corruption.' The Prime Minister picked up the document, held it out two feet from his face, hooded his eyes and said very slowly, 'I don't know about that. We already have the Toby Belch vote. We must not antagonize the Malvolio vote.' There were dutiful chuckles round the table. Then the Chief Whip, Ted Heath, ever business-like and forceful, intervened by pointing out that we had committed ourselves to such reforms. 'Well,' said Macmillan resignedly, 'this is your province, Rab. I suppose you think it's all right.' I indicated that I did, and without further discussion we passed on to less contentious matters.

Of course, even for unadventurous spirits the Home Office can never provide a rest cure. It is residuary legatee of every problem of internal government not specifically assigned to some other department, and many of these problems are politically sensitive, straddling the controversial borderline between liberty and order. I had not been long in office before I found the department in very hot water indeed because of just such an issue. The Bar Council had requested assistance in inquiries they were making into complaints about the professional conduct of a particular barrister, and had had the transcripts of intercepted telephone conversations made available to them under the authority of a warrant from the Home Secretary. This provided a field day for the champions of liberty in the House of Commons, who protested that it was a monstrous state of affairs and heatedly demanded, 'Are we now living in a police State?' Within twenty-four hours the temperature had dropped several degrees with the disclosure that the telephone tapped was not the barrister's but that of the self-confessed criminal—one of the knife-slashing gangsters of Soho—who was his client, and that the authorization had been granted not by me but my predecessor. However, I was not prepared to leave the matter there. I advised the Prime Minister that there should be immediate consultation with the Opposition party leaders and that, if they agreed, the whole question of telephone tapping should be investigated by an independent committee under the chairmanship of Norman Birkett, who had recently retired as a Lord Justice of Appeal. The Birkett Committee carefully defined the conditions and safeguards under which these intrinsically objectionable but occasionally necessary powers should be used. Their recommendations were accepted, and there was no further crisis in that quarter. But the incident taught me a useful lesson. Thereafter I used to go into the Smoking Room practically every evening to smell out rats— incipient causes of trouble that might blow up on the floor of the House at a few hours' notice and, if badly handled, could affect the standing and reputation of the whole government. If any appeared, or even if there were the smell of one, however faint, I would ring the Permanent Secretary at once and arrange a talk then or next morning. Thus, to use a celebrated Irish mixed metaphor, the rats were nipped in the bud, and for five years we successfully anticipated or avoided serious trouble.

My Permanent Secretaries were Sir Frank Newsam and Sir Charles Cunningham. Some time before I arrived at the department Newsam had almost literally taken charge of the country on the occasion of the East Coast floods, when he ordered the military about in the most efficient albeit peremptory manner and secured achievements that would have surprised Canute. Newsam was a powerful man and an 'original', but he was near the end of his career and his health and the age limit rendered a change inevitable after a few months. Cunningham, his successor, had made his name in Scotland and was very rapidly to make it in England and Wales. Like Lushington, Digby and others before the turn of the century, he was a great centralizer and signed every submission to me himself. This was quite different from the procedures at the Foreign Office where the young men submitted their views which were capped by their seniors. However, I certainly received excellent advice; nor was there ever any difficulty in my seeing the able juniors, two of whom were attached to my private office—T. A. Critchley, historian of the police, and Arthur Peterson, whom I later made Head of the Prison Commission in succession to Sir Lionel Fox. With the aid of these and other modern-minded officials, I was able to bring into the work of the Home Office the same spirit of reform and zeal for progress as had called into being the Education Act of 1944. A start was made soon after my appointment when the

House of Commons debated penal reform. There was a thin attendance, but I was able to outline a constructive approach to the problems presented by increased crime and to stress how the overcrowded state of the prisons, many housed in ancient and unsuitable buildings, must be remedied. Taking account of two reports from my Advisory Council—one relating to discharged prisoners and the other to the treatment of young offenders— I had managed by the beginning of 1959 to publish a White Paper of comprehensive scope, *Penal Practice in a Changing Society*, on which all subsequent improvements have been based, and later to provide better conditions and higher pay for the prison officers, the probation officers and the police.

The White Paper emphasized the need for research, to increase knowledge both of the causes of crime and of the effectiveness of the various forms of treatment and training. A research unit was set up in the Home Office, and I encouraged it to carry out, in collaboration with the universities and other research organizations, a wide-ranging programme. Later on, with the generous help of Isaac Wolfson, it was possible to found the new Institute of Criminology at Cambridge over which Professor Leon Radzinowicz has presided with such unqualified success. Side by side with this expansion of research, the White Paper outlined a £20 million building programme—the largest for one hundred years—to help relieve (or so it was hoped) the grave overcrowding of prisons and to provide accommodation suitable for modern training requirements. In particular, my programme stressed the need for more Borstal accommodation and Young Prisoners Centres and for developing the detention centres where constructive short-term training could be provided for those between 16 and 21 under rigorous conditions and strict discipline. In face of the great increase of crime amongst the young, comprehensive legislation was prepared in line with the best modern thought. It was here that I had my main controversy with elements in the Conservative party ('Colonel Blimps of both sexes—and the female of the species was more deadly, politically, than the male') who thought me soft in standing out against the reintroduction of corporal punishment. Twenty years earlier the Cadogan Committee had reported as follows: 'After examining all the available evidence, we have been unable to find any body of facts or figures showing that the introduction of a power of flogging has produced a decrease in the number of the offences for which it may be imposed, or that offences for which flogging may be ordered have tended to increase when little use was made of the power to order flogging or to decrease when the power was exercised more frequently.' But though I used up-to-date statistics and other evidence to confirm this finding that birching was not an efficient deterrent, blood-curdling demands were annually made for its restoration and quite clouded my time as Chairman of the party. Indeed I did not gain an ascendancy over the critics until 1961 at the party conference at Brighton where, following on a decisive and unanimous report from my Advisory Council, I spoke for forty minutes and carried the whole audience after a prolonged debate. Iain Macleod had tears in his eyes when he came up to congratulate Mollie. But, though they hesitated to return to the assault, many members of the party continued to hold this stand against me.

In relation to capital punishment, the law was in process of being modified when I arrived at the Home Office, and I thus inherited the rather curious Homicide Act of 1957 which restricted the death penalty to certain specified types of murder. These were not necessarily the types regarded as the most wicked, but rather those on which the deterrent effect of capital punishment was believed to be most likely to operate and those striking especially at the maintenance of law and order. They included, for example, murder of a police officer or a prison officer acting in the execution of his duty, and when I first assumed office my concern about attacks on the police and prison officers was a principal factor in persuading me that the modified law should be retained. It was the long-established practice for the Home Secretary to review every capital case before the law was allowed to take its course and to consider whether there were grounds for advising the Crown to exercise the prerogative of mercy. This was a hideous responsibility. On my desk, in the Home Secretary's massively dreary room, Sir John Simon had placed a grisly text reminding himself and his successors of their duty when considering a capital sentence. I had this removed immediately, even though there were several years of such decisions before me. Each decision meant shutting myself up for two days or more, with only the Office, the Judiciary, and occasionally my old friend David Kilmuir, the Lord Chancellor, to counsel me.

Having studied past cases, and bearing in mind the ambiguous state of the law in relation to capital punishment, I exercised my discretion in several cases to commute and reprieve. In one case at Winchester Prison the documentation submitted to me showed that there had never been a medical examination. My advisers and I were horrified by this omission: the examination was held and the prisoner was found to be mentally unbalanced and was immediately reprieved. On another occasion I reprieved a young man who had shot a taxi driver, and I am convinced he will make a good citizen. But the most difficult decision I had to make was whether to reopen the case of Timothy Evans who had been hanged for the alleged murder of his wife and child. I made a speech in the Commons declining to reopen the case but acknowledging for the first time my own belief, now generally accepted, that a jury would not have convicted in later days when they knew all the truth about Christie. Whatever view may be taken of the statistics relating to homicide and the death penalty, there can be no doubt that the possibilities of judicial error raised by the Evans case provided a weighty argument for abolition. By the end of my time at the Home Office I began to see that the system could not go on, and present-day Secretaries of State are well relieved of the terrible power to decide between life and death.

I was fortunate during my years at the Home Office to be aided by a succession of capable and energetic junior Ministers. Without their parliamentary skills I should scarcely have been able to undertake, along with all my other responsibilities, as large and varied a legislative programme as I wished and as the country required. 'I find that much of the legislation for which the Home Office is responsible was drafted and carried through in the emergency of wartime or laced in Victorian corsetry', I told a Conservative Political Centre meeting in London early in 1959; and added: 'Here I believe there is scope, if not for the Prince Rupert, at any rate for the Norman Hartnell of debate. A promising start has been made.' During the early days Patricia

Hornsby-Smith, a bonny fighter and very good 'about the House', helped me to put through some important children's legislation and also the Maintenance Orders Act 1958. The former improved and strengthened the law relating to the welfare of foster-children and the procedures for adoption; the latter gave the courts a sensible and much needed power to attach part of the wages of those who default on maintenance order payments, as an alternative to sending them to prison. In the following Parliament David Renton, the shrewd and much respected National Liberal M.P. for Huntingdon, successfully undertook the exposition of the Home Office proposals for the appointment of traffic wardens and the introduction of a ticket system of standard fines for certain minor traffic offences. This experiment has passed the test of time, though I make no claims for it in terms of public popularity. Dennis Vosper, later Lord Runcorn, whose early death was a personal and political tragedy, had a particularly good manner in the House and took off me much of the load of the legislation on gambling and drink. The licensing legislation, though certainly not the last word on the subject, has so far lasted intact: it introduced more flexibility into the hours during which public houses can open and removed a considerable number of irritating and sometimes ridiculous anomalies. The betting and gaming legislation, passed in response to the advice of the Royal Commission presided over by Sir Henry Willink, was not so successful. It drove betting off the streets, where it was illegal and strained the police, but the House of Commons was so intent on making 'betting shops' as sad as possible, in order not to deprave the young, that they ended up more like undertakers' premises. The gaming sections, designed to purify this occupation and remove the pecuniary profit of third parties, did not prove strong enough, and Jim Callaghan later had my support and encouragement in bringing in fresh legislation.

The three most important Acts I put through Parliament in these years have still to be mentioned. First in point of time was the Street Offences Act 1959, which took account of the recommendations of the Wolfenden Committee in so far as these related to prostitution. The Act substantially increased the penalties for soliciting, with imprisonment as a possible penalty for repeated offences, and increased the maximum prison sentence for those convicted of living on the immoral earnings of prostitutes. I was moved to take such action by the condition of the streets around Mayfair and Piccadilly which were literally crowded out with girls touting for clients. This gave a very unhealthy look to the centre of our capital city. But my position in clearing up this state of affairs was made peculiarly difficult by the fact that I was related to Josephine Butler, the great social reformer who in 1870 had founded the Association for Moral and Social Hygiene of which I was a Vice-President. It had been her cardinal principle that in matters of prostitution the woman is not alone responsible and must not be the target of punitive action; the responsibility of the man must be established. I pointed out to the Association that there were provisions in my Bill against pimps, but could not convince them, as the Commissioner of the Metropolitan Police had convinced me, that whereas the police knew and could trace the women who had regular abodes, they simply could not identify the men, who were unknown, transitory and very often from out of town. Alas, the Association for Moral and Social Hygiene called for my resignation from its ranks. I was sorry to have to comply, for I had great admiration for the saintly and courageous career of Josephine Butler. But I consoled myself with the knowledge that the Act achieved in a very short period exactly what it set out to do—not, of course, to end vice, but to make it no longer a shameful and open nuisance in the life of a great city. Between 16th August, when the Act came into operation, and 31st December 1959, the number of convictions in the metropolitan district for the offence of loitering and soliciting was less than 10 per cent of what it had been in the same period a year earlier. The streets were in fact cleared.

The second decisive measure of this period was the Charities Act 1960, which modernized the administration of charity law. This was the first major legislation on the subject for almost a hundred years, and it was designed to deal with the novel situation charities had been presented with by the advent of the Welfare State. In many instances their primary objects had been overtaken by statutory services; yet the importance of their work in promoting social progress through voluntary action was as great as ever. The problems arising from this situation had been sympathetically considered by the Nathan Committee which reported in 1952, but the Committee's proposals for some control of charities by central or local authorities had been, I think rightly, rejected by my predecessor in 1955. This did not seem to me to rule out other recommendations for change. Accordingly we swept the statute book clean of all the charity legislation since 1853 and of other enactments relating to mortmain which dated back to the sixteenth century. One modern consolidated measure was put in their place which has given the Charity Commission the responsibility to assist charities but without power to administer them. This assistance is of three types. First, free advice is given to trustees of charities, particularly regarding schemes to modify their trusts and purposes when necessary. Secondly, a central register is maintained, thus not only ensuring that the institutions so registered are recognized as charities both in fact and in law, but also facilitating reduction in the degree of overlap between individual charities' objectives. Thirdly, a greater measure of voluntary co-operation between charities and State services is encouraged —and indeed achieved. All this has reflected great credit on the Charity Commissioners.

The last and by far the most controversial of the measures for which I took responsibility as Home Secretary was the Commonwealth Immigrants Act 1962. In view of all that has happened since, it is necessary to see this Act in its true historical perspective. For decades, many thousands of West Indians, lacking opportunity, jobs and money at home, had emigrated to the United States. In 1952 Congress virtually blocked this channel when it passed the McCarran-Walter Immigration Act. Other countries on the American mainland were also operating immigration restrictions. Britain alone provided an open door for West Indians, as for all other Commonwealth peoples. We did so because we believed in the motto 'Civis Britannicus sum'— that is to say, because the historic right of every Commonwealth subject, regardless of race or colour, freely to enter and stay in Britain was prized as one of the things which helped to bind us together. When public opinion on the issue was tested by the Gallup Poll as late as the summer of 1961, 21 per cent of people in this country still favoured the continuation of unrestricted entry. But by that date more than three times as many—67 per cent—advocated the imposition of some restrictions. The motives of this decisive majority were doubtless mixed, and not all were honourable; but in the circumstances of 1961 it was natural even for the liberal-minded to believe that immigrants could be integrated into our community with tolerance and without friction only if the potential size of the social difficulties involved was reduced.

Its size was the essence of the problem. The number of Commonwealth immigrants from the under-developed countries—still mainly from the West Indies, but also from India and Pakistan, and to a lesser extent Africa and elsewhere—rose from 21,000 in 1959 to 58,000 in 1960 and to 136,000 in 1961. In certain fields of employment, notably public transport and the hospital service, the immigrants had made a most valuable contribution to our labour force; but it was, to put it mildly, questionable whether we should be able to absorb largely unskilled immigrant labour in such huge and uncontrolled numbers. Moreover they were concentrated in particular areas of London and a few big provincial cities, where a great influx of newcomers inevitably imposed strains on local services and even provoked isolated anti-racial manifestations. As Home Secretary I had been gravely troubled by the Notting Hill riots in 1958, and I cannot praise too highly the determined action of the Judiciary in the person of Mr. Justice Salmon who pronounced the most stringent sentences on the racist trouble-makers. But whilst disturbances on this scale did not recur, I was by 1961 persuaded that the rise of racial tension could be avoided only if it were anticipated. This in essence was the argument for the Commonwealth Immigrants Bill which controlled entry by a system of labour permits that in practice approximately halved the rate of net immigration.

It is a fact of history that the Labour Opposition, led by Hugh Gaitskell, launched the most infuriated attack on the Bill which they labelled as cruel and brutal anti-colour legislation. Indeed had they persisted through the committee stage, which was taken on the floor of the House, we might not, in the view of Philip Allen (now head of the Office), have got the measure through at all. It is also a fact of history that when the general election came in 1964 the Labour party manifesto promised to retain immigration control and that in the following year the new Labour government, having turned a complete somersault, intensified the restrictions their predecessors had introduced. To ardent idealists this appeared a betrayal of principle; to hostile polemicists it provided grist for the mill. But to me it gave a ray of hope. Would not the two major parties, by drawing closer together in espousing the twin policies of control and integration, make it more difficult for the candidates of either to exploit colour problems for political advantage? It may be less easy to entertain this hope today. But I do so—not only for the sake of the immigrants themselves, but for the sake of the nation's political health.

CHAPTER TEN

LARGE ELEPHANT

M Y LAST years in the House of Commons were devoted increasingly, and at the end almost exclusively, to overseas policy. Although I remained at the Home Office until July 1962, I had already in March taken on responsibility for Central African affairs. Sir Charles Cunningham, the head of the Office, regarded it as quite natural for the Home Secretary to be given this 'residual' problem. I found his view rather touching, even inspiring. The problem involved the livelihood and liberty, the expectations and emotions, of nine million people, governed under what was at one and the same time the most ambitious and the most anomalous of the constitutional improvisations of our rapidly evolving Commonwealth. This improvisation, dating from 1953, had tied together the self-governing settlers' colony of Southern Rhodesia with the two African protectorates of Northern Rhodesia and Nyasaland. The arguments for Federation were primarily economic and, on that level, cogent. It could scarcely be disputed that the economies of the three countries were complementary, that the potentialities of the larger unit made it more credit-worthy and attractive to external capital, or that a common market was highly desirable for the development of the region as a whole. Remarkable economic advance did in fact take place under Federation—of which the great Kariba Dam was an outstanding symbol and the 23 per cent increase in the real value of African wages a representative statistic. Yet when the Monckton Commission published its review of Central Africa in 1960, it reported that sincere and long-standing opposition to Federation among Africans, particularly in the northern territories, remained widespread and had become 'almost pathological'. In the colourful phrase used by Monckton's biographer, it was 'a matter of indifference to them that the cage in which they were trapped was gilded'.

Though as a senior Minister I obviously accepted collective responsibility, I should make it plain that I never supported the Monckton Commission's appointment. The arguments which persuaded the government were largely couched in terms of our own domestic politics: that is to say, it was held to be for the good of the Federation if Church and middle-of-the-road opinion at home could be reassured by a dispassionate and widely-based inquiry, and if the Labour party could be dissuaded meanwhile from any firm commitment to break it up. In fact, a comprehensive inquiry followed by maximum publicity was bound to highlight, without solving, the Federation's central political dilemma. This dilemma lay in two related phenomena. First, the 'plural' nature of its racial composition—an overwhelming African majority, small Asian and Coloured communities, and a very sizable body of Europeans upon whose capital, skill and enterprise, economic development largely depended. Secondly, the marked disparity that existed between the ratio of Europeans to Africans in each of the three territories—in Southern Rhodesia 1 to 13, in Northern Rhodesia 1 to 30, in Nyasaland 1 to 300. It was legitimate in 1953 to hope that Africans' suspicion of the Federal idea might evaporate if, against a background of rising prosperity, room was given to them to play their parts in the territorial and Federal governments. Indeed, the exalted concept of a partnership within a multi-racial community was sincerely held up not only as a moral idea and a Commonwealth necessity, but as a counter to the beguilements of Communism. By 1960, however, these hopes, though not extinguished, had grown dim. With the nationalist tide coming in, and independence being given or promised to more and more African countries, it began to appear to Africans, in Nyasaland particularly but also in Northern Rhodesia, that only the Federal Constitution stood between them and the form of freedom accorded to their fellows elsewhere on the continent. In these circumstances, it was predictable that the issue of secession from the Federation should have loomed so large in relation to the Monckton Commission's composition, remit and report. Its conclusion on this subject—

namely, that if the U.K. government said it would in principle permit a right to secede, this would actually discourage extremism and secure a fair trial for some new form of association —was well-intentioned; but in practice it cut the ground from under our feet.

When Lord Birkenhead came to write Monckton's biography, he was told by Sir Alec Home that after the Monckton recommendations had failed to gain acceptance 'Home abandoned all hope for the Federation and considered it doomed'. My memory is somewhat different. I recall that, during the short period when I was considering the Prime Minister's offer, I went to see Alec at the Foreign Office and felt much comforted by his intense conviction that I should accept and by his expressed hope that there was still at least a chance of saving something from the Federation. Harold Macmillan himself had painted an even rosier picture. It had proved increasingly impossible, he told me, to run a co-ordinated policy for Central Africa when two of the territories concerned were the responsibility of the Colonial Office and one of the Commonwealth Relations Office. The P.M. recalled that he himself had made his name after being 'put out on a limb' during the war as Minister Resident in Northern Africa, and implied that I could do the same in Central Africa. Personally I inclined to Alec's more cautious view. It seemed rather simple to suppose that there were any runs to be made. It occurred to many commentators that there was a reputation to be lost. However, I accepted out of a sense of duty and also, I think, out of a sense of adventure.

My appointment was well received by the Federal government and by public opinion at home. The new Central African Office began its Whitehall career on 19th March, and on 8th May I was ready to make my first statement to the House of Commons. Nine months had already passed since the Malawi Congress Party, led by Dr. Hastings Banda, had won an overwhelming victory under the new Nyasaland Constitution, and its protagonists had continually claimed that this was in effect a mandate for secession. I therefore thought it prudent to acknowledge their unpreparedness to remain 'in the present Federation', but carefully added that before any firm conclusion was reached there should be a full examination both of the

GHANA INDEPENDENCE CELEBRATIONS: THE AUTHOR WITH
PRINCESS MARINA, DUCHESS OF KENT

OCTOBER 21, 1959.
AFTER THEIR WEDDING:
THE AUTHOR
WITH MOLLIE

1960 AT STANSTEAD

consequences of a withdrawal for Nyasaland 'and also of possible forms of association with the other two territories'. I added that it remained the government's view that there were great advantages for all the peoples of Central Africa in such continued association. My purpose in making this statement was twofold. First, to show the Federal government the realities of the situation before I arrived in Africa, instead of waiting till I appeared to be subjected to pressures on the spot and then to lose height. Secondly, to keep the situation sufficiently open to enable some kind of union between the three states, particularly on the economic side, to be created if that proved at all possible.

My wife and I were welcomed at Salisbury airport by a nationalist demonstration designed to convince me that the end of the Federation (of which the first sign would be the secession of Nyasaland) was inevitable. I certainly did not get this advice from the central government who were still as optimistic of saving their bacon as I was. The Federal Cabinet, under Sir Roy Welensky, met in a small long upper room (ανωγεον) in the middle of Salisbury. Outside the window fluttered a Union Jack, a sight no longer to be seen in that capital. I watched it with nostalgia and a hope that it might last. My first *rencontres*, with Sir Edgar Whitehead's territorial government as with the Federal government, were met with friendliness, though not without strong warnings. I then left for Zomba to stay with the Governor of Nyasaland, Sir Glyn Jones.

Hardly had we arrived at Government House than he informed me that Dr. Banda had already had a governmental assurance that the right of secession would be granted to his country. Neither the Governor nor I subsequently mentioned this to Banda. But Sir Roy Welensky is right in his memoirs to show some sympathy with my finding this situation an awkward one. Jones warned me that we would get nowhere if Dr. Banda were provoked into a fury. We therefore arranged that the Governor should hold a handkerchief in his hand and, if he were to raise it to his face, I should check my course and lay off the pressure. In the event Jones blew his nose only once and I left Banda with a friendly impression. He agreed to my proposal for an examination of the consequences of the secession, and I invited him to London shortly for further talks on the territory's future. Jones advised me that I could not do less, unless I wanted to arouse a country which was almost totally African to a state of rebellion. The Europeans then amounted to a few thousands: businessmen at Blantyre, the tea planters and other settlers, and a few important and valuable civil servants. As seen from the air, the country was covered with small huts, shacks and tents of the African natives—and what a beautiful country it is with its great lake and mountains and rolling downland.

When we got back to Salisbury, having also visited and held discussions in Lusaka, the press releases assured me a very hard reception from the Federal Cabinet. I had, however, made clear that it was my intention, or at least hope, to create a constructive solution for the Federation. So the result, after much indoor fireworks, was that Welensky issued the following press statement which showed that I had not only done the right things by Nyasaland but had so far kept the Federal government with me:

'The Federal government have completed their talks with the Secretary of State, Mr. R. A. Butler, and my colleagues and I are glad to have had the opportunity for full and frank discussions on a wide range of subjects.

'The Federal government will co-operate to the full with the committee of advisers the Secretary of State proposes to appoint to investigate the economic effects on Nyasaland which would result were the territory to secede from the Federation, and the future form of association between Northern Rhodesia and Southern Rhodesia.

'We have long been concerned that the harm to Nyasaland which would stem from secession has not been fully appreciated; apart from obligations to the civil service and the problem of the apportionment of the national debt, it is not generally realized that another source would have to be found to finance over 50 per cent of Nyasaland's recurrent expenditure.

'For some time, therefore, the Federal government have urged the government of Great Britain to make a full examination of what the consequences of the secession of

Nyasaland would be and we welcome the Secretary of State's decision to have this examination made.

'The Federal government is glad to note the statement made by Mr. Butler, that no decision has been made other than to undertake an appraisal of the situation by means of a committee of advisers.'

The following eyewitness description of the episode was sent to me:

'Sir Roy Welensky held a short press conference at 10.30 a.m. on the 26th. It was very fully covered by television, film and radio, and about forty correspondents were present. Sir Roy started by issuing the short statement which precedes this. He prefaced this statement by the remark that he had not intended to give a press conference but had been urged to do so by the press.

'In answer to questions Sir Roy expressed considerable doubts as to whether a purely economic association could work effectively and expressed the view that such an association would have to be accompanied by political ties of one form or another. He said that he would be willing to continue to serve any Federation in a political capacity, but not in either a purely economic capacity or any single territory.

'He repeated on several occasions his willingness to consider any reasonable suggestions for an adjustment of the Federation and expressed the view that the Secretary of State's visit had achieved a great deal of good. He said that the Secretary of State, in his view, possessed one of the best minds in H.M.G. and that his seniority and wisdom had been of great assistance. He said that there were no easy solutions to the problems involved but that if anyone could find a reasonable solution it was likely to be Mr. Butler.

'On being asked whether relations as a whole with H.M.G. had improved as a result of the visit, he stated that he had for a long time been propagating the idea of one Minister being in charge of the Federation and in this sense he was extremely glad that this had now happened. . . .

'The Prime Minister was in a very affable mood and the tenor of the whole occasion was one of approval for the

appointment of Mr. Butler and for the results of his visit as a
whole. He expressed his intention of full co-operation in every
way with the advisers whom the Secretary of State intends to
appoint.'

I had spent much of my Ministerial and early experience
visiting India or handling Indian affairs, and I was now fascinated
and excited to smell the smells and listen to the sounds of the
African continent. I was impressed with the comparative
inhospitality of the soil and, except in Nyasaland, by the
sparseness of the population. I found a fundamental difference
with India largely due to the difference in time, centuries as
opposed to years, for which in some parts of Central Africa the
native population with their culture had been *in situ*. We
enjoyed the quiet and dignity of Government House, Salisbury,
and the welcome given us by the Dalhousies. I was also pleased
to receive the following telegram from Governor Jones in
Zomba, particularly its opening metaphor:

'You will wish to know first reactions to your visit conveyed to me from several sources.

'African leaders are thoroughly satisfied because they consider you to be a person whom they can trust and also to be
a wise administrator. We understand that you have been
referred to as NJOBVU YEIKURO. This literally means "large
elephant" but the implied meaning is "sagacious beast". The
elephant is a beast of honour locally and appears as a symbol
of chieftainship and hence wisdom in many parts of Africa,
including Barotseland. Here the title is definitely an honourable one.

'So far as the general European reaction is concerned you
have given them some comfort. They begin to accept that
Nyasaland must secede but feel that the British government
will negotiate for them satisfactory safeguards such as a Bill
of Rights and they still hope for an alternative form of
economic association.

'I do not consider you need feel anxiety on the score that
you have not been tough enough with Banda. As you know,
I and my advisers feel that there is only one course that
Britain can take if bloodshed is to be avoided in Nyasaland.

That course must be orderly although the brakes can be only lightly applied. You are holding the position until midsummer. You have not given way to extravagant and immediate demands and you have succeeded in influencing Banda to keep his public utterances fairly moderate for the time being. I therefore think that you are entitled to be satisfied that you have achieved some considerable success in holding a most difficult situation in Nyasaland. . . .

"MOVE UP, MALCOLM, RAB'S MAKING A HURRIED ASCENT, TOO!"

'Banda has just been to see me and sends you his best wishes. I have impressed on him the need both to give very serious attention to your economic enquiry and also to ensure that he says when he gets to England things which will inspire confidence in his sense of responsibility.'

The *Rhodesia Herald* summed up on 28th May:

'So far he has not put a foot wrong. . . . His public utterances have been chosen with extraordinary care.

'The possible lines on which he is thinking are—
(1) Federation should be prescribed in a form stronger than that of a mere economic union;
(2) that a different relationship must be established between the two Rhodesias on the one hand and Nyasaland on the other.'

I thus ended the first round without having lost too much breath or taken too much punishment. The credit for this belongs to a large extent to Sir Glyn Jones and Sir Evelyn Hone, the quite exceptionally efficient Governors of the two northern territories, and to the High Commissioner in Salisbury, Lord Alport. It was indeed a fortunate stroke of fate that had caused 'Cub' Alport's path and mine to cross once again, after our early association in the Conservative Political Centre, and enabled my wife and myself to enjoy the hospitality of Mirimba. The four of us had met in England so as to prepare, for our own guidance and that of the British government, what we called 'the composite approach'. This was designed not to leave any one territory out on a limb—creating an explosion in Northern Rhodesia, for example, because I had gone too far in Nyasaland —and to keep the territories as far as possible together, economically if not politically. I was also stoutly supported in this work by my two principal civil servants, Mark Tennant and Duncan Watson. Our little Central African Office was at Gwyddyr House, Whitehall, and there I gathered together an able collection of advisers, principally from the Colonial and Commonwealth Offices. Tennant and Watson themselves had remarkable capacities for work and in all my long experience of government office I never benefited from better briefs.

In July my advisory team assembled in Salisbury, travelled the Federation for three weeks, and set about drafting a report with rare gusto. The idea of appointing this small posse sprang from the hope that we might plan some association between Nyasaland and the Rhodesias. For chairman of this body, I had begun by thinking of Sir James Robertson, first Governor-General of Nigeria, or of Lord Howick. I had registered with regret that it would be impossible to wean my old friend Burke Trend from the government machine. Then Alec Home most nobly

offered to release Sir Roger Stevens from the Foreign Office. To
him I added Arthur Brown, Professor of Economics at Leeds,
and David Scott, the Deputy High Commissioner at Salisbury,
a man of outstanding ability, and as constitutional adviser was
lucky enough to secure Major-General Sir Ralph Hone. Looking
back, I feel I may not have paid enough tribute to this distinguished body of men. Roger Stevens was decidedly the best the
Foreign Office could provide, and Brown's lucid and imaginative plan for an African Common Market was my constant
study. Yet such constructive ideas were, alas, engulfed in the
torrent of racial nationalism. Although I could not accept
my advisers' advice, this is no reflection upon their idealism,
industry or contribution. They performed an invaluable service
in keeping the atmosphere hopeful in 1962. And though the
more constructive hopes were disappointed, their report,
particularly with its documentation notably on Nyasaland, was
of the greatest assistance when it came to arranging an orderly
winding up of the Federation.

Meanwhile Dr. Banda had visited me in London, and pronounced himself satisfied with my proposal that there should
be a Nyasaland Constitutional Conference in November. Banda
has proved, as I expected, quite one of the most stable rulers on
the African continent. As has been seen, he does not brook
opposition lightly. He is determined and loyal to his friends.
His long residence in London had accustomed him to trusting
the British word, and I returned him 'the right side up' to his
expectant country. I did not want to hurry Nyasaland too much
for fear of losing the links which I desired to keep between
Northern and Southern Rhodesia. That is why I resisted any
early plan to replace the Federation, and in this respect I
differed both from the High Commissioner, Lord Alport, and
from the team of four advisers. The former recommended, in a
very valuable and full document, which is referred to in his
book *The Sudden Assignment*, what amounted to a Transition
government for a five-year period. The latter recommended a
'Commission' to take the place of the Federal government. At
that stage I preferred to stall on the High Commissioner's plan
and to put my doubts to Sir Roger Stevens so that he could take
account of them before submitting his final report at a later date.

I have done no more than summarize the advice given me in
August. But my view was that the general disruption it could
cause would actually be more than what actually occurred in
the end, that is to say dissolution.

I set out my attitude in a personal letter to Alport on 23rd
August:

'I have hitherto only acknowledged your long letter
describing your ideas on a transitional plan. . . . I have now
had some limited opportunity of conference with the
Advisers. I do not propose to regard their present ideas as
final. Nor would they wish me to do so.

'There is one similarity between your ideas and theirs,
namely that you both consider that the present Federation
should come to an end. You replace the present regime with
a Transitional Council and they with a High Commission (as
I call it).

'My preliminary talks with the Prime Minister confirm my
first reaction, namely that H.M.G. cannot envisage any action
which could be interpreted as shooting the Federal government dead. You refer to Edgar Whitehead's warning that
Welensky might "do a Samson". While we must not give way
to threats we must respect the very strong feelings of the
Federal Ministers in favour of the retention of a positive
association of at least North and South Rhodesia.

'I can see the force of my Advisers' argument that the
Federal Prime Minister and his friends should be brought
along to see the realities of the situation in N. Rhodesia; and
that this should be done in such a way that the facts speak for
themselves and that H.M.G. does not appear unilaterally to
bring to an end the euphoria under which they are living.

'The Advisers are keen that a North and South Rhodesian
Conference should be held early in 1963 to achieve this
purpose. I have not made up my mind on this, but I see the
force of their arguments. What I am not prepared to do at
present is to make up my mind as to future action. I am not
prepared at present to chart action beyond November, when
we have agreed to hold the Nyasaland Conference. I must see
and gauge the results of the N. Rhodesian elections.

'My own personal inclination is that any association which can be achieved should retain external affairs and defence. Both the Advisers and you yourself recommend splitting defence. I have asked Stevens to look further into this, and to obtain guidance in Whitehall.

'I think it would be a good thing if the Advisers could see a little more of the Federal Ministers. They are fully seized of the position as seen from Lusaka and there is not much to add on Nyasaland. During the next weeks and months prior to the end of October let us continue to exchange views.

'Owing to the undoubted pain involved in passing from the present Federal regime to a new one, my government colleagues and the party would probably be less worried by a Transitional Plan, than would business, the Africans and Whitehead. The latter want an early solution.

'I will mull over the question whether we aim at a transitional period or not. This raises the question whether the Federal government would remain alive during the transitional period. Please understand that I realize, whether the Federal government remains in existence or not, that an early decision must be accepted by all concerned including Federal Ministers, that a new chapter is being opened and a new form of association sought. Welensky has indicated that he will look at fresh ideas. If he does he should be encouraged, if he doesn't it makes H.M.G.'s moral position stronger in eventually taking a line without his full agreement.

'Up to now I have not dealt with the eventuality in which both units North and South opt for secession. We would have to deal with such a situation if it arose.

'Finally, you may be interested in my attitude towards Welensky's visit next month. Subject to any comments you may make, I would propose:

(a) to prepare him for a statement on Nyasaland's secession in November:

(b) to throw a fly over him about the best way of seeking to preserve some form of association between North and South. Here I should warn him of what I believe Kaunda's reaction will be. This is about as far as I can go, simply adding that a further plotting of ideas cannot take place till after the N. Rhodesian elections.

'Do you yourself think I can go further than this beyond asking Welensky what his constructive proposals are? If I warn him of the likely African reaction I believe I shall have preserved my integrity and this is vital.'

Roy Welensky has been kind enough to pay me a number of tributes in his book *4000 Days*. We had met one another first in 1958, in company with Sir Stephen Courtauld and his wife, benefactors of the art and culture of Rhodesia. Roy has a warm heart for his friends and his pugnacity concealed a wide human understanding. But his political range was more limited. He represented very adequately in the Rhodesian Parliament the small non-commissioned officers of the Copper Belt in Bulawayo and in the railway yards at Umtali. They did not want changes. They did not welcome the Africans coming to the front. Neither did he. Though never tiring of recounting how, when a lad, he 'swam bare-arsed in the Makabusi with the piccanins', he was bored with Africans. This was one reason why the Federation never matched in the political sphere its otherwise grand achievements, social and economic. Roy was a very considerable boxer in his earlier days. His footwork and his eyes remained quick. Many a punch landed on me, but then I felt the benison of the boxing glove. He would always answer to the bell and retire to his corner when the round was over. By September of 1962 he had in himself accepted the inevitability of Nyasaland's secession. But he still came back for a further round in December. He had a great sense of humour, robust and salty. When he attended the Commonwealth Prime Ministers' Conference in 1962 he said: 'Fortunately we have a fine juicy rabbit for the African States to sniff up, that is the Common Market. If there were no Common Market, I would be the rabbit.' Later on the rabbit turned out to be Southern Rhodesia, where in my time Sir Edgar Whitehead was struggling with United Nations resolutions. Roy and he were not always on good terms. I remember Roy saying of Edgar, before Edgar's defeat by Winston Field, 'He has as much chance of being elected as a snowball in Beira.'

Roy Welensky may be described as a natural statesman. He had not had the benefits of prolonged or profound training or education for the task, but he possessed an innate capacity to command men and earned the respect of his Cabinet colleagues —in particular Julian Greenfield, a man with a good legalistic brain, Malcolm Barrow, an able Home Minister, and 'Pop' Caldicott, a sound Finance Minister. He had a combative power of speech and frequently put his case with great effect to the Federal Parliament. Perhaps too often he painted the British government as the arch-enemy and creator of all confusion. It was no good trying to do business with Roy in a hurry and this was the mistake made by Harold Macmillan's tour organizers in 1960 when they did not give him sufficient time in Salisbury. Quite apart from the mistake of short interviews, Roy did not appreciate the Whitehall-drafted telegrams which rained in on him at the time of the Monckton Commission's report. These were not the type of missives that his mind readily feasted upon.

Following my diagnosis I always gave Roy plenty of time, and this was especially so when he came for a weekend to Stanstead in September 1962. This was one of the few occasions when I was able to extract from him his constructive proposals to meet the situation. Usually in public postures or conferences he kept up his guard like a boxer and confined himself to attacking the British government. My advisers and Lord Alport—who himself never curried favour with Roy and had many blows aimed at him, most of which he succeeded in parrying—got quite understandably tired of these attacks. I remained stoical. What emerged at Stanstead was that he would like to see a Union of the two Rhodesias, leaving defence and foreign affairs to the Union, the other subjects to go to the States. He would not accept an economic union, on which *The Times* had published a leading article. He must have a political content to the Union. As I have said, Professor Brown, the chief economic adviser, produced a masterly plan for an African Common Market, but neither this nor Roy's idea of a Union saw the light of day owing to the depth of racial feeling between Northern and Southern Rhodesia. If Southern Rhodesia had, under Whitehead or Field, adopted a liberal constitution which gave a hope of Africans in the government, the whole story of an economic or indeed political Union between the Rhodesias would have been different.

Roy Welensky also confessed to me at Stanstead that he would not mind retiring from public life, if he could find a successor. He mentioned the continuing effects of his wife's illness, and said that he had really had enough. The next three months were to rain a succession of blows upon his head. The elections in Northern Rhodesia resulted in the formation of a new Executive Council involving a coalition between the two African nationalist parties under Dr. Kenneth Kaunda and Mr. Harry Nkumbula. In the Southern Rhodesia elections in December, a clear-cut victory was won by the Rhodesian Front, which was not committed to Federation and was widely characterized as a 'White supremacy' party. Meanwhile the Nyasaland Conference which met in London from 12th to 23rd November moved to a smooth and unanimous conclusion which paved the way for Dr. Banda to become Prime Minister. It created a form of internal self-government, and included a Bill of Rights to safeguard the interests of the Europeans. Thus, of the four governments concerned in Africa itself, only one—that of the Federation, under Sir Roy Welensky—was any more in the hands of the United Federal Party and desirous of maintaining the federal association. The secession of Nyasaland was now indeed inevitable, and I had great difficulty in holding a statement conceding secession until 19th December, a short time before my second visit to the Federation. I used the expression that 'we were not to be put off our duty to Nyasaland'. The attempts to put me off were comparatively mild in the Commons, but very severe both in the Lords and in a special two-day session of the Rhodesian Parliament which Welensky called. The Federal Prime Minister quoted pledges given by Lords Swinton and Chandos at the inauguration of the Federation in 1953. These were said to be to the effect that the Federation could not be disbanded, for example by granting the right of secession, without the consent of the units of the Federation. Lord Malvern, who flew back specially for the Lords debate, made a characteristic speech accusing the British of betrayal and of paying more attention to 'a Messiah', that is Banda, than to the white population. Lords Salisbury, Chandos and Boyd were concerned and certain voices, including Lord Salisbury's, were raised encouraging me to salvage what I could for the future by means of association between the two Rhodesias. The press next day reported almost entirely the attacks on the government and not the considered defence of the Lord Chancellor that the Imperial Parliament had a perfect right to legislate for the Federation if it so wished. Roy's onslaughts in Salisbury were very fierce and accused us of 'ratting' and 'treachery'.

Accordingly, before leaving for my second visit to the Federation, I launched with the Lord Chancellor the preparation of a White Paper refuting the attacks made upon the government for alleged breach of pledges given in 1953. The White Paper continued to be drafted while I was in Africa from the third week of January to early February 1963. What emerged in short was that no pledge in the literal form expressed by Sir Roy Welensky could be established. There had arisen in 1953 a series of discussions opened by a Mr. Eastwood about the credit of the Federation and the holding of a Review Conference which was envisaged for 1960. Oliver Lyttelton (now Lord Chandos) said then that the Constitution could not be liquidated at such a conference unless all four governments were agreed, to which Mr. Greenfield, later Federal Minister of Justice, added a fifth government—the United Kingdom. He further said that in his view the fifth government, the United Kingdom, having created the Federation, could terminate its existence. This last point is made clear by Article 29 (7) of the Constitution of the Federation which provides that 'nothing in this Constitution shall affect any power to make laws for the Federation or any of the Territories conferred on Her Majesty by any Act of the Parliament of the United Kingdom'. This really ended the juridical, though not the political, controversy.

My visit to the Federation passed off very quietly. I was, of course, the conquering hero in Nyasaland but had some difficulty in holding the Kaunda supporters in Lusaka, who naturally wished to obtain the right of secession for themselves. Mr. Nkumbula told the press that I had promised such a right and this infuriated the Federal government. But I was able to explain that the report was untrue. I carried with me during my second visit to the Federation a note advising me that I would have to choose between an initiative such as my advisers under Sir Roger Stevens and the High Commissioner had suggested, or leave the units, that is the territorial governments, to make the running. Now I had decided in August and September that I would not set up a Commission or interim government alternative to the Federation. This seemed to me a course which would alienate and indeed exacerbate the Federal Cabinet and all the territorial governments. During my visit I therefore worked patiently away at finding links between the units and in particular between Northern and Southern Rhodesia. I purposely did not make public speeches and my most useful talks were with Roy at his own home outside Salisbury. He sat in his shirt sleeves slumped in an armchair. Despite his previous furies he was calm and courteous. He told me of his farming ambitions and his charming wife fed us with tea. During all my time as Minister for Central Africa Roy avoided putting forward constructive ideas in public. I went on three occasions to his home and he did say again that he would support a political nexus between Northern and Southern Rhodesia, reserving to the centre defence and foreign affairs. But I never got him to go further than this or to acknowledge the deep sense of nationhood springing up in Northern Rhodesia. Before I left for home I gave a press conference on 2nd February, in which I explained that my whole time had been taken up with private political discussions. I wanted to find for those who had made Central Africa their 'home' some sense of certainty. How little any statesman has succeeded in finding 'certainty'!

In March I was to be visited in London by a deputation from the Federal Government, a mission led by Kaunda from Northern Rhodesia, and the representatives of Southern Rhodesia. The latter were to arrive on 21st March, the Northern Rhodesians on 24th, and the Federal Ministers, Greenfield, Caldicott and two Parliamentary Secretaries Lewanika and Chipunza, headed by Sir Roy, on the 26th. I had informed Parliament that the object of the talks was to arrange a future association between the territories. I had in mind a conference in London or in Salisbury. I found these few days in March some of the most laborious and painful of my career. At my first meeting with the Northern Rhodesians they all marched out of the room saying they would consider no association until they had been granted the right of secession and assumed their independence. The Southern Rhodesians similarly demanded independence. I made it clear that until there was an end to discrimination by a repeal of the Land Apportionment Act, until there was a blocking third of Africans in the legislature to deal with attempts to reform the Constitution, and until there was an enlargement of the A Roll, independence would be impossible, since there would be no outlook of or for a future African government.

On the 28th my government colleagues and I had a re-appraisal of the situation assisted by the Governor and Deputy Governor of Northern Rhodesia. We decided that the situation could not be held without conceding the request for secession. The galling part was that, so frenzied were they to set up the State of Zambia, that they gave little or no hope for association with their neighbours; certainly the idea of a political nexus with Southern Rhodesia was excluded. All this led to a most painful interview with Sir Roy and his Ministers on the 29th. He says in his memoirs that I looked grey. I certainly felt it. This was in fact the end of the Federation which had been built up with such high hopes since 1953. I informed Sir Roy that I would be making a press statement and a broadcast that same evening. I would start by adhering to our aim of an association between the territories. I would state that we had come to the conclusion that no territory could be kept in the Federation against its will and thus that any territory must be allowed to secede if it so wished. We looked forward to a conference preferably in Africa to work out the new relationship. I ended: 'I realize the importance to you, Sir Roy, of what I have just said. I assure you that it has cost me and my colleagues a great effort to arrive at this decision.' Roy, who was by now boiling, asked me to send an immediate message to the Prime Minister refusing Macmillan's invitation to lunch for himself and his Ministers 'since the food would choke them'. After a fruitless discussion of Barotseland and a loyal outburst by Caldicott in support of his chief, the meeting came to an abrupt and gloomy end.

At the conclusion of his book Roy Welensky said that on

thinking it over he did not feel 'harsh or bitter' about me. He was to carry forward this magnanimity during the Victoria Falls Conference of June–July 1963 to which in his book he makes hardly any reference, and which in its turn conducted the operation of winding up the Federation with dignity.

After the drama in March the question remained as to whether a conference should be held to establish new links, or whether a major reunion should be brought about which would at one and the same time end the Federation as it existed and endeavour to establish relations between the independent territories. Northern Rhodesia seemed so absolutely determined on independence that the latter course began to emerge as the most appropriate. The task of statesmanship was thus to bring the four governments concerned to the conference table. Winston Field, who became a friend and whose untimely demission of office and later demise I so much regret, for long refused to attend a conference. He wished, as a prior condition, to have a guarantee of the independence of Southern Rhodesia. But the same facts stared me in the face then as confronted the Labour government later: to give independence to an administration unprepared to open multiracial paths to government is contrary both to British tradition and to Commonwealth unity. Field subsequently claimed that I had actually offered him independence before the Victoria Falls Conference opened, and the story is reproduced, with embellishments from Ian Smith, in Kenneth Young's book *Rhodesia and Independence*. The story is not accurate. I know perfectly well that I did not give the Southern Rhodesians an assurance of independence, and so does Sir Roy Welensky. On the contrary, I *asked* for assurances in terms which the Southern Rhodesian Prime Minister was unable to accept. In the end, and almost literally at the end, Winston Field agreed to come to the conference. Nyasaland sent official representatives, and Sir Evelyn Hone came with a bevy of Northern Rhodesian politicians. Finally, the lion of the piece, Sir Roy, intimated that he and some of his Ministers would attend in order that the affairs of the Federation, including the future of the debt and of the public servants, might be fairly settled.

The *Rhodesia Herald* of 29th June reported that my 'feat' in

FRACHADIL, MULL, WITH RHUM IN THE BACKGROUND
(from an oil painting by the author)

WITH MOLLIE, HER
DAUGHTER SUSIE, AND
SOME GRANDCHILDREN

1963 MR. HAROLD MACMILL

MAY 1962 IN SALISBURY, RHODESIA, WITH (*above*) SIR ROY WELENSKY, AND (*below*) LORD ALPORT (BRITISH HIGH COMMISSIONER) AND AFRICAN CHIEFS

bringing all the delegates to agree immediately to the broad
principle that the Federation should transfer its powers to the
territorial governments 'in an orderly and speedy manner' had
astounded observers at the conference. Its report went on:

'Undoubtedly the tremendous amount of quiet ground-
work put in by Mr. Butler in the past forty-eight hours has
brought this about. A month ago the Falls Conference was
regarded as impossible. First with Mr. Field, then with the
Northern Rhodesian leaders, and finally with a highly
suspicious and sensitive Sir Roy Welensky, Mr. Butler has
exercised his extraordinary charm and logic to produce this
result within an hour of the conference opening.

'Mr. Butler is believed to have inferred that while discussion
should range widely, rules for debate will include keeping to
the point. This is an obvious hint that territories must mind
their own business and keep to the business in hand—a
restriction on possible trespass by one territorial politician
into the politics of another territory.

'Sir Roy, who is reported to have spoken in a genial fashion,
although he has described the occasion as "melancholy", was
the first on his feet after Mr. Butler.

'The subtle moulding influence of Mr. Butler appeared to
show itself again because the five speakers who followed him
all followed broadly the same line in spite of their varied
standpoints.

'After Sir Roy, Mr. Field spoke, followed by Sir Evelyn
Hone (the Northern Rhodesian Governor), and then by Dr.
Kaunda and Mr. Nkumbula.

'Observers remarked on the note of goodwill and modera-
tion in all the speeches which developed Mr. Butler's theme of
getting on with the job in hand "in an orderly and speedy
manner".'

The conference ended on 4th July. On the same day I received
this telegram from the Prime Minister and the Cabinet at home:

'The Cabinet at their meeting this morning asked me to
send you their warmest congratulations on the way in which
you have handled the Victoria Falls Conference. It was not

a happy occasion—the ending of a noble experiment—and it might well have ended in a mood of bitterness and determination not to co-operate. But your skill, experience and resourcefulness have won the day. You have instilled into the governments taking part in the Conference a sense of dignity and a sense of responsibility. If in the future the countries of Central Africa grow closer together this will be due to your conduct and leadership.'

Two months earlier it had seemed impossible that an orderly dissolution of the Federation could be achieved. It appeared that Winston Field was determined not to attend any conference unless he was granted independence and it appeared that Sir Roy was so angry about the March incidents in relation to the granting of the right of secession to Northern Rhodesia, that he would not assist in any orderly attempt to regulate the future. Both Prime Ministers seemed to be sitting pretty, since if I did not concede the demands of Southern Rhodesia they could literally have obstructed events for months ahead. However, Field realized the pressures within his own territory to attend a conference and to attempt to get the best terms possible out of Northern Rhodesia, and Welensky, realizing the game was up, did not want to continue what he called an undignified posture and remain as Prime Minister of an undertaking which was on its way out. Both therefore came together to attend the conference.

The Northern Rhodesians had a dangerous attitude, in that they were demanding as machinery a Commission to take the place of the Federal government. Perhaps the turning point of our discussions was when I made it clear in the conference that I could not accept the Northern Rhodesian position. It would have been very blind for the British government not to accept Sir Roy's co-operative mood and to have established a Commission. Sir Roy would certainly have gone into direct opposition to our plans although I heard from the Federal Public Service that they would have worked for a Commission. The Governor, Sir Evelyn Hone, on the critical day of the conference, proposed an adjournment for half an hour to cool down his Ministers and this, together with the time-table, namely a date for the dissolution of the Federation at the end of the year, brought the Northern Rhodesian Ministers along.

The British delegation, thanks to the efforts of Mark Tennant and Duncan Watson, produced the most massive briefing for the conference. The papers themselves occupied the whole of an official bag. This briefing was carefully co-ordinated in Whitehall and comprised papers from the Treasury, the Department of Technical Co-operation, the Commonwealth Relations Office and the Foreign Office itself. The contents of these papers were used by my advisers to provide the frame-work of my speeches. At one session Sir Roy objected to the set of speeches made by the Chairman and said the British govern-ment was taking an undue advantage. This was rather typical of his dialectics at their worst since the Federal government had already issued a variety of papers of a voluminous character demanding, *inter alia*, that we should accept the whole of the debt burden. Besides, my set speeches had to be circulated to the conference as documents and if I had not prepared them they could not have been so handled. The report itself, which can be read as a White Paper, indicates the immense amount of work we got through. In particular the agreement on defence was a remarkable one because the Northern Rhodesians accepted that Southern Rhodesia should keep the R.R.A.F. intact, as also they accepted that the U.K. government should come in and be the authority in the two Northern territories in control of defence up to the date of independence.

The atmosphere of the conference was confused by Sir Roy's decision that business meetings should be reduced to a mini-mum and that his Ministers should neither attend receptions nor eat any meals with the British delegation. I remembered again the phrase about 'the food choking them'. We thus used to pass each other in silence in the restaurant. It must be realized that the Federal Ministers were suffering from a long-drawn-out sense of bitterness and sorrow at the break-up of their form of government and their life. I had been very conscious of this for a long time. The Federal idea, had it really blossomed, could have provided an example of racial co-operation which might have altered the face of the southern part of the conti-nent. All such hopes were now discarded. It was therefore generous of Roy to pay a series of private visits to my wife and myself later in the evenings. He not only discussed his own personal future, saying (like Cincinnatus) that he would grow asparagus and strawberries 'as the poor always had enough money for luxuries'; he also spoke of the conduct of the conference and his anxiety for the public servants. On one occasion when there was a report of trouble in Nyasaland he threatened to send in Federal troops. But I warned him that those days were over. He thought it most unlikely that he would make a comeback by entering Southern Rhodesian politics and he has been, as one would expect, as good as his word.

Politics is the art of the possible, and what I found it possible to achieve was an orderly dissolution of the Federation, the establishment of two new states in Zambia and Malawi, and the chance given to Southern Rhodesia to have a strong army and air force, with the opportunity for its ruling clique to open their doors to Africans if they paid any heed to world opinion. The present outcome of a white minority drawing up a republican Constitution and excluding Africans does not surprise me; but it does deeply offend me as a negation of human liberty and dignity.

CHAPTER ELEVEN

CUSTOMARY PROCESSES

WHEN I RETURNED from the Victoria Falls conference in July 1963, I found it widely assumed among the back-benchers that in a matter of weeks or months Macmillan would have to make way for a new leader. A general election could not be postponed beyond October 1964, and the Prime Minister was already in his seventieth year. His Labour rival, Harold Wilson, was twenty-two years Macmillan's junior, and ever since the election of President Kennedy there had been growing feeling that in Britain, as in America, the torch should pass to a new generation. These sentiments might not have made headway but for a persistent slump in the government's popularity which began with the economic crisis of 1961. Until that year Conservative stock, so low in the aftermath of Suez, had steadily improved, and in the 1959 general election the parliamentary majority inherited from Anthony Eden had been substantially increased.

During 1960, when Harold made a change at the Foreign Office, I would like to have gone there and assumed one hat instead of three. But Alec Home was chosen and became in a short time a marked success. He has a particular genius for writing out speeches on Basildon Bond writing paper in a shorthand of his own, and then delivering them without a flaw.

In 1961 Harold decided to move Iain Macleod from the Colonial Office and offered him the Chairmanship of the party. I had then done two years and was glad to comply, but I was more than sorry to relinquish to him the leadership of the House which had a particular fascination for me. When I handed over, the Speaker, Harry Hylton Foster, and the Clerk, Sir Abdy Fellowes, wrote to me, the first saying, 'I shall miss your own particular way of doing it in just the right fashion; with judgement, charm and unassailable good humour and thank you for your support to me as a new Speaker.' My friend Abdy, who was at my first school, said, 'It will be a long time before the House is led with the same "feel" for it as you had and who could soften the most pertinacious and obstinate by a touch of humour or an individual approach.'

From 1959–61 by-elections and opinion polls faithfully reflected the government's successes and Labour's divisions; but following the summer of 1961 so marked an economic and political deterioration took place as to cause the Prime Minister to make in July 1962 the most drastic reorganization of a government ever undertaken within the lifetime of a modern parliament. The end result of this latter-day 'night of the long knives' was the creation of one of the strongest young Cabinets of the century. That, to do him justice, was Macmillan's aim. But the spilling of so much blood did serious damage to the Prime Minister's hitherto unbroken image of 'unflappability'. The Gallup Poll reported that only 36 per cent of the electorate now expressed approval of his performance.

The principal victim of the massacre was the Chancellor of the Exchequer—'*Selwyn Lloyd ausgebootet*' ran the headline in one German-language newspaper—and many echoed, privately or publicly, Anthony Eden's view that he had been 'harshly treated'. Selwyn's tenure of the Treasury had been distinguished by major innovations, including the introduction of economic regulators, which gave the Chancellor power to vary indirect taxes between Budgets, and the acceptance of 'indicative planning' through the National Economic Development Council. These were certainly important gains. But his management of the economy had proved much more controversial. The 'pay pause', announced with the approval of his colleagues in July 1961, had brought extreme odium on the government and in the Prime Minister's view, shared by several of us in the Cabinet, both the working out of a longer-term 'incomes policy' and the modification of the rigours of deflation had been unduly delayed. Macmillan was particularly sensitive about the latter. In 1958 he had accepted the resignation of all three Treasury Ministers, Thorneycroft, Birch and Powell, because, as he put it, 'I had a feeling that the strict puritanical application of deflation was in danger of being developed into a sort of creed.'

Now he determined to move Selwyn Lloyd, largely so that the Treasury brief against rapid reflation could be re-written. In both instances the loss of talent was regrettable; on the latter occasion it was avoidable. The speed with which government changes were finally made on 13th July stemmed from the Prime Minister's fear that Selwyn Lloyd's natural reaction in 'cutting up rough' might cause his administration to collapse. As I wrote at the time: 'He should know by now how to handle Selwyn. He has favoured him and cared for him for six years. He has made Chequers available for him. And now he has made him a martyr. This is a pity because it all tends to get things out of proportion. The man Selwyn is probity and sense itself and this is of great capital value. His success has been in the proud role of service. His future may now be re-elevated into spheres unknown and by him uncharted.' None of this can be gainsaid, least of all my prophetic conclusion.

These were not merely retrospective reflections. I had first been brought into consultation about government changes on 6th July when I lunched with the Prime Minister and the Chief Whip at Admiralty House. They had asked me what I would do if I were Prime Minister and forming a new government, since, said Macmillan, 'That is what I virtually want to do now.' I replied that it would be easier for someone starting from scratch. On being cross-examined about the Treasury, I said I would make a change but we would miss the Chancellor from the government altogether. The question then arose whether Maudling would be the best successor, or whether he was insufficiently senior. It seemed to me on reflection that his ideas, as set out in a recent letter to his constituents at Barnet, should put doubts at rest. Reggie has a rare talent for writing Pauline Epistles, not to young churches but to old Conservatives. Discussion then turned to Conservatives, old in experience though not always in years, who had indicated a willingness to go at some time—David Kilmuir, Percy Mills, Harold Watkinson and Jack Maclay—and to others, including David Eccles and Charles Hill, whom the Prime Minister seemed disposed to drop. I questioned whether Eccles, whose intellect was valuable in any Cabinet and who had rendered distinguished service in a variety of posts, could be spared; and eventually he was offered, but refused, the Board of Trade, thus retiring from public life until his imaginative recall in 1970 to be Minister for the Arts. I was particularly sorry about the move of David Kilmuir from the Woolsack. He had been with me all my political life and had helped me to reform the Conservative party; he represented, with the Prime Minister and myself, the only remaining link in the Cabinet with the Churchill era. As the talk progressed after lunch I fell into a profound depression, not only about individual fortunes but about the future of the party bereft of senior statesmen. My solemn reverie was interrupted by the Prime Minister suddenly turning to me and saying, 'Do cheer up, Rab. Why are you so melancholy?'

I was personally unwounded by the night of the long knives or Massacre of Glencoe, as I call it. Nominally, indeed, my position was enhanced: I gave up the Home Office but was named First Secretary of State and invited to act as Deputy Prime Minister, a title which can constitutionally imply no right to the succession and should (I would advise, with the benefit of hindsight) be neither conferred nor accepted. Save only for the Central African Office, whose activities have already been recounted, I had no executive department to control; my responsibilities were, so to speak, supernal—specific or general, as the Prime Minister might from time to time determine.

Admiralty House,
Whitehall, S.W.1
May 29, 1963

'Dear Rab,

'I told you today that I am hoping to go to Scotland by the night train on Thursday, May 30, and will be returning to the South on the morning of Monday, June 10, and that I should be grateful if you would take charge of the Government while I am away and take the Chair at any meeting of the Cabinet that may be necessary.

'I do not think we need issue a formal Press Notice about this but I will ask Harold Evans to tell the Lobby that you will be looking after things while I am on holiday.

Yours ever,

I am most grateful for this.   Harold'

The government of which I was, for this brief and disagreeable period, to take charge yet again had scarcely enhanced its fortunes since the purge of the previous summer. *The Times* was persistent in opining that, 'The country has moved near enough to a presidential form of government to mean that only a change of Prime Minister will persuade people that they are looking upon a new Ministry.' This view was not contradicted by the adverse results of by-elections in Scotland and in England. Governments cannot be held responsible for the weather, but this one was certainly blamed for mounting unemployment—3·9 per cent by February—which was greatly aggravated by the worst winter since 1881 and only gradually subsided as the reflation of the economy and special regional measures took effect. Of less immediate electoral importance, but of far greater significance to the long-run strategy of the government, was the veto by de Gaulle on Britain's move into Europe—the major premise of the Prime Minister's forward thinking. As if this external blow was not enough, the government's standing at home was deeply harmed, first by the Vassall case which cast doubt on the efficiency of the security services, and then by the Profumo affair which seemed to call in question the very standards of our public life.

Within a few days of Macmillan's departure to Scotland at the end of May, I was informed that the Secretary of State for War had admitted he had misled the House in his statement at the end of March about the nature of his association with a model. I talked to Martin Redmayne, the Chief Whip, and the Prime Minister's Parliamentary Secretary and it appeared that there was no alternative to accepting the Secretary of State's resignation. Macmillan rang from Scotland to ask whether we could not fight back, but we thought that we must immediately let Profumo go and he was accordingly seen by the Chief Whip. I had more than an hour with the Prime Minister directly he got back from his holiday. He was in a somewhat euphoric state and said that everything looked so different in the north that he could hardly believe the trouble into which he was coming. It was only during the following week that he realized the extent of the tragedy that had occurred and, as he told me after the Commons debate on 17th June, his heart was broken but his spirit was still strong. The result of the debate was more devastating than I had anticipated. While the Prime Minister's honour shone clearly throughout, his lack of knowledge of what had happened made a disagreeable impression upon backbenchers and, combined with a series of criticisms over the months, led to a crisis of confidence which raged through the House all through the 18th June. As Baldwin used to say, it is always difficult to assess the rages of the Tory party in the House. I spent some time assessing opinion and could not but register that there was a very strong tide flowing in favour of a young man of the new generation, with Maudling's name being the most frequently mentioned. At 11 p.m. John Morrison, Chairman of the 1922 Committee, called on me at Smith Square and confirmed my view. He advised me strongly to take part in any government formed by a new man whoever it was, though he added that he would understand if after all I had gone through in 1957 I decided to do no more. I gave him no answer except to say that I was surprised at the Conservative Private Members' rush to get rid of a trusted leader in a moral crisis, and one who had proved himself a great Prime Minister. Indeed, when I had visited the Prime Minister that evening he was more worried about the continued revelation of moral disturbance than he was about his own future. He said that he would not wish to resign on the basis of this one sordid case but would wish to do it in an orderly manner with a view to giving way to another man before the next election. He gave no indication at all of who he thought the other man should be, nor did he show interest in any subject I raised except those affecting the immediate situation. I accordingly went off to Africa without the benefit of the Prime Minister's counsel, but with the knowledge that the party had been temporarily calmed by the tactics employed by John Morrison and Derek Walker-Smith at a meeting of the 1922 Committee on 20th June.

A month later, after my return from Africa, I wrote the following short assessment of the political situation, which did not appear to me to have altered greatly:

'I have been very pleased to receive so many acknowledgments of the success of the Falls Conference from M.P.s and others, and this will always be a source of satisfaction since the job itself was so difficult. Judging by the attendance at the debate yesterday I do not think however that the whole episode has made much effect on the Conservative party. They are only too ready to object when there is trouble and it was typical that there were so few present and that they ignored the occasion.

'On coming back I agreed to do the *Panorama* programme which might have been worse although I was not keen to comment on the leadership stakes. What I really had in mind in answering the questions was not so much to enter into competition but to show that I was in a sufficiently strong position to take a generous line later about a younger man if that should prove necessary.'

I added:

'This is because my diagnosis shows that there is a very strong movement in favour of somebody not too closely associated with the Establishment. What is really happening in the party is that the herd instinct is unleashed and that they are tending to attack anybody in authority starting with the Prime Minister, including the Chief Whip, Martin Redmayne, and also embracing the leaders of the 1922 Committee, who are thought to be too old-world. These in their turn are not making much stand against the herd and are tending to accept the drift. There is not so much positive approval of a younger man as there is a recognition that this may make a clearer picture for the next election. They ignore the argument that a younger man may be there too long and then might be hurt by the election. That they do so was confirmed to me in a talk by the Chief Whip who said there was a move to make a caretaker government under me but that strong preference was to go for the next generation.

'When I talked to the P.M. he was not in a happy mood and was resigned to the fact that he would probably have to go. His own preference was for waiting some time, perhaps even until the party conference. His anxiety, he said, was to retain the discretion of the Crown so that the Crown could choose whomever she wished.

'There is considerable discussion going on as to the method of choosing a leader. If there is clearly a big majority for one candidate then I think the rest of us should pull in and help. I think a leader in the Conservative party, as Pretyman said in 1921, should *emerge* and that is the only lasting way of achieving a result.'

The process of emergence had got no further when I went down to Chequers to dine with the Prime Minister on 11th September. We talked together for four hours and, with the exception of four minutes on Central Africa and Southern Rhodesia (about which his only observation was that I had appeared worried in the early summer), the conversation was devoted to his personal prospects. As we approached my bedroom door, he said that since my own prospects were uncertain in regard to the leadership I should do well as a king-maker. But my private diagnosis was that at this point he hoped and intended to remain as leader. I wrote a letter to the Foreign Secretary, Alec Home, in the following terms:

'You asked me to let you have a line after spending last evening with Harold. His state of mind is as follows: his aim for us is either to defeat the Socialists at the next election or so to achieve an election result that they have no overwhelming majority and can be turned out within the space of one Parliament.

'He realizes that a state of indecision is bad for the party and has been so warned by Oliver Poole [the joint Chairman]. He therefore considers that he has the choice of two speeches to make to the party conference. One would indicate that, after dealing with the Denning report [on the security aspect of the Profumo affair], etc., he would contemplate retirement say at the end of the year. That is after seven years as P.M. (He has not formalized the wording in his mind but the idea would be to give the impression that *he* would not lead the party at the next election.)

'The alternative speech would be a challenging one saying that he felt that his work and contribution were unfinished and that he proposed to remain as Leader. Here he told me he depends for his decision on a diagnosis as to whether there is constructive work to be done with the President of the USA and the Kremlin in the field of foreign affairs. He is therefore looking forward to his talk with you. He realizes that if he does decide to stay he will have to take on and defeat a section of the party, who feel that there should be a new Leader for the Election.

'He has by no means made up his mind. I noticed the same hankering as I have seen in P.M.s' minds before, especially Churchill before his retirement, to stay in office and achieve something lasting. We know how difficult this is. I indicated that it might not be possible to be so definite at the party conference. (He has since told me that this impressed him.) It might be necessary to assess the feeling of the party in November after he had dealt with the Denning report. I said that it would be tragic if after seven successful years there should be a big break with the party in the House. He himself realizes that it would be a thankless task to remain P.M., fight an election, perhaps lose and then have to submit to a change. He expressed some doubt whether he was in the mood for another election. What is clear is that probably owing to privilege the publication of the Denning report may be delayed till the House meets. But whatever happens there it won't be debated till November.

'I asked him if the question of the succession was affecting his mind. I think it clearly is to the extent that he thinks that the succession is "open". He is not reconciled to the suggestion of some backbenchers before we rose that the present Chancellor of the Exchequer [Maudling] is ready for it, in the foreign sphere. (Here we come back to his hankering after the foreign situation.) He thought that any of the rest of us who might be thought of were not certain to emerge. He wants to preserve a proper degree of the Queen's choice and does not want a diktat from the 1922 Committee. However we cast our minds back on history, and agreed that almost no P.M. had chosen his own successor, and that this issue might have to be thrashed out, if he decided to go, without his having the final word. So much for the succession, or as far as we got with it.

'My conclusion is that his mind is turning on whether he can make any contribution further next year in the foreign sphere. What we have all to avoid is any chimera and any resultant tragic split with the party. I am sure you will respect my writing. I look forward to seeing you next week.'

In the following week I discussed the leadership problem separately with Alec Home, Oliver Poole, Quintin Hailsham, Martin Redmayne and Reggie Dilhorne. One feature of all these talks was a frank appraisal of the succession including the less favourable aspects of my own chances. There was, of course, difference of emphasis between the different personalities. The Chief Whip said that he thought a rallying could be created round me. Certain doubts were being expressed as to whether Maudling was ready, having not held office for long. My defect was that, having been in office for so long, I had more opponents than the others—a point confirmed by the Lord Chancellor— but that might be overcome. Maudling had seen him and vowed friendship to me. There were critics of Hailsham. On the other hand Poole was running Hailsham strongly. This was confirmed in my talk with Poole which was as usual ani- mated by deep friendship. He even told me that a seat in the Commons, namely St. Marylebone, was being kept on ice. Poole said that if I came out on top he would be quite reconciled, but he thought Quintin was the man to win the election. Alec Home, by contrast, said he saw distinct advantages in moving to a younger generation. He wanted to know if I were a candidate, and I said, 'Yes, up to a point, but not to the extent of having a vote on the matter.' If things got to that pass I would opt for the Leader whom I saw emerging as the party choice.

On the morning of Monday, 7th October I had an hour's talk with the Prime Minister, during which he expressed his desire not to announce a final decision when he addressed the party conference at Blackpool the following Saturday. It was, how- ever, increasingly clear to me that he wished to stay on. In the evening there was a meeting of Ministers and other leading Conservatives at which much plain speaking was heard. The Lord Chancellor and Duncan Sandys took a very strong line in favour of the Prime Minister's staying on; Alec Home, with great good humour and courage, described the numbers of what he called the ordinary members of the party who wanted a change, and Oliver Poole and I spoke in the same sense. Oliver, I was later told, continued to argue the case over dinner, but no decision was taken that night. The following morning, Tuesday 8th, there was a Cabinet at 10 o'clock. Macmillan looked exceedingly ill, and half-way through the morning he suspended business and left the room, remarking philosophically that his body had given him trouble from time to time in his varied life and he must see his doctors. A long and informal discussion then took place around the table, led by Iain Macleod who opted for Harold staying. There was quite a strong reaction against my suggestion, supported by Alec Home and Reggie Maudling, that the P.M. might temporize in his Conference speech on Saturday. Ministers as a whole wanted a clear decision and most were for his staying as Leader.

I reported this to the Prime Minister at 5 o'clock. It was an ironic message. He was in great pain and showed me clearly that neither he nor his doctors felt he could fight the next election. I was very moved. First Winston in 1953, then Anthony in 1956, now Harold in 1963, had called upon me to act in an incapacitating illness. When I left Downing Street a communiqué was being prepared. It said: 'The Prime Minister has tonight been admitted to the King Edward VII Hospital for Officers for an operation for prostatic obstruction. It is expected that this will involve his absence from official duties for some weeks, and he has asked the First Secretary, Mr. R. A. Butler, to take charge of the government while he is away.'

Mollie and I arrived in Blackpool on Wednesday 9th and proceeded to the Conference headquarters in the Imperial Hotel. I was at once apprised by my friends Toby Aldington and Peter Goldman that there was opposition to the idea of my standing in for the Prime Minister on Saturday to make the traditional wind-up speech. They counselled me to bring this matter to a head immediately, and I was disposed to do so as acting head of the government rather than as a candidate for the succession. An official invitation was therefore sought from the Conservative National Union and its acceptance was endorsed by a meeting of Ministers that evening. I had a more serious difference of opinion with my colleagues on arrival, since the hierarchy were particularly keen to hurry on the P.M.'s retirement, whereas I was equally keen to give him a chance to recover and not to have to take vital decisions while he was an invalid.

I think that my judgement was correct and altogether more kindly to Macmillan. It would have been better for him and for everyone else if the decision had been taken at a less preposterous time. Less harm would have been done to the Conservative party, and dignity, which was altogether lost during the ensuing days, might have been preserved. However nobody seemed to share my views, least of all Macmillan, who was by then so anxious to support Hailsham that he was not thinking, or probably even informed, of loyalty from me.

As Randolph Churchill so eloquently described in *The Fight for the Tory Leadership*, Macmillan had seen Hailsham on the Monday before the Conference and indicated that in the event of retirement he would support his candidature. Accordingly the 'cohorts'—including the family, especially Maurice Macmillan and Julian Amery—warmly urged the case for Hailsham at the Imperial Hotel. Randolph himself returned from America with hundreds of badges marked Q for Quintin. He came up to my room and obligingly handed me some for my wife, myself and friends. These I consigned to the waste-paper basket.

Meanwhile Home with great determination had been to the hospital in London and obtained Macmillan's written resignation, which was read to the Conference on Thursday afternoon: 'I hope that it will soon be possible for the customary processes of consultation to be carried on within the party about its future leadership.' Alec Home obtained this and himself read it out. The fact that the P.M. asked for the processes of selection of his successor to be undertaken in the middle of a party conference was bound to create consternation, confusion and intrigue, and indeed it did. I cannot imagine an atmosphere less suited to such a declaration with scores of journalists, television interviewers, *et hoc genus omne*. It turned Blackpool into a sort of electoral Convention *à l'Américaine*. After that there was no peace.

The effect of Macmillan's encouragement was that Quintin Hailsham announced to the C.P.C. meeting on the Thursday night his determination to renounce his title. When I entered the Winter Gardens he was emerging surrounded by an hysterical crowd, having been greeted by a demonstration described to me by a hostile witness as 'reminiscent of a Nuremberg Rally'. He had been up to my room that afternoon and asked my advice. I had recommended him to say he was considering his position and no more. He said he thought it very good advice but would not take it. Alec Home gave him similar advice. Home's biographer implies that if Hailsham had taken it and not publicly shown his judgement faulty, Home would have supported Hailsham as Macmillan's designated heir.

We had frequent opportunities for meeting the Homes, who had the next-door set of rooms. He told us on more than one occasion that he could not himself contemplate coming down from the House of Lords and denuding it of himself as well as its leader. He appeared to Mollie and me to stick to that view during the Conference until the Saturday when he told us he was consulting his doctor. The Lord Chancellor, travelling down with us in the train, took Mollie a bet of £5 to 5s. that he would not stand. At that time the Lord Chancellor seemed fairly sure that, with the slump in Quintin's stock, my position was good. He was, however, extremely discreet and did not tell us any results of the Cabinet soundings in detail.

It became clear to me at Blackpool that there was considerable support for Alec, partly because he made a good speech on foreign policy, partly because he took the chair at my meeting in his capacity as President of the National Union, and partly because of lobbying by back-benchers who saw him as the best compromise candidate. His wife, Elizabeth, has told Mollie that they did not really get the view that it was coming their way until the next week; but, in fact, it was. My speech to the party conference on the Saturday had a good reception, but those who favour 'democracy by decibels' noted a victory for Home on points.

I had taken great pains with this speech, and its centre-piece was a deliberate attempt to bring the philosophy of the Charters up to date and to project Conservative social policy into the next decade. No one who studies it today can doubt its long-run influence, and I attach more importance to that than to its immediate effect:

'The kind of society we Conservatives are developing must

derive its motive power, not from the commands of the planners, but from the character of the people. We shall, therefore, march forward to victory and beyond with an imaginative and far-reaching "Programme for People"—not a programme that is concerned solely to line their pockets and satisfy their material needs, but a programme that inspires their sense of service and dedication, develops their intellectual potential, and raises their economic status.

'A first feature of this programme is a new and exciting break-through on the educational front. For on the future of education not only the efficiency of our society but the fulfilment of our ideals depends. In the nineteenth century a Conservative government completed the process of making primary education free and compulsory for all. In 1944 I played my part in opening the doors of secondary education to all. Now a fresh challenge and opportunity await us. Already seven new universities are being created, and plans are in hand to increase substantially the capacity of existing universities, colleges of advanced technology and teacher training colleges. These programmes will be developed, in the light of the Robbins Committee Report. Our aim is higher education for every boy and girl in the land who can benefit from it.

'We believe that these policies can succeed only if parents and children are assured that the extra talent and skill that they gain from education or training will bring them extra reward. In a Socialist society they could never have that assurance. Under Socialism the fruits of individual effort, enterprise and sacrifice would be plucked and harvested not by the people but by the tax gatherers. Under Socialism, the room at the top would be reserved for the Gentleman in Whitehall who is always supposed to know best. In a Conservative society, by contrast, we mean to see that incentives are maintained and improved, that initiative and skill are rewarded, that there are a variety of ladders to the top and that positions of responsibility are not reserved for one coterie or class or brand of education.

'This Programme for People must also be extended, in the spirit of our Conservative Industrial Charter, to the factory and workshop floor. Our future economic opportunities will yield barren fruit unless human relations in industry develop alongside scientific and technological advance. We must give up thinking of sharply defined spheres of responsibility, let alone of conflicting interests or separate "sides". In a modern industrial Britain, increasing its wealth as we wish to do by at least four per cent each and every year, there can be only one side—and all of us are on it. In concrete terms, this means that we must look for a marked reduction in the four million days lost on average each year through industrial disputes and strikes. We are intent on making a new approach to the abandonment of outdated, irrelevant and unnecessary restrictive practices, whether indulged in by management or by labour. And we are working out wider social and financial measures to rehouse, resettle and retrain workers and tide them over the period when they are changing jobs.

'In each of these areas of policy, then, the government and our party are staking out new frontiers. But unlike the Socialists, we do not regard a Programme for People as an indiscriminate distribution of expensive presents by a profligate Santa Crossman. We believe that social benefits and social subsidies should go first and foremost to those who really require them, and that those who are able to stand on their own feet and make provision for themselves should be allowed and encouraged to do so.'

After references to housing and health policies, I ended:

'Above all, never let us get into the frame of mind where we can believe that we have fulfilled our social responsibilities when we have finished paying our rates and taxes. We still owe our service, our compassion and our Christian duty. Our Programme for People therefore rests on the belief in the infinite capacity of the individual to rise and meet these challenges. It carries with it the urge to ambition, to success and also to responsibility, and it is not an incitement to envy, malice or uncharitableness. It is a creed for the young and for the young in heart, and it is not a repository for the disgruntled in spirit.'

I returned to London and the Prime Minister made clear what I had always known, that, had he not been stricken down, he would have made a speech on the Saturday at Blackpool saying that he was going on. This would have avoided all discussion of the succession. Rather to my surprise popular support, especially in the *Daily Express* of the 16th, showed me to be in the lead—Butler $39\frac{1}{2}$, Hailsham $21\frac{1}{2}$, Maudling 11, Home $9\frac{1}{2}$. I also had many more letters than usual and much assurance from Michael Fraser at the Research Department that the national polls really indicated a very considerable measure of support in the country. The situation was not however quite the same in the Parliamentary party. There was an element of criticism there of which I was informed by the Chief Whip and the Lord Chancellor, just as there was an element of criticism of Hailsham, and it seemed quite possible that the Whips would prefer a compromise candidate. On the other hand I was assured by the Lord Chancellor and by the Prime Minister that the Cabinet would be perfectly happy to work either under me or Alec Home.

I think that Harold himself always had a feeling, despite the nine years between us, that my succession would not make enough difference between his regime and the next, and he mentioned this argument to me on the 17th. I pointed to the fact that I was younger than when he took over. I also pointed out the difficulty of bringing a peer down from the Upper House—not only the short-term difficulty of the delay but also the psychological impact on the country. I therefore did my best to keep the doors open. Despite the unpleasantness of the situation personal relations were maintained. I saw Alec Home, Reggie Maudling and Quintin Hailsham. In my talk with Alec he himself expressed grave doubts whether he wished to take it on. He said his wife was encouraging him, but that he realized the difficulties of coming back to the Commons and of the years after the election if we were in office or even more if we were in opposition. He said he would be perfectly happy to back me. I got the impression that he was personally not keen to stand himself but could be persuaded. He said he hoped that if he had to do it he could count on me. My talk with Reggie was very short. He simply said that he did not know how the M.P.s would react in his favour but that he counted on me to work with him. My talk with Quintin had more content since he said that if another peer came down from the Upper House he would withdraw from public life whether he was in the Upper or Lower House. He would then go back to the Bar and try to make a living there. I reminded him of my advice that he should not have renounced the Upper House so speedily. He agreed that this advice had been good but said that things had now gone too far. I besought him if the decision went against him to return to the Upper House and do his bit there. He said he would be perfectly ready to serve with me.

There then followed the inquiry by the Whips in the Commons about whom M.P.s wanted as Leader. I have never seen the result of this operation. I simply heard from numerous of my friends that they were rung up by quite junior Whips who stressed that Alec was standing, having decided to renounce his peerage. The Whips had a difficult job and were as usual a good body of men, but the accounts sent in to me showed me that each man in conducting this inquiry adopted a different emphasis according to his own character. At any rate we were informed that the Chief Whip had carried a document to the sick Prime Minister showing the majority preference.

By the Thursday afternoon the newspapers had smelt that things were going Home's way. A meeting took place that night at Enoch Powell's house at which Toby Aldington, Iain Macleod, Reggie Maudling and Freddie Erroll were present. They were later joined by the Chief Whip. This was a meeting of revolt against the choice of Home. They telephoned me at the St. Ermin's Hotel, where Mollie and I were staying while our house in Smith Square was under repair, to pledge their support. Quintin himself rang saying 'This simply won't do' and Mollie answered him. She was superb throughout, counselling me to stay out, and this made my eventual decision all the more poignant. Other members of the Cabinet who were friendly to me were Henry Brooke, Edward Boyle and John Boyd-Carpenter. I was also spoken to by the Chief Whip who reiterated that the majority of the party were for Alec. One presumes and hopes that the Chief Whip informed the Prime Minister, as he was requested to do, that seven or eight members of the Cabinet were opposed to the choice of Home. What is certain is that Macmillan decided to ignore this powerful objection and acted (as he had done in 1962) with utter determination and dispatch, making a definite recommendation of Home.

The next morning I had to preside over a meeting of Ministers, and then at 11.30 had time to look after my own affairs. I telephoned the Lord Chancellor and asked him to take an initiative in getting together the rival candidates—Hailsham, Maudling and myself—since, if there were serious opposition to Home's succession, Macmillan and his friends should know. I have in my records a minute by the Lord Chancellor describing how he rang both the hospital and No. 10 to obtain approval for taking the chair at such a meeting, but no reply was vouchsafed to him. Meanwhile Iain Macleod had by his own arrangement come to my office in the Treasury building with Quintin and Reggie. Both made it clear that they were willing to support me, Maudling calmly, Quintin with characteristic fury. By this time Alec Home had been to the Palace and had been invited to attempt to form an administration. Mollie and I lunched at the Carlton Club where I was approached by William Rees-Mogg and a variety of other young supporters, beseeching me to hold out. A notable exception to this advice was provided by James Ramsden, later Secretary of State for War, who thought very definitely that I should co-operate in the new government. I needed time to think about this and not be rushed into a decision. Immediately after lunch Alec moved into No. 10 and I was invited to see him. He assured me that everything depended on my decision and Maudling's; he wished me to go to the Foreign Office and Maudling to stay at the Treasury. I replied that I must reserve my position on two grounds: first, whether it was right for an hereditary peer to succeed at the present time; secondly, whether he could command enough unity in the Cabinet. On the first count, I said that much depended on character but that even if he could get himself across to the public, the difficulties of the peerage remained and spoilt the image of modernization. On the second count, I described the efforts made during the morning to get people together and pointed out that matters had been rushed and insufficient consideration given to the difficulties. I gave him particulars of the Ministers who stood out against his leadership, and said that it was now up to him to see if he could secure the necessary unity. Until I had the answer to this question I could not respond to any suggestion he had made for my future, honoured though I might be by it. I added that I was, of course, not presuming that I personally would have all the support. I was trying to seek a solution which would obtain the maximum unity.

I later took up a suggestion by Hailsham that the 'triangular' meeting we had in the morning should be followed by a 'quadrilateral' meeting with Home. This took place in the evening and was attended by the Chief Whip. It then appeared that while Hailsham would prefer to serve with me, he had also come round to the idea of serving under Home. Reggie Maudling, who reserved his position till next morning, used the expression that 'things were closing in'. The number of Ministers supporting me was eroding. I had a long and difficult discussion in the evening and night with Geoffrey Lloyd and others who came in, and with Mollie. She naturally thought I was the better man for No. 10 and for the next election, so it was very difficult to be persuasive about there being in my view a majority for Alec in the Cabinet as well as in the party. In my talk with him I had put the need for unity first and it seemed to me that the most unselfish way of achieving unity was to serve with a friend rather than to force the issue the other way. This was a consecutive attitude of mind.

The Lord Chancellor and I had a talk in which we agreed that there were no differences of policy between Alec and me and that a resignation really ought to depend on a difference of policy. He wrote to me in this sense after it was all over on 23rd October. 'By your action you have held the Tory party together at a very critical time. I do not doubt that if you had refused to serve, Alec would have failed to form a government and if you had then been sent for, which seems most likely, I think you would have started under very heavy criticism, for it would indeed be hard to justify a refusal to serve on the ground of policy—for there was no difference of policy—and differences of policy are really the only justification for refusing to serve a colleague. Many would have thought that you had refused to serve Alec only to secure your personal advantage and that would certainly have done serious harm to your standing. As it is your reputation stands tremendously high for the way in which you behaved in a situation of the very greatest personal difficulty.'

The Chief Whip said to me later that it would have been possible to alter the whole decision in my favour, but that he thought I would never have been happy again if I had done so. With this diagnosis I agree. As I said to Kenneth Harris on the B.B.C. in early 1966, one cannot alter one's nature. I had always worked for the unity of the party and I did so on this occasion. I had always had wonderful friends especially Mollie and I did not lack them on this occasion. 'My own view', Quintin wrote to me when Randolph Churchill's account was published, 'is that the four of us who were principally concerned come rather well out of the story, both as it really happened, and as it is told by Randolph. I do not think that any of us behaved dishonourably or without dignity (I would not say this for all the other, but minor figures) or in such a way that any need feel less affection or confidence in one another. Equally I am sure that both you and I did right at the critical time to support the new regime. As you know, I wish Harold had made you Foreign Secretary in 1957. I now feel certain that that is one department of state which will be handled with rare distinction. I hope I shall enjoy the House of Commons whatever the future holds. I was miserable at losing my leadership of the House of Lords, but one of the prices the party must pay for treating some of its leading figures a little roughly is to recognize that their self-respect sometimes makes it impossible to act as the party would like. At all events there are interesting times ahead. . . .'

CHAPTER TWELVE

PASTURES NEW

QUINTIN'S LETTER was perfectly correct. In politics, and out of them, there were interesting times ahead. I would have been glad to become Foreign Secretary in 1957. I was gratified to get my wish at the end of 1963, though I realized that there would be a difficult election within a year. When in Moscow the following summer I jokingly told my opposite number, Gromyko, that after the election I would learn Russian—if I happened then to have more time on my hands. But since 1964, despite the excelling facilities available in Cambridge, I have been too absorbed to commence this labour.

The Office and the foreign scene had changed greatly since I had served Edward Halifax and Anthony Eden as junior Minister. In this earlier period the world was being shaken to its foundations and the country was split by the issue of Munich. It was not till 1940 that a truly National government was formed and Britain passed through the most important solitary year of her history. The Office in that year braced itself to face the war which it had long regarded as inevitable. When I took over in 1963, by contrast, there was a variety of local conflicts in Borneo (the Malaysian 'confrontation'), Cyprus, South East Arabia and Guiana, but in Europe the skies were comparatively clear. Ever since the war Britain had proceeded systematically to 'de-colonize' its dependencies. The first major move was the Indian Act of Independence in 1947, to be followed by action in Ceylon, Africa and elsewhere. In addition to five years' work for India, I was myself responsible, as I have recounted, for granting independence to Malawi and Zambia. As I said in my broadcast to the Soviet people from Moscow on 31st July, 1964, Britain had freed over 650 million people in a span of fifteen years. The Commonwealth creation itself was without precedent in world history and a tremendous act of faith. Not only was there a big change in Britain's world position, but foreign policy itself had become more attuned to the economic facts of life. I found a new and large economic section presided over by Sir Charles Johnston. Much of my work was concerned with trade and finance, such as the progress of the Kennedy round of tariff reductions and the economic preliminaries of going into Europe. Ernie Bevin had realized that a country's foreign policy depends as much on its economic as its strategic strength. Speaking to me of the staff at the Office, he said in 1947, 'I want them boys to think as much of sums as they do of treaties and protocols.'

Of course treaties and diplomatic usage rightly remained of the first importance in the sixties, and Talleyrand's description of the ideal foreign secretary remains apt to this day:

> 'A minister for foreign affairs must be endowed with a sort of instinct which gives him such quick warning that it prevents him from compromising himself in any discussion. He must have the faculty to appear open while remaining impenetrable, he must be reserved yet capable of letting himself go, he must be subtle even in choosing his methods of amusing himself. His conversation must be simple, varied, unexpected, always natural and sometimes naif. Put shortly, not once in the twenty-four hours must he stop for a moment being Minister for Foreign Affairs.'

I am told that my conversation corresponds tolerably well to Talleyrand's requirements. But Lord Malmesbury's advice to one entering diplomacy was to listen, not to talk. In his view English reserve and ill manners are less harmful than 'premature and hollow civilities'.

Fully armed with all these precepts I wasted no time and attended the Western European Conference at The Hague on the 24th October. My main object was to meet Couve de Murville and to attempt to establish closer relations with France which had never really mended since the head-on collision at Brussels over the Common Market. Couve had certainly read and digested Malmesbury's advice about listening, not talking. The delegates were received by the Queen of the

Netherlands at an evening party. Her arrival was delayed and the interval gave opportunity for conversation. I drew Couve into an alcove and started to talk French. This took him by surprise. He confessed that he almost invariably talked in English to British public men and seemed surprised at my fluency in his own language. Without giving me any positive hope about the attitude of the Six he spoke with unaccustomed warmth about the importance of British presence in the Western European Union. Next day he was more guarded and had re-captured his *sangfroid habituel*. I was, however, able to establish that future W.E.U. meetings should be held, to help 'consolidate the political and economic unity of Europe which was a funda-mental aim of British policy'. I had the benefit of the advice of Sir Con O'Neill, then Ambassador to the European com-munities. I was accompanied by Lord Hood, my private sec-retary Oliver Wright (now Chief Clerk) and others, and saw once again how well the Office cares for its Secretary of State. Dr. Luns, the 'perpetual' Foreign Minister of Holland, lived up to his reputation as a host and greeted me immediately with a selection from his inexhaustible repertoire of stories. He said 'I hear you have been in Africa. Do you know about the tribal chief who said "My wife makes good soup. I miss her." '

When I arrived at the Foreign Office I had some preconceived ideas of what I wanted, not so much to achieve (owing to the shortness of time), as to probe. I also wanted to profit by the example of two of my predecessors, Ernie Bevin and Anthony Eden. From the first I had the ambition to try and look after the well-being of the staff. Ernie had told me, 'When I was a trades union leader I used to stay with various branch union secre-taries and their wives. That's how I learned how to help them in their family problems.' I did my best to help the Service by putting into force the Plowden Committee's reforms for im-proved conditions and allowances, travel facilities for families and many other points for which the members of the Service showed great appreciation.

From Eden I had attempted to learn something about the art of negotiation. To understand Anthony you must read a fascinating classic by his brother Timothy called *The Tribulations of a Baronet*. This describes Anthony's parentage—a choleric artistic father who beat the plants in his greenhouse to smithereens because they were the wrong colour, and an exquisitely beautiful mother. Walking across the Park one day Anthony said to me, 'Those blue distances remind me of my father's watercolours'. Anthony's own temperament was a mixture of the charm of his mother and the artistic impetuosity of his father; the combination gave him a particular talent for sharp perspicacity in negotiations which culminated in his success in Indo-China in 1954. His temperament suited the Foreign Office, where he had so many devoted friends, better than No. 10 where he was much more isolated. I was not able to reach any climax such as Anthony did in 1954 or Austen Chamberlain at Locarno; but by patient negotiation between Greeks and Turks my colleagues and I were able to bring the critical situation in Cyprus nearer to a peaceful outcome, as we did also with the confrontation in Malaysia.

My first objective of bringing European Union closer was started at The Hague meeting which I have mentioned and continued in two other Western European gatherings. But of course the atmosphere was not nearly so favourable as it has seemed since the change of leadership in France. I wanted to achieve a step forward in disarmament since Alec Cadogan had told me when I was in the Office before that the bitterest disappointment of his public life had been the failure of the disarmament conference before the 1939 war. There is no one I admired more in the transaction of foreign affairs than Cadogan. My desire to ease the warlike or semi-warlike situations in Cyprus and Borneo and Aden was achieved with the aid of the Commonwealth Secretary, Duncan Sandys, since the Foreign and Commonwealth Offices were not then united. I wanted to test the reality of our special relationship with the U.S.A., and lastly to find out from the Soviet leaders what chance there is or was of relaxation of tension in the nuclear age. These, then, were my objectives.

When the Prime Minister told the Commons that I was going to Geneva to make a pronouncement on disarmament, there were raised eyebrows in Washington. However, when I arrived in Switzerland, I found Mr. Foster, the acclaimed American expert, unperturbed. A major speech on disarmament in the midst of my short tenure of the Office was something of a feat. Latterly it became fashionable to have a Minister in charge of this subject alone. I am not surprised that this assignment kept Lord Chalfont busy in the Labour Government, for I have never come across such intricacy of detail in any other field. After stressing that there must be a true balance between the nations

"AH, NOW THEY WANT ME TO ACT IN GREEK TRAGEDY AND WHITEHALL FARCE."

involved in disarming, that there must be verification and (I stressed) international machinery for keeping the peace, I went on to define the following points on which agreement should be sought. First, observation posts in the NATO and Warsaw Pact areas, then a comprehensive nuclear ban treaty combined with the banning of further dissemination of nuclear weapons. I then recommended a freeze of nuclear delivery vehicles and the early physical destruction or 'bonfire' of some armaments. This met with a series of 'niets' from the Soviet representative, who seemed huffed when I pointed out that his nation's defence expenditure had increased by 43 per cent in the previous four years, while we had cut ours, as a proportion of the national product, by 1·8 per cent since 1952. I mention these points since they were to come up again hour after hour in my talks with Gromyko. The impasse in the field of disarmament and the immense size of the Soviet and American programmes must be a principal heartache to anyone with a sense of realism and a sense of idealism about the allocation of the world's resources.

When I went to America in May of 1964 I sought the truth about the special relationship. The Secretary of the State Department, Dean Rusk, immediately reassured me about its reality. He said, 'We have our NATO and our CENTO but without Britain these would all mean less to us. We like to feel we can always rely on you, that is why we are critical of your trading with the Iron Curtain and with Cuba.' During my visit I explained to Dean that I was not personally pressing to see the President. The Embassy and Harold Caccia, the Permanent Secretary, thought this an odd attitude since the Head of the Executive is everything in the U.S.A. But my political nose proved to be right since the talk did not help me at home. It took place in a small study with only President Johnson, McGeorge Bundy, David Harlech (who still felt deeply the loss of Kennedy, but whose value in Washington was as great as ever) and myself. Dean only attended for a few minutes and had shown previously great unwillingness to come. The President launched immediately into Cuba trade. He explained that Nixon or some other Republican opponent would take full advantage of the fact that he, L.B.J., was giving me coffee and I was trading with Castro. He besought me to send the bill for the Leyland buses and other items to his ranch in Texas and he would pay the account. Alternatively I was to invoice the material to Bundy and he would pay up. After he had been going on somewhat violently for five minutes a telephone flashed. Disregarding us, he spoke firmly into the receiver for a long stretch of time, apparently giving instructions to a political boss to get something through the Senate or House. He kept using the expression 'fix him' or 'send him to see me and I will see him whoever I am with and whatever I am doing'. This call took up quite a part of the interview and revealed the man's intense political preoccupation. I believe that he never let up at all and that politics was his hobby and his life. It was difficult after this to make much further progress, but he did say, before we adjourned, that I must understand that he had the highest regard for Britain and all her history and all we stood for. I was glad to hear this tribute to Britain. It confirmed what the Secretary of State had said about the close relationship.

The Americans were usually, but not invariably, sympathetic about areas where British troops were involved in action or in peace-keeping roles, namely Cyprus, Borneo, Aden and Arabia, and Guiana. I was helped by two first-class deputies—Lord Carrington and Sir Harold Caccia. Peter Carrington was especially useful in the wide range of problems which lay between the Foreign and Commonwealth Relations Offices. Telegrams dealing with trouble spots were usually drafted in one or other office but they had to be approved by both Ministers. This involved much labour since the Commonwealth Secretary was a punctilious and cautious draughtsman. Peter Carrington spent much of his time circulating between the two departments and only occasionally was it necessary for the great white chiefs, Sandys and me, to meet formally. Charles Douglas-Home reported on the 29th January that I had taken over Cyprus but this was not precisely accurate: prior to the amalgamation of the two offices there was always dichotomy. This was also the case in respect of Aden and South Arabia. I answered for British policy in my wind-up speech in the sole foreign affairs debate of my time on 17th June. I had made what Ernie Bevin would describe as a 'tower d'horizon' in my opening and this was poorly received, but in describing the rulers of the Federation at the end of the second day, their various escapades and imprisonments, I said 'Sheikhs I believe they are called.' I then went on to defend British policy to the satisfaction of my supporters. The impasse in Malaysia was marginally helped by my visit to Japan and Manila in May when I secured the agreement of both governments to intercede in the struggle with a view to securing a peaceful settlement. It cannot, however, be too clearly stated that the presence, often in action, of British troops was the most powerful factor in restoring order.

My most ambitious objective was to explore world issues with the leaders of the Soviet Union. In so many of the post-war governments in which I served, the illusion of the 'bear hug' hung like a sort of mirage before various Prime Ministers' eyes. I mean by that the hope that a summit meeting between Russia and Britain, or Russia and the West, should determine and check the possible use of the nuclear weapon, protect its proliferation and guide humanity towards peaceful ends rather than annihilation. In my many meetings with the eighty-year-old Churchill before he retired, this was his dominant theme. Macmillan's most intense moments as Prime Minister were spent with Kennedy and by himself in pursuit of the same mirage. I myself was not astonished at the absolute negation of any such hopes when I met with Khruschev and Gromyko. Dean Rusk had described Gromyko to me as a 'brave type'. He did not seem to me so sinister as Litvinov or Molotov, but his capacity for saying no seemed equally unbounded. Alec Home did not have the 'bear hug' complex. He had read deeply about Marxism and distrusted the possible expansion of the Soviet system into world revolution. For myself I think the truth lies somewhere between Alec Home's caution and Churchill's aspirations. In essence Russian foreign policy has been the same under the Soviet as under the Czars.

My visit to the Soviet Union was really the last big effort I was able to make before the general election. Mollie came with me and we were accompanied by Harold Caccia and a strong team —including Nicko Henderson, now our brilliant Ambassador in Warsaw, who had been for six months my Private Secretary. When we all paraded at the Kremlin, Khruschev accused one of the party of having a Cuban goatee beard. Humphry Trevelyan, the Ambassador, and his wife received us with rare hospitality, giving up their own rooms to us. We enjoyed the view of the Kremlin over the river from the Embassy. We were conducted on a comprehensive tour later in the visit. We saw the astonishing treasures, ranging from jewellery to coaches. While we were visiting Lenin's apartments I sank, out of exhaustion, on his dingy desk, only to be pulled off in fury and astonishment at my sacrilege. The desk was then dusted down and we were allowed to proceed. We saw there and at the tomb in Red Square what Lenin means to the revolution and how Stalin is treated only as an episode.

1964. THE AUTHOR, AS FOREIGN SECRETARY, WITH (*right*) MR. DEAN RUSK IN WASHINGTON AND (*below*) MR. KHRUSCHEV IN MOSCOW. NEXT TO THE AUTHOR SIR HUMPHREY (NOW LORD) TREVELYAN AND SIR HAROLD (NOW LORD) CACCIA. KARL MARX IN THE BACKGROUND

Keystone

OCTOBER 1965
MASTER OF TRINITY
COLLEGE, CAMBRIDGE

ON THE YORKSHIRE MOORS
WITH LORD SWINTON (*right*)
AND MR. CHRISTOPHER
SOAMES

Press Association

The Soviet leaders were quite aware that a British election
was looming and did not feel disposed to reach conclusions. On
several occasions they assured us that they did not wish to
separate us from our allies, although when I left him at the
Kremlin, Khruschev did say, 'If you would only give up NATO
I would make a lasting treaty of friendship between Britain and
the Soviet Union.' From the twinkle in his eye I could see that
he knew my answer before I gave it. I first met Khruschev with
Bulganin in Britain in 1956 when Eden asked me to join the
negotiations. I held him in quite a friendly regard and feel
certain that his memoirs, serialized in *The Times* recently, are a
genuine reflection of the man, as in part tape-recorded. I was
sorry when Khruschev was deposed later that year. His colleagues distrusted more and more his peasant intelligence and
spontaneity and did not find in him sufficient background of
economics. Certainly I confirmed that the agricultural policy
was falling behind when I was there. Khruschev was less
mercurial than George Brown but with a similar natural genius.
He was also more accustomed to the orthodox and less given to
whimsicalities. His overthrow was achieved by presenting him
with a front of unanimity among his colleagues. He saw that he
must either go quietly or end up in Central Asia.

Both Khruschev and his Foreign Minister refused to answer
my appeal to help intervene in the Laos tangle. At lunch on the
second day Gromyko asked me to sit next to him and said quite
spontaneously, 'You are continually trying to involve us in
Indo-China.' I replied that 'Under the 1954 agreement you are
Chairman with us of the Convention.' He said, 'Our enemies in
the United States are deeply bedded down there with men and
munitions and we do not wish to interfere.' I discussed with
Khruschev the non-dissemination of nuclear weapons in connection with the Western proposal then made for a multi-
manned nuclear sea force. Despite his dislike of this idea
Khruschev promised to keep open the desirability of non-
dissemination especially in the Middle East, but this is as far
as we got in an approach to any nuclear *relâche*. When the
Labour leaders visited Moscow earlier in the year they took
eleven points with them and claimed to have brought them
back. In our debate in the Commons in the middle of June I

twitted Harold Wilson with having brought down from the mount one more point than Moses. I do not really remember how many points we discussed with Khruschev, I do know however that Soviet policy has remained unalterably cautious of upsetting the balance of strength between the Soviet Union and the West. They are still frightened of a resurgence of German might and this we noted when we were taken to visit the great cemetery at Leningrad, a memorial of the terrible suffering of that city.

This visit to Leningrad, with a short view of the priceless Hermitage, was the climax of our tour and we returned to an uneasy August and September before the general election. I certainly enjoyed my time at the Foreign Office even though my objectives were still dancing as mirages on the horizon. In this I felt, however, that my vision was no more or less distorted than my predecessors'. I had had a short but useful innings. Alec asked me to shadow the Office in opposition and I did so for a few months until I was offered and accepted the Mastership of Trinity College, Cambridge.

*

Trinity was not exactly a strange place to come to. I already knew many of the Fellows, and of course my family has had roots here for many years. Following the Trinity tradition of alternating between a humanist and a scientist as Master, my great-uncle Montagu was succeeded by J. J. Thomson. Then came Trevelyan and after that my predecessor, Lord Adrian. I am a humanist in so far as I am anything, although not as distinguished academically as the others. But I was a Fellow of Corpus Christi, Cambridge, so I am moderately respectable.

Shortly after my arrival, soundings were taken about the entry of the Prince of Wales as an undergraduate. The first proposals for him were that he should have a special course and not risk taking a degree. A witty cartoonist depicted me as saying that I would frame him a course of history in which I became Prime Minister! However these expedients were quickly abandoned and the Palace was weaned from a two-year to a three-year stay. The first was spent on archaeology and anthropology and this is the time when the Prince was most at Trinity ending up with a first division of the Second Class in the result.

The Prince's grandfather had lived a life aloof from the college in a boarding house in the company of the Duke of Gloucester and an equerry. Edward VII had lived at Madingly Hall, even more remote than George VI. Our Prince shared the

"Ask his Royal Highness to come to my office when he's finished his solo flight"

whole life of the college and was frequently seen taking his luck dining in Hall. His only complaint was that friendships made overnight were very difficult to maintain. He followed up his good result in archaeology by getting a second division Second Class in history. This means that he was the first heir to the throne to take a degree. An important personage had said to me, 'It will be a scandal if you cannot guarantee him a good First.' But, of course, all the candidates for examinations work under numbers. The examiners mark the papers and only later look up the names. The Prince therefore survived his ordeal triumphantly. He has a love of books and was to be seen on many an evening in an alcove in the historic Wren Library. He had great powers of concentrating his work. One of his main talents is histrionic. He worked and played with our Dryden Dramatic Society and excelled himself in their performances.

This has helped him to become a national TV personality. He wishes to use these outstanding gifts to show the country that the monarchy is 'with' the young people. Already at his young age he has not only charm but a mission and it is indeed fortunate for the monarchy that he is richly endowed.

Trinity has proved to be more absorbing even than I had forecast. The young men, together with one hundred and fourteen Fellows, come to close on a thousand souls and they must have due care and attention. Those who have student trouble are those who spend the least time with their young people. There is much detail to attend to and many meetings. The very size and tradition of the place leads to a marked urbanity and broadmindedness among the Fellows. Our Lodge looks out over Great Court with a very beautiful view. I had a letter from one of my friends in the Commons which said, 'My dear Rab, It's never totally possible to be absolutely unhappy looking out on Great Court.' In short, it is very rewarding to be Master of Trinity. The happy discharge of this duty demands the close application of all the faculties which may have been developed over a lifetime of public service. It is no longer to enjoy a sinecure but rather, with the young problem as it is, a further opportunity to test one's nerve, and to explore and practise the art of the possible.

INDEX